What People Are Saying About
Chicken Soup for the Gardener's Soul . . .

"From the time of Adam and Eve, we have all been required to be gardeners. Read and enjoy the fruits of the tree of knowledge and of life."

Bernie Siegel, M.D.
author, *Love, Medicine and Miracles* and *Prescriptions for Living*

"*Chicken Soup for the Gardener's Soul* captures the spirit of the millions of people who garden. The inspirational messages easily explain why gardening is America's favorite leisure activity. While the 245,000 members of the National Council of State Garden Clubs, Inc., will enjoy this wonderful addition to the *Chicken Soup for the Soul* series, this book is certainly a great read for anyone."

Deen Day Smith
president, National Council of State Garden Clubs, Inc.

"On days when it's raining and your back hurts and you can't be out in the garden doing battle with the weeds, here's just the book to curl up with—a reminder of why you would never be without a garden, despite the backaches."

Martha Smith
author, *Beds I Have Known: Confessions of a Passionate Amateur Gardener* and *My Floral Roots: A Scottish Garden Odyssey*

"A superbly rewarding read. Each and every story reveals a discovery of the real meaning of gardening as a regenerative act of hope and love."

Tom Powell
editor and publisher, *The Avant Gardener*

"A must-read! Every story will inspire and nurture your soul."

Donna Dawson
master gardener and owner, *ICanGarden.com*

"As someone whose life work is sharing and promoting the joys of gardening with seeds, this book has been a way for me to reacquaint myself with how critical and deeply fundamental gardening is to everything that brings out the best in us. A treasure!"

Renee Shepherd
owner, *Renee's Garden Seeds*

"Gardening is so centering for mind, body and spirit. How wonderful to finally have a book of stories where gardeners share this special connection with nature to move and inspire us all."

Tracy DiSabato-Aust
author, *The Well-Tended Perennial Garden*

"A wonderful book that will warm the heart of any green or brown thumbers."

Roger Dawson
author, *Secrets of Power Negotiating*

"In *Chicken Soup for the Gardener's Soul* you will reap an un-limited harvest of faith, possibility and love that will inspire you to plant anew by sharing the stories with everyone you know!"

Brian D. Biro
motivational speaker and
author, *Beyond Success* and *The Joyful Spirit*

"*Chicken Soup for the Gardener's Soul* conveys what we gardeners either sense intuitively or know unequivocally . . . that our gardens grow us even more than we grow them."

Arlene Bernstein
author, *Growing Season*

"My mother taught me that chicken soup was a great healer for the body. Now I've discovered something that heals the soul—the right brew of stories in this very special book: 101 stories that feed our yearning for harmony with nature and nourish our hungry spirits."

Connie Goldman
coauthor, *Tending the Earth, Mending the Spirit—The Healing Gifts of Gardening*

"Sometimes you water and grow flowers; sometimes they water and grow you. This book will bless you in a mighty way. Read it and share it with people you love. They'll be glad you did."

Willie Jolley
author, *It Only Takes a Minute to Change Your Life* and *A Setback Is a Setup for a Comeback*

"Just what this Northwest gardener's soul needs for those 'why-do-I-bother-gardening' kind of rainy days!"

Ketzel Levine
National Public Radio correspondent and author, *Plant This! Best Bets for Year-Round Gorgeous Gardens*

"A must-read! Fascinating, heartwarming stories about people and their gardens!"

Ed Hume
host, *Gardening in America*

"Stay healthy. Take chicken soup if the flu bug strikes. Read *Chicken Soup for the Gardener's Soul* for peace of mind."

Doc and **Katy Abraham**
syndicated columnists and authors, *The Green Thumb*

"This spirited and heartfelt compilation will take its rightful place in every gardener's library."

Davis Dalbok
founder, Living Green Plantscapes, San Francisco

CHICKEN SOUP
FOR THE
GARDENER'S
SOUL

101 Stories to Sow Seeds of Love, Hope and Laughter

Jack Canfield, Mark Victor Hansen,
Cynthia Brian, Cindy Buck, Marion Owen,
Pat Stone, Carol Sturgulewski

Health Communications, Inc.
Deerfield Beach, Florida

www.hci-online.com
www.chickensoup.com

We would like to acknowledge the following publishers and individuals for permission to reprint the following material. (Note: The stories that were penned anonymously, that are public domain, or that were written by Jack Canfield, Mark Victor Hansen, Cynthia Brian, Cindy Buck, Marion Owen, Pat Stone, or Carol Sturgulewski are not included in this listing.)

Love and Daffodils Forever. Reprinted by permission of Nicolle Woodward. ©2000 Nicolle Woodward.

The Garden Guard. Reprinted by permission of Tom R. Kovach. ©2000 Tom R. Kovach.

To Own Something Beautiful. Reprinted by permission of Jonita Mullins. ©2000 Jonita Mullins.

Blossie. Reprinted by permission of Dan Barker. ©1999 Dan Barker.

Planting Day. Reprinted by permission of Beth Pollack. ©1999 Beth Pollack.

(Continued on page 377)

Library of Congress Cataloging-in-Publication Data

Chicken soup for the gardener's soul : 101 stories to sow seeds of love, hope and laughter / [edited by] Jack Canfield . . . [et al.].
    p. cm.
    ISBN 1-55874-886-5 (trade paper) — ISBN 1-55874-887-3 (hardcover)
      1. Gardening—United States—Anecdotes.   2. Gardeners—United States—Anecdotes.   3. Gardening—Anecdotes.   4. Gardeners—Anecdotes.   I. Canfield, Jack.

SB455.C475 2001
635'.0973—dc21

00-047175

©2000 Jack Canfield and Mark Victor Hansen
ISBN 1-55874-886-5 (trade paper)   ISBN 1-55874-887-3 (hardcover)

Publisher: Health Communications, Inc.
      3201 S.W. 15th Street
      Deerfield Beach, FL 33442-8190

R-04-01

Typesetting by Lawna Patterson Oldfield
Cover photo by Dick Tracy

We dedicate this book with love
to everyone who helps make the world
a better place through gardening.

"Well, I've tried everything else!"

Contents

2. BLOSSOMING FRIENDSHIPS

3. LOVE IN BLOOM

4. MAKING A DIFFERENCE

7. OVERCOMING OBSTACLES

8. THE FAMILY TREE

Acknowledgments

From the first day the seeds of this book were planted, *Chicken Soup for the Gardener's Soul* has been an exciting, challenging and joyous adventure. But it would not have been possible without the help of many, many people. We would like to thank them all for their dedication and contributions.

First, a huge thank you to our families, whose faith and love sustain us always.

A huge thanks to Jack's and Mark's wives and children—Inga and Patty, Oran, Kyle, Christopher, Travis, Riley, Elisabeth and Melanie—who supported us by reading many stories and sharing their lives with this project without complaint.

To Cynthia's husband of twenty-five years, Dr. Brian Richard Sheaff, her son, Justin David, and her daughter, Heather Brittany, for their patience, love, and support during this growing season. Thanks to her brothers, Fred on the farm and David in heaven, and her sisters, Debbie and Patty. And sincerest gratitude to her parents, Al and Alice Abruzzini, who instilled in their children a love of the land and appreciation for nature.

To Cindy's husband, Rob, for his dear love and constant support. To Charly for adding so much happiness.

Heartfelt thanks to her parents, Paul and Priscilla Jevne, for their love and goodness. To her brother, Paul, and his family for much-needed fun and relaxing times. And special thanks to her sister, Suzanne Jevne, for invaluable feedback on stories. . . and everything else.

A big hug and thanks to Marion's husband, Marty, for his patience, support and willingness to mow the lawn. Love and appreciation to Art and Darla Allen, the rest of her family and friends, and, of course, the spirit of her garden.

To Pat's wife, Becky, for being his best friend, lifemate and greatest blessing of his life. And to his four children, Nate, Jesse, Sammy and Tucker, for being such wonderful people and joys to live with and help raise.

To Carol's husband, Roe, for his unconditional love and unhesitating belief in all she does. To her sons and chief mailing crew, Ben, Ted and Hugh, who patiently suffered through too many pizzas while Mom was on deadline. To her parents, Frank and Nancy, and all the Murkowskis, for a loving life rooted in Alaska. To Arliss Sturgulewski and the Gore girls and friends, for their unfailing support and good cheer.

Many others have been instrumental in the development of this book. We owe a special debt to Patty Aubery, who had the foresight and faith to match five people, who had never met or worked together, to work with Jack and Mark on this book. Thanks from the bottom of our hearts for believing in us and the project.

We thank Heather McNamara, senior editor for the *Chicken Soup for the Soul* series, and her assistant D'ette Corona, for tirelessly working with us throughout the entire process of compiling this book, and for preparing and editing our final manuscript. We appreciate your hard work and hearty laughter.

Praise, too, to Nancy Mitchell Autio, for managing the monumental task of obtaining permissions for the stories and cartoons used in this book. Thanks for your love and invaluable help. You're a class act!

Leslie Riskin was always there and kept us on track with quick responses and an upbeat attitude. Veronica Romero, Robin Yerian, Vince Wong and Cindy Holland kept the wheels turning smoothly in Jack's office. And Deborah Hatchell was there to listen, calm us with gems of wisdom and coordinate countless details. Thanks, Deb, for your love and unfailing support through the entire process.

A heartfelt thanks to Patty Hansen for handling the behind-the-scenes details that are so vital to the book. Patty, a special hug for putting your inner vision on the cover.

Thank you to Trudy Marschall, Michelle Adams, Tracey Smith, DeeDee Romanello, Joy Pieterse, Lisa Williams, Kristi Knopp and David Coleman for working to make sure Mark's office runs smoothly.

Mark and Chrissy Donnelly and Maria Nickless earn our praise for applying extraordinary creativity and energy to marketing and promotion. Thanks, too, to Laurie Hartman and Lois Sloane, for extending the *Chicken Soup for the Soul* mission with your licensing expertise.

There are many others who loaned their time, talent and hearts to this project. Many thanks to Penny Boschee and the staff at the A. Holmes Johnson Memorial Library in Kodiak, Alaska (the little library that could) for their outstanding research assistance.

Applause goes to Chris Ellis and his can-do staff at Print Masters, in Kodiak, for taking care of our last-minute printing jobs with a smile. Kudos to Brian O'Leary and Robert Pletnikoff of the St. Mary's School mailing crew.

We are grateful to David and Betsy Hinchman for their creative vision for this book and their willingness to share

it with us, and to Penny Porter, for her loving encouragement and assistance in getting the word out to writers in
the Southwest. Thanks to Cary and Barbara Wolinsky for
great story ideas.

Our thanks to Beverly Merson, Carol Kline, Marci
Shimoff, Jennifer Read Hawthorne, Bryan Aubrey, Steve
Zikman, and Sid and Ilene Slagter for gladly sharing their
wealth of experience and expertise in creating *Chicken
Soup for the Soul* books. Thanks also to all of the coauthors
in the *Chicken Soup* series, for your caring and your great
generosity, and making it a joy to be a part of the *Chicken
Soup* family!

Peter Vegso, President of Health Communications, Inc.,
for his continuing support in the publication and distribution of the *Chicken Soup for the Soul* books all over the world.

Tom Sand, who has worked so hard to get our books
distributed more thoroughly around the globe.

Christine Belleris, Lisa Drucker, Allison Janse and
Susan Tobias, our editors at Health Communications, Inc.,
and Kathy Grant, administrative assistant, for their generous efforts in bringing this book to its high state of
excellence.

Thanks to the art department at Health Communications,
for their talent, creativity and unrelenting patience in producing book covers and inside designs that capture the
essence of *Chicken Soup*: Larissa Hise Henoch, Lawna
Patterson Oldfield, Andrea Perrine Brower, Lisa Camp,
Anthony Clausi and Dawn Grove.

Randee Feldman, *Chicken Soup for the Soul* product manager at Health Communications, Inc., for her masterful
coordination and support of all the *Chicken Soup* projects.

Terry Burke, Kelly Maragni, Kim Weiss, Maria Dinoia,
Irena Xanthos, Jane Barone, Lori Golden, Karen Ornstein,
and Kimberley Denney at Health Communications, Inc.,
for their incredible publicity and marketing efforts.

Claude Choquette, who manages year after year to get each of our books translated into over twenty languages around the world.

Special thanks to Erin Saxton and all of the talented and hardworking folks at Newman Communications, for their passion in promoting the book and ensuring its maximum success. Also, a hug to our attorney, Anthony Berman, for his generous help and excellent advice.

Much gratitude goes to the many volunteers of Be the Star You Are! nonprofit organization, who spent countless hours gathering, reading and acknowledging stories, as well as arranging hundreds of radio interviews around the country. Special thanks to Rebecca Schmidt, Patricia Hallberg, Sara La France, T. J. Van Buren, Dr. David Loveall, David Marten, Shaya Nelson, the Campolindo High School cheerleading squad, Business Radio 1220 AM KBZS in San Francisco, Father Patrick McGrath of Ireland, Eleanor Dugan, Paul Bogle, Barbara Gabriel, Rocky and Louise Elia, Jerry Ackerman, Norbert Brein-Kozakewycz, Ed Silver and Jo Ann Germaine Deck.

Thanks to all of the people who were willing to find time to read the 180-plus stories that were finalists for our book. Their insight and suggestions were invaluable. They include Carla Thurber, Linda O'Connor, Angela Belford, Janet Jensen, Barbara Godsoe, Martha Lange, Miggs Hubbard, Marki Stephens, Ron Nielsen, Patricia Hallberg, Kim Carlson, Autry Henderson, Carol McKinnon, Judy Green, N. E. Winters and Ben M. Winters, Mary Gagnon, Elinor Hall, Betsy Hinchman, Suzanne Thomas Lawlor, Holly Manon Moore, Maria Sears, Bette Starr, Julie and Xan Coghill, Monica and Gwendolyn Luther, Kenneth Smith, Anne Gore, Eileen Van Wyhe, Mary Judson, Marlene Ratzlaff, Christine Gallis, Sharon Ward, Julie Wander, Kim Thompson, Martha Hunter, Ruthie Hunter, Nancy Quinn, Art and Darla Allen, Sue

Jeffrey and Mary Jane Krajnak.

Thanks to our clients at Starstyle, Plantamins Inc., GreenPrints and everyone else for their enthusiasm for this project, even when it meant less time for them. To the radio stations across America who invited us on their programs to talk about gardening and this book, and to the newspapers, newsletters and chat rooms that shared our stories, we send our gratitude.

Heartfelt thanks to the more than 5,000 people who submitted stories, poems, cartoons and other pieces for our consideration. You know who you are. While it wasn't possible to use everything you sent, we were deeply moved by your generosity in sharing stories of love and inspiration in the garden.

Because of the huge scope of this project, we may have left out the names of some of the people who helped us. If so, we are sorry. Please know that we really do love and appreciate all of you. Thank you for sharing the gardens of your heart.

Introduction

A book is like a garden carried in the pocket.

Arabian Proverb

Anyone who has ever selected the perfect rose for a sweetheart . . . picked corn in Grandma's backyard . . . or walked in the peace of an ancient forest . . . understands the inspiration that is rooted in the earth. We are all soothed and renewed by nature's gifts, whether by a pot of African violets, a grand formal garden or a humble patch of peas and tomatoes.

Chicken Soup for the Gardener's Soul shares the rich rewards of gardening—the joys, the hearty laughs, the inspiration and the solace. It shares the friendships, the family bonds and the love that comes from caring for— and about—plants. Whether you're a master gardener, a novice struggling to nurture a green thumb, or simply an admirer of flowers and green growing things, you will love these stories. They are sure to moisten your eyes and warm your heart, lift your soul and tickle your ribs.

As stories have poured in from around the world, we've found that the gifts of the garden are more numerous and profound than we ever imagined. Gardening has helped people reach out to loved ones and heal or deepen family relationships. It has provided a way for people to serve their communities and help others grow in courage, self-esteem and pride of achievement. It has given people the strength to face the toughest challenges life has to offer. And it has applied a healing balm of comfort to many a grieving heart. In many of the stories, gardens serve as a touchstone to a simpler, quieter time. We find in them a refuge and a refueling of our souls. After a day filled with phone calls and traffic jams, many of us feel an almost physical need to get out in the garden and sink our hands in the rich, cool earth. And, perhaps most importantly, our gardens connect us with the ones we loved most in those simpler days. Many writers recounted their most cherished memories of the time spent with their mom or dad, grandma or grandpa, working away in the garden.

So many stories moved us to tears or made us laugh out loud, we wish we had room for 1,001, instead of 101! But we've done our best to choose the absolute best of the thousands we've received. Stories about a determined woman who planted an entire mountainside with daffodils, and a little boy who tried to grow doughnuts using Cheerios as seed. Stories about a man who refused to die until he had left the world a more beautiful place, and a Vietnam veteran who had to learn how to talk to plants before he could relearn how to talk to people.

Chicken Soup for the Gardener's Soul shares these true and heartfelt stories and many, many more. It has been nearly two years in the making, involving countless hours of reading, writing and editing—a task we wouldn't have traded for the world. It's been our privilege to be the ones gathering and sharing all the hope, humor and inspiration contained in this book. Creating it has been, like gardening itself, an act of love. But now the harvest is in—and you hold it in your hands.

Join us in the garden and share the bounty.

Share with Us

We would love to hear your reactions to the stories in this book. Please let us know what your favorite stories were and how they affected you. We also invite you to send us stories you would like to see published in future editions of *Chicken Soup for the Soul.* Please send submissions to:

Chicken Soup for the Soul
P.O. Box 30880-GA
Santa Barbara, CA 93130
Fax: 805-563-2945
www.chickensoup.com

You can also visit the *Chicken Soup for the Soul* site at *www.chickensoup.com* or at America Online by typing the keyword: *chickensoup.*

We hope you enjoy reading this book as much as we enjoyed compiling, editing and writing it.

1

THE JOY OF GARDENING

He who plants a garden plants happiness.

Chinese Proverb

Love and Daffodils Forever

It is better to remember our love as it was in the springtime.

Bess Streeter Aldrich

Bill and Constance had just celebrated their thirty-ninth anniversary when Bill went for his annual checkup. Always in perfect health, he was unprepared for what the doctor found. Symptoms Bill had ignored as "old age" led to questions, palpations, more questions, and finally instructions for a battery of tests.

"Just to be on the safe side," the doctor said. When Bill took the news home to Constance, she refused to consider that it could be something serious.

Fortunately, it was April and the gardens beckoned. Preparing the beds for the coming season, Bill and Constance threw themselves into the now-familiar yearly routine. They spent their days, as always, surrounded by trays of flowers and bags of mulch, wielding their favorite trowels.

As the summer progressed, thirty years of gardening rewarded them with a showplace of color. Benches and birdbaths were placed amid the bounty of flowers, and they spent nearly every evening during the summer relaxing and basking in the beauty. The old swing hung from their favorite oak, and they held hands, swinging like teenagers and talking until long after the sun set and the fireflies flickered.

By summer, Constance began to notice a subtle change in Bill. He seemed to tire more easily, had difficulty rising from his knees and had little appetite. By the time the test results were in, she was no longer so sure of a good prognosis.

When the doctor ushered them into his office, she knew. His demeanor was too professional, too unlike the friend they had known and trusted for so many years. There was no easy way to say it. Bill was dying, with so little hope of curing his illness that it would be kinder not even to try. He had perhaps six months left, time enough to put his house in order, but little time for anything else.

They decided he would stay at home, with help from visiting nurses and hospice when the time came. Their children were both far away, one in Oregon and the other in Chicago. They came for extended visits, but with jobs and children, neither could come permanently. So Bill and Constance spent the ending time as they had spent the beginning time, alone together. Only now they had their beloved gardens, a great comfort to them both for that entire summer.

By September, Bill was fading fast and they both knew the end was near. For some reason Constance couldn't understand, he seemed to be pushing her to get out more. He urged her to call old friends and have lunch, go shopping, see a movie. She resisted until he became so agitated that she conceded and began making her calls. Everyone was more than willing to accompany her, and she found she did take some comfort in talking over lunch or during the long ride to the mall.

Bill passed away peacefully in October, surrounded by his family. Constance was inconsolable. Nothing could have prepared her for the emptiness she felt. Winter descended upon her with a vengeance. Suddenly it seemed dark all the time. Then the holidays came, and she went to Oregon for Thanksgiving and to Chicago for Christmas. The house was cold and empty when she returned. She wasn't quite sure how she could go on, but somehow she did.

At long last, it was April again, and with April came the return to longer and warmer days. She would go from window to window looking out at the yard, knowing what needed to be done, but not really caring if she did it or not.

Then, one day, she noticed something different about the gardens. They were coming to life sooner than they had in the past. She went out and walked all around and through the beds. Daffodils were peeking up through the soil; hundreds and hundreds and hundreds of daffodils. She and Bill had never put many spring plants in their gardens. They so enjoyed the colors of summer that they had only a few spring daffodils and hyacinths scattered here and there.

Where did they come from? she wondered as she walked. Not only did the blooms completely encircle each bed, they were also scattered inside, among the still-dormant perennials. They appeared in groups all over the lawn, and even lined the driveway to the street. They ringed the trees and they lined the foundation of the house. She couldn't believe it. Where on earth had they come from?

A few days later, she received a call from her attorney. He needed to see her, he said. Could she come to his office that morning? When Constance arrived, he handed her a package with instructions not to open it until she returned home. He gave no other explanation.

When she opened the package, two smaller packages were inside. One was labeled "Open me first." Inside was a videocassette. Constance put it into the VCR, and Bill appeared on the screen, talking to her from his favorite chair, dressed not in pajamas but in a sweater and slacks. "My darling Constance," he began, "today is our anniversary, and this is my gift to you."

He told her of his love for her. Then he explained the daffodils.

"I know these daffodils will be blooming on our anniversary and will continue to do so forever," Bill said. "I couldn't plant them alone, though." Their many friends had conspired with Bill to get the bulbs planted. They had taken turns last fall getting Constance out of the house for hours at a time so the work could be done.

The second package held the memories of all those friends who so generously gave of their time and energies so Bill could give her his final gift. Photographs of everyone came spilling out, images captured forever of them working in the garden, laughing, taking turns snapping pictures and visiting with her beloved husband, who sat bundled in a lawn chair, watching.

In the photo Constance framed and put by her bed, Bill is smiling at her and waving his trowel.

Nicolle Woodward

The Garden Guard

What wisdom can you find that is greater than kindness?

Jean-Jacques Rousseau

Both my parents, Hungarian immigrants, were born with green thumbs. Our family of ten depended on the food we grew in our huge vegetable garden. My mother canned much of the produce for winter, and my father sold potatoes and cabbage to the local stores and high schools. Our garden was the pride of the neighborhood.

But then, one summer when I was quite young, we had a problem. Someone was stealing some of our vegetables. My parents were dumbfounded. "I don't get it," my father said. "If someone wants vegetables from us, all they have to do is ask. If they can't afford to pay for them, they could just have them."

Then one of the neighbors tipped us off that an old bachelor who lived a short distance from us was seen selling some vegetables in a nearby town. It didn't take long for my parents to put two and two together. Benny did not have a garden. So he was obviously getting his vegetables from someone else's garden.

Now, Benny was not a bad old fellow. My dad often hired him for haying and other odd jobs just to help him out. Benny had no steady job and lived in a small cabin that looked rather bleak to me. My parents figured he was taking our vegetables to earn a few extra dollars. But stealing is stealing, and it just isn't right. My father decided to handle this situation his own way.

"I'm going to hire Benny," he announced one day.

"What?" my mother exclaimed. "Joseph, we don't have enough money to hire anyone. Besides, why would we hire the man who's taking our vegetables?"

My father only smiled and said, "Trust me, Mary, I've got a plan."

"What are you going to do?" my mother asked.

"I'm going to hire him to guard our garden."

My mother shook her head. "What? That's like hiring the fox to watch the henhouse. I don't understand."

"Well," my father said, "here's what I think. Benny's got himself backed into a corner. And I'm going to give him a way out. The way I figure it, he can't turn me down. And he sure can't take the vegetables that he's guarding."

When my father approached him about the job, Benny was obviously a bit shocked. But Dad handled it pretty well.

"Benny," he said, "someone—probably some kids—has been taking vegetables out of our garden. I wonder if I could hire you to guard it for me?"

Benny hemmed and hawed for a bit, but after Dad explained that he would also be eating supper with us (and Mom's cooking was legendary), he finally agreed.

Needless to say, there were no vegetables missing the next day. Whether or not Benny slept most of the night was not important. The fact was that Dad's plan was working. We were not missing any vegetables and Benny had a job . . . of sorts. I don't think my folks could have been paying him much. But he was being paid. And just having a job gave Benny more than a little pride.

That solved our problem. But that wasn't the end of the story. Things worked out even better than my father had planned. You see, each morning, after Benny got done sleeping—er, guarding the garden—he'd stick around long enough for breakfast and then follow us around in the garden.

Now, Benny got to kind of liking this garden business. He'd ask questions like, "Why do you plant these carrots here? How come some of these peas are growing faster than those over there?"

My parents were patient with him, answering all his questions. Then my father suggested something. "You know, Benny, the growing season is just about over, but I could take my team of horses over to your place and plow you up a nice patch of ground where you could plant a garden next spring."

"You would do that?" Benny asked.

"Certainly," my father replied. "That's what neighbors are for."

By the following spring, Benny had his garden spot, all plowed, disked and ready for planting. In fact, my parents gave him various seeds that he could use: corn, peas, pumpkins, potatoes and such. Benny caught on to gardening as if he'd been a born farmer.

As we drove by his place in our old rattletrap car one day, Dad slowed down and pointed at Benny's garden. "Look at that, would you? He's growing nicer sweet corn than we are. And he's so busy gardening that he doesn't have time to guard our garden. Of course . . . for some reason, we don't need a garden guard anymore."

We all chuckled a little at that. But our smiles lingered for a long time after—smiles of pride in the new gardener we had helped create, and pride in our remarkable father.

Tom R. Kovach

To Own Something Beautiful

A thing of beauty is a joy forever.

John Keats

During the days of the Depression and World War II, my mother was raised by her Grandma Wilson, a widow with no pension and no Social Security. Their huge vegetable garden was a necessity, not a luxury, often providing them with the only food they had to eat. They survived by harvesting their own vegetables and renting out three rooms of their small five-room house.

One day, Grandma Wilson was out working in her yard when a neighbor walked by and stopped to admire a beautiful clump of irises growing artfully along the edge of the property. Grandma called them "flags" and took special pleasure in them because they bloomed faithfully year after year. She couldn't afford to buy flowers to plant, so she lovingly nurtured the few perennials that she had.

The neighbor, an older woman, walked by Grandma's house each day on her way to and from work. She, too, enjoyed the bright cheerfulness of the flags at a time when the whole world seemed to be struggling. She stopped at the edge of the yard that day as if on impulse.

"Would you be willing to sell me those flags?" she asked. "I surely do admire them."

Grandma looked up from where she knelt in the soil but hesitated before speaking. Sell her flowers? How could she sell them? They were one of the few patches of beauty in her hardscrabble existence.

"I'll give you a dime for them," her neighbor continued, opening her worn purse and fishing among some coins she kept tied in a handkerchief.

Grandma hesitated just a moment longer as she stood and wiped her hands on the apron she always wore. She hated to part with her flowers, but a dime was a dime and heaven knows she needed the money. She also realized that her neighbor needed that dime every bit as much as she did. She must really want those flowers. Perhaps she needed them more than Grandma did.

"You can't transplant them now," Grandma explained. "Not until after they quit blooming."

"I know," the woman replied. Then she held out the dime.

"Oh, you can pay me when you come to get them," Grandma said. She'd feel guilty taking the money now.

"No," her neighbor answered with a chuckle. "I'd better pay you now while I've got the money."

So Grandma took the dime and thanked her, trying to still the regret rising in her heart.

A few weeks passed and the blooms on the irises were fading. Grandma expected her neighbor to come any day and claim her purchase. With guilt, a tiny part of her hoped that the woman would forget, but Grandma knew that wasn't right. She decided that the next time the woman walked by she would remind her to dig up her bulbs.

A day or two later, Grandma spotted her neighbor coming up the street. She was walking with one of her daughters, and they were engrossed in conversation.

As they approached, Grandma heard the woman tell her daughter, "See them flags? They're mine."

"What do you mean, they're yours?" the daughter asked. "Did you ask Miz Wilson for them?"

"No, I bought them," the woman said.

"Then why are they still in her yard?" the daughter asked.

"Oh, I couldn't take them away," her mother answered. "She don't walk by our house. But I come by here every day."

The daughter looked puzzled, and Grandma was, too.

"This way," the woman explained, "we both can enjoy them. I don't have the time for working in a flower bed, but Miz Wilson takes mighty good care of them." She smiled at Grandma. "I just wanted to own something that beautiful."

Jonita Mullins

The Wedding Gift

A gift, with a kind countenance, is a double present.

Thomas Fuller, M.D.

I had picked out the flowers in my wedding bouquet carefully, with thought for the meaning of each one. There was blue iris, my fiancé's favorite flower; white roses, symbolizing purity; and strands of green ivy, to represent faithfulness.

Midway through our wedding reception, I found myself breathless and happy, chatting with friends and juggling a full champagne glass and my flowers. Suddenly, I felt a hand on my shoulder. I turned to see a woman I had met only briefly, a friend of my new mother-in-law. In her hand, she held a tendril of ivy.

"This fell out of your bouquet when you were on the dance floor," she said. I thanked her and began to reach for it, when she added, "Do you mind if I keep it?"

I was startled at first. I hadn't even tossed my bouquet yet. And I barely knew this woman. What did she want with my ivy?

But then practicality kicked in. I was leaving on my honeymoon in the morning and certainly wouldn't take the bouquet along. I had no plans for preserving it. And I'd been given so much today.

"Go ahead. Keep it," I said with a smile, and congratulated myself for being gracious in the face of a rather odd request. Then the music started up, and I danced off in the crowd.

A few months later, the bell rang at our new home. I opened the door to find that same stranger on my porch. This time, I couldn't hide my surprise. I hadn't seen her since the wedding. What was this all about?

"I have a wedding gift for you," she said, and held out a small planter crowded with foliage. Suddenly, I knew. "It's the ivy you dropped at your wedding," she explained. "I took it home and made a cutting and planted it for you."

Years ago, at her own wedding, someone had done the same for her. "It's still growing, and I remember my wedding day every time I see it," she said. "Now, I try to plant some for other brides when I can."

I was speechless. All the quirky thoughts I'd had, and what a beautiful gift I'd received!

My wedding ivy has thrived for many years, outliving any other effort I made at indoor gardening. As the giver predicted, a glance at the glossy green leaves brings back memories of white lace and wedding vows. I treasure the ivy's story and have shared it many times.

Now, nearly twenty years later, I'm the mother of three growing sons. Someday they'll be married, I know. And although I don't want to be an interfering in-law, surely the mother of the groom can suggest that the bride's bouquet contain a bit of ivy?

I know just the plant to cut it from.

Carol Sturgulewski

Blossie

You don't have a garden just for yourself. You have it to share.

Augusta Carter

I build gardens for people. In the past twelve years, I've built about 1,400 vegetable gardens in Portland, Oregon, almost all of them for people who didn't have the money to start a garden themselves. I bring everything in on a pickup truck—raised-bed frame, trellises, cages, seeds, starts, instructions, even the soil itself. Then I build the beds right on top of the people's lawns.

I figure each garden costs about $500, most of which is covered by the grants I get for my foundation, The Home Gardening Project. And my wife and I don't mind living pretty frugally. Actually, we're as poor as church mice. But when you compare people's lives before they had gardens to their lives after, well, you know this work just has to continue.

With each garden, I meet people who are in tough situations. An old woman who is nursing her stroke-victim husband. A young and inexperienced mother, with no husband around but several hungry children to feed. A poor woman who voluntarily cares for five abandoned children, all born with spina bifida or other congenital defects. I think I've gotten used to meeting people who have it hard.

Still, sometimes the ravages of life take my breath away. I'll never forget a woman named Blossie.

On the phone, she told me she was alone, on Social Security, and crack-addicted kids routinely broke into her house. She heard about the program, and she said she'd love a garden. She sounded very tired and rapidly aging, like many of the other 150 callers I responded to that spring.

She was slow to answer the door when I arrived. It was a struggle for her to wheel herself backward with one hand and pull the door open with the other. First I saw the wheelchair, then her eyes—eyes that looked to have absorbed more pain than a combat surgeon's. Her face and hands were swollen. She had tried to cover her knees with a tattered towel, but I could see the white bandages caked with splotches of dried blood. Then I noticed the wheelchair again—quite clearly . . . because she had no calves or feet to obstruct the view.

She'd just had her legs amputated, after a lifetime of aggravating her diabetes with poor diet and bad habits. She told me she wanted a vegetable garden to help improve what remained of her health. She wanted a garden so she could go outside for a reason, get a little exercise, and have something to care for besides the little terrier at her side.

Her house was embarrassingly messy and smelled of uneaten food and old bandages. She plaintively invited me in, but I politely excused myself.

"I'm busy," I said. "I'll just go out back and site the garden." She insisted that she wanted to come with me, or at least shout from the backdoor where she wanted the garden built. I made a mental note to call the Senior Job Center and ask them to build a handicapped ramp for her the day after I build her garden.

Blossie's need seemed critical, so I bumped her up on my waiting list and told her I'd be by in two days with her garden on the back of my truck. For a second, her brave forbearance changed to a smile, and her hands fluttered in anticipation. The garden was going to connect her to life. She could hardly wait.

I'd have to build five gardens that day—and break my promise to my wife that I'd make that spring an easy season. But my wife never expected me to keep that promise anyway. Facing Blossie, how could I say no?

When I returned, I built Blossie's garden in the sunny strip behind her backdoor, with easy access from the ramp that was scheduled to come in the next day or two. (Hooray for the old guys from the Job Center, with their hammers, tapes, saws and hearts!)

I built the three frames of her garden double high, filled with six cubic yards of premium soil, so she could easily reach it from her chair. I also supplied her with some tools I picked up at Goodwill, the handles cut to half-length. She watched from the backdoor. Soon she was on the phone to a friend, telling her the news.

"I know you want to get started as soon as you can," I said, handing her the seed packages and tray of starts. She took them into her lap like a Christmas present, her eyes lighting up in hope. Suddenly she wasn't listening anymore; she was ahead of herself, in the future, picking delicious tomatoes and basil for her summer salad, perhaps her only meal that day. She didn't seem to hear me say that I'd be happy to send someone around tomorrow to plant if she didn't feel like she had the energy to do it herself. The thought of needing such help didn't seem to cross her mind. She looked up and pointed to the old laundry sink out by the bushes. Would I mind filling that up with dirt, too? She wanted to grow some flowers, "just for pretties, you know."

When I drove past her place the next evening, she was heading down her new ramp, wheelchair in high gear, and she had the seeds and starts in her lap. Nothing could stop her now. It looked like another success story, similar to many others.

It wasn't until summer rolled around that Blossie's story became different. While monitoring the gardens that August, I stopped in to see her. I expected to find her as I usually had, housebound, in pain, hungry for some human contact, especially contact that wouldn't hurt her.

I was surprised by noise—the chatter and laughter of women coming from the backyard. I peeked over the back gate. Blossie was holding court from her wheelchair over six other aged women. She spotted me looking in and ordered me front and center—right that minute! She was exuberant, talking a mile a minute, her hands waving like a girl's. The ladies were with her every step of the way, and they were all talking about the garden.

Blossie introduced me. I offered the women free gardens, since they seemed to like Blossie's so much. They made appreciative sounds, but all said no. Then one of them explained, "We already have a garden—this one. You see, we all live down at the housing project, the nine-story one. There isn't anything but a parking lot around it, no place for a garden."

Blossie had called one of them weeks before, asking for some help and companionship. Pretty soon all six of these residents were coming down twice a week to help Blossie with her garden, weeding, fertilizing, replanting and watering. The garden, amazingly, was able to produce enough food for all of them to share. One of the women went inside and emerged with a tray of tea service, a gesture that made them laugh at themselves. After such long, hard lives, pretending to be genteel is silly—but fun. Looking around, I saw the garden itself was splendid, crowded with the vegetables Blossie likes to eat.

Soon the women stopped noticing me. I left them to their happiness and occupation, glad to have had a hand in it. Blossie's garden had grown up and spread out, helping six people in need besides herself. It was a wonderful sight.

People are always asking, "What is the purpose of life?" That's easy. Relieve suffering. Create beauty.

Make gardens.

Dan Barker

Planting Day

Do not squander time, for that's the stuff life is made of.

Benjamin Franklin

When I was little, I often helped my mother plant our family's garden. As soon as the chilly winds of Chicago winter gave way to spring, Mom would be outside with a spade, seed packets, gardening gloves and a secret smile that had been hibernating all winter. That smile never seemed to shine as bright as on those first few days in April when she squatted in the mud with tiny seeds in her hands.

I would pull on my grubbiest jeans, choose my shovel with care, and bound across the yard before Mom could say, "You forgot a jacket!" I would kneel by her side for hours, carefully digging holes and cautiously pushing seeds into the earth with my chubby fingers. We spent hour after hour repeating the process, until the formerly snow-smothered area barely knew what hit it!

Unfortunately, I grew up. Somehow, I found better ways to spend the first days of spring, and I threw my

annual April morning job into the growing pile of childish, outgrown activities. After all, I was too old to kneel in
the dirt all day planting some silly seeds. I came to the
conclusion that the shopping mall needed my assistance
more than Mom did.

Surprisingly, my mother never said much about my
decision until two years ago, the spring I turned fourteen.
I was on my way to a friend's house when Mom stopped
me.

"Would you please help me with the planting today?"
she asked.

"Oh, Mom, I was just getting ready to leave," I pouted.
"I'll probably be gone most of the day."

"Well, could you possibly come home a little early and
join me in the fresh air?" Mom asked.

I mumbled something along the lines of, "Uh, maybe . . .
I'll see."

By the time I left the house, Mom was already in the
garden. She looked up for a moment as I walked past, and
from the corner of my eye I saw a certain pain and sadness in her gaze. At first my heart told me I should stay
to help, but as I got farther from home and closer to an
exciting day of hanging out with friends, I forgot my
impulse.

A few hours later, as the sun started to fall from its place
in the warm, spring sky, I decided to leave my friends a bit
early and head back home.

Mom usually finishes planting around six, I thought. *If I get
back soon, I'll still have an hour or so to help her.* I felt very
noble for my selfless decision. But when I reached home,
there were Mom's dirty boots by the door and a small pile
of empty seed packets on top of the garbage can. I was too
late.

I didn't think much about that day until nearly a year
later.

One of my father's good friends suddenly lost his wife to cancer. The doctors hadn't discovered Sara's illness until it was too late. She died shortly after the diagnosis, leaving behind her husband and two small, confused children.

Right away, Mom went south to visit the family and see how the children, David and Rachel, were coping with the sudden loss of their mother. She spent a few hours with little Rachel. When she came home, she told me this story.

When Sara had received her terminal diagnosis, she asked her husband, "What should I leave our children? How do I give them something to remember me by, a symbol of my love for as long as they live?"

Mom learned the answer from Rachel.

"Mommy made me my own garden," Rachel said proudly, as she tugged on Mom's hand and led her outdoors. Sara had decided to plant her children something that would live on long after she was gone.

Although the children had helped with the original planting, it was obvious that most of the work had been patiently completed by their mother. The result was a masterpiece, with so much more among the leaves and petals than simple foliage. A piece of Sara's heart and soul was left in full bloom for her children.

As I listened to my mother tearfully tell Sara's story, I realized the true power of a garden. How had I missed it? Our annual planting was not about kneeling in dirt, throwing in some seeds and hoping for the best. It was about kneeling there *together*, planting potential life and creating the best memories possible out of those moments together. I was so lucky to have a healthy, vibrant, caring mother who was always there for me. As I suddenly realized how badly I missed seeing her soft hands place seeds in mine, many things became clear. I began to understand that the pain I had seen in her eyes that day a year ago had come from missing the little girl who was once at her side.

A few weeks later, I came home to find several bags of seeds on the kitchen table. I knew spring planting was near. The following Sunday, I woke to rays of sunlight streaming through my window. I looked outside to see a figure stooping in the dirt. I threw on the first clothes I could find and ran outside.

The first rays that encircled me were the ones streaming from my mother's smile. The first water our seeds encountered were the teardrops sliding happily from my eyes. We worked together all day and didn't stop until nightfall.

I won't ever miss planting day again.

Beth Pollack, age sixteen

Street Smarts

I live in the garden; I just sleep in the house.

Jim Long

When my husband and I married, we moved to Frankfort, Kentucky. Since our yard was within view of our state's capitol building, many tourists passed our house.

My elderly neighbor got me interested in gardening, and within a few years, our yard was a wonderland of flowers. People would even stop and peek through the fence to see all the blossoms that were not in plain view.

As time went by, I found I was working in the gardens from sunup to sundown. I loved being outdoors, and the gardens were so large, there was always more to do. I also enjoyed sharing my flowers. I loved the surprised look on strangers' faces when I impulsively picked a bouquet and gave it to them as they passed by. Sadly, our neighborhood also had its share of street people, but I was happy to share my flowers with them, too.

One morning, around 7:00 A.M., I was out in my gardens next to the sidewalk when one of the "usual" street persons approached. Most days, he just ambled past me, picking up cans and trash. Today, though, he suddenly stopped.

He looked me square in the eyes. "Excuse me, lady," he said. "Can I tell you something?"

"Sure," I said, expecting the usual compliments.

"Whoever owns that house works you *way* too hard!" Then he went on his way.

I laughed to myself all morning.

Lucy B. Richardson

A Veteran's Garden

The best proof of love is trust.

Dr. Joyce Brothers

My uncle was with the 8th Air Force in World War II. After the war, he got into growing gladiolas. My dad was a Marine in Korea. When he got out, fruit trees were his thing. I was a Marine in Vietnam from 1968 to 1969. When I came home, it took me years to realize what plants can do for you.

I never could talk about the war. Neither could Dad or Uncle Louie. But I was worse. I couldn't talk about anything. My wife said over and over, "You never say anything!" I couldn't. I didn't know how. I lost that skill in Vietnam. I don't know how or why I lost it. I had it when I got there. But it was gone when I came back. I just stuffed things inside and let them eat at me.

A lot of the Vietnam vets I know have a problem getting close to people. When you're in combat, you form fierce bonds with your squad members. You get closer than you were with your own brothers. After a few of these people get killed, the loss is so great, you're afraid to get close to other people. You love your wife and children, but you're so afraid you might lose them you can't express it. At the same time, you get protective, very protective, maybe controlling at times. You can't relax and be normal.

That's how I was: wound-up, tight, silent, a mess. Then one day I heard my dad talking to his apple trees. Well, I want you to know it is very impolite to listen to a man talking to his plants. So I didn't. But it got me to thinking. I started my garden the very next day.

The first year I didn't talk to my plants like my dad. I *yelled* at them. "How can you be so dumb?" I'd shout at the tomatoes. "What's wrong with you?" I'd rant at the sunflowers. "Lighten up, would you?!" "It's over, okay?!" "Who do you think you are?!" I was like a drill instructor swearing at his recruits. Only when I was yelling at the plants, I was really yelling at myself.

Those days of yelling at my poor plants let me sort out the things that were bottled up in me. Sometimes I watered my plants with tears. Going to war isn't nice. It's a time where, on one hand you are a god, and on the other you are a scared high-school kid. Then, when I got back from 'Nam, some people spat on me and called me a "baby killer." I was so mad, so frustrated, so empty inside I didn't know what to do. So I yelled at my plants.

It's hard for a combat vet to ask for help. But my plants gave it to me. My garden became my community. I cared for my plants. I brought them things like water and compost. I protected them from weeds and insects. I read about gardening and learned how you could plant flowers to attract "good" insects that would help with the "bad" ones. And they responded. They grew—wonderfully.

After that first season, I got so I could *talk* to my plants. I could even sing to them, stuff like show tunes and the Marine Corps Hymn. I would say things like, "How's it going?" "You need anything?" "You look good today." I learned patience from plants—you can't hurry a carrot. I got to feel pride again—I have the best Early Girl tomato you ever tasted! And I wanted to talk to people again—to tell them about my garden and share my harvest!

Then I started to think about communicating my inner feelings with my three children. By this time my wife was gone, and I deeply wanted a real relationship with my kids, one where we could talk about life and ideas and feelings, not just school and the weather. So I practiced with my plants. "I want you to know how important you are to me," I'd say. "I'm trying." "Sometimes I get so mad I just want to shout and I don't know why." "I want you to read this book. I think it would explain how I feel about this."

That made all the difference in the world. Today I am friends with all my children. We can talk in an equal person-to-person way. My oldest, Nikki, is an adult now. We talk each week. She and I can talk about anything. Garrett, my son, will finish college this spring. We are good friends. Whitney, my baby, just got back from a ten-city concert tour with her college singing group. She called on her first day back to tell me all about it.

After I was able to connect with my children, I met Charmaine, the woman I want to spend the rest of my life with. And the garden was right there waiting for me when I wanted to practice what I'd say to her.

I'm proud now to be a Vietnam vet. I wasn't a baby killer. I was a guy like my dad or Uncle Louie who got his country's call and answered it. And I can talk to people now. I've learned that people are just like plants. You treat them nice, and they will do the same for you.

The Marines sent me overseas. But it took gardening to bring me home.

James P. Glaser

Gardening in Our Blood

In the spring, at the end of the day, you should smell like dirt.

Margaret Atwood

When autumn time arrived last year,
I said, "I've really had it, dear!
I've raked and hoed and picked and canned;
Just see that callus on my hand!
You know what I've been thinking, dear?
Let's let our garden go next year.
We'll buy all those things in the store—
They wouldn't cost us too much more.
When summer comes I'll sleep till ten,
Get up and clean the house, and then
I'll make a glass of lemonade
and go and sit beneath the shade.
When you come home at night from work,
I'll put the coffee on to perk,
Then we'll sit down and talk or read
And never think of garden seed."
Remember how you smiled and said,

"I think you've really used your head
To save us all this work next year.
I'm sick of gardening, too, my dear."

But then one day, the sky was blue,
The sun was warm, the tulips grew.
The April days grew long and free,
The ground lay waiting patiently.
The sleeping grass awoke to green,
And then in every magazine
Were ads for bulbs and plants and seeds—
In fact, for all your gardening needs.
One day you picked me up downtown.
With bundles I was loaded down.
No need to try and hide the facts
With "Burpee Seeds" stamped on the sacks.
Remember how your face got red
And how you turned away and said,
"When we've unloaded all that junk,
I have a few things in the trunk.
I'll need some help, for it is hot
And seed potatoes weigh a lot."

So now we stand here, hand in hand
And gaze at our productive land.
The berry beds are weeded clean,
The vegetables are tall and green.
We love our land in drought or mud,
For we have gardening in our blood.

Jean Little

Butter Beans and Bulldogs

More in a garden grows than what the gardener sows.

Spanish Proverb

I shared so much with my husband, but *not* his passion for his vegetable garden. When we moved into the neighborhood in Lilburn, Georgia, back in the seventies, most everyone had a small garden. Jerry said that we should plant one, too.

"No, thanks," I declared. "I'm not a garden person." Undaunted, he went out and bought seed and an old, used tiller and began to till a corner of our backyard. He was so optimistic, he even bought a small freezer for storing the bounty. I threw a couple of loaves of store-bought bread into the shiny new freezer—all I ever intended to contribute. Smiling, Jerry raved on about how great it would be to have homegrown vegetables year-round.

"Who's going to pick them and put them in the freezer?" I asked, arms folded stubbornly.

"You might learn to enjoy it one day," he said.

I knew better.

Jerry spent countless hours in his garden. One night, when he had to work late, he came home and tended his tomato and bean plants by moonlight, whistling "Blueberry Hill." I watched from an upstairs window, convinced he was wasting his time and energy.

His garden was the talk of the neighborhood. Everyone came to marvel and sample. The green bean stalks were so tall, I had to look straight up in the sky to see the tops. The tomatoes were deep red, perfectly round and juicy.

Everything grew well in Jerry's garden, but the butter beans were his favorite. Homegrown butter beans—some people call them limas—and the University of Georgia Bulldogs football team were two of the most exciting things in his life. I cared about football and the Georgia Bulldogs about as much as I cared about that darn garden.

The years passed, and Jerry went on picking butter beans without me. Often our children helped him shell them and together they placed package after package in the freezer with all the fanfare of people putting the Hope Diamond in a vault.

In 1982, Jerry became sick rather suddenly. He'd always been incredibly healthy and assured me he was all right. Nothing unusual turned up on the tests at the hospital. But I couldn't shake the feeling that we were dealing with a biggie. On the fifth CAT scan something showed up. Exploratory surgery revealed inoperable cancer had spread throughout his brain.

Jerry and I had been together for twenty-five years, and I had no idea how I was going to live without him. I was so afraid I hardly ate or slept, barely talked, couldn't even cry. I just stared at my husband, willing him to hang on, begging God to let life make sense again.

The doctors wouldn't permit Jerry to work or drive. After a while, he couldn't have anyway. Jerry went on like always, laughing, whistling "Blueberry Hill," rooting wildly for the Bulldogs, playing with our collie, signing our twin sons up for Little League and, of course, tending his garden. He'd never been a worrier. I don't think he even knew how to worry. Never mind—I could do it for both of us.

One day we came home from one of his hospital stays and plopped down on the sofa. "What do you want to do?" I asked, staring straight ahead, thinking, *This can't really be happening.* "I think the Bulldogs are playing," I said. "If you want, I'll watch the game with you."

I turned to glance at Jerry. He gave me his big, easy smile. "I'm going to pick butter beans," he said, as if this were just another early-autumn Saturday.

I looked at him. Really looked at him. He wasn't afraid. He didn't ask, "Why me?" He wasn't faking it. He wasn't even being brave for me. He was just very simply excited about his butter beans.

He stood up to go outside, and I stood, too. "I'll go with you," I said, still terrified of what my future held without him.

"You don't like to pick butter beans!" he exclaimed. Then he burst out laughing like he always did when he was really happy, his arms resting on my shoulders.

"I changed my mind." I'd never wanted to do anything so much in my whole life as pick butter beans with my husband.

Out in his tall, green garden we went to work under the broiling Georgia sun. Creepy things crawled over my feet. I'm sure I saw at least one snake. I got so hot I saw spots, and my back, arms and legs ached. I sweated. But every time my gaze met Jerry's, he smiled enormously. Once he winked at me. Finally, he announced that we were through in the garden, and we carried our reward inside.

Sitting at the kitchen table, Jerry and I began shelling the huge mound of butter beans. *I could do this every day for the rest of my life and be happy and content,* I suddenly realized, as my eyes lingered on my husband's large, square, freckled hands easing the beans out of their shells.

Jerry left this life the following summer. We still had some of those butter beans in the freezer.

The memory of that hot, early fall day we picked them together has stayed with me, one of the highest points of our long marriage. It helped give me the strength to go on, to see that the life God had given me made sense after all.

Now I love gardens. I have a small plaque that says, "Life began in a garden." For me, courage began in a garden, the courage to face life without my partner. It was a tiny seed at first. But like everything in Jerry's garden, eventually it grew and thrived.

Marion Bond West

Reprinted by permission of Mark Parisi.

Ladies of the Garden Club

*Let us be grateful to people who make us happy;
they are the charming gardeners who make our
souls blossom.*

Marcel Proust

"Me? Join a garden club?" I asked my boss in amazement. "Why in the world would I do that?"

I was a career-oriented woman in my early thirties. I
had no time for a garden. And unless it was a business
networking group, I had no interest in clubs.

"As employees of the community health department,
our mission is to make the city a healthier place to live,"
Mrs. Hubbard informed me. I had no idea how joining a
garden club would accomplish that. And I had no idea
that Mrs. Hubbard's mother was the club president. All I
knew was, the boss said "Go"—so I went.

My first meeting was on a Wednesday morning.
Looking for the address, I was captivated by the beautiful
gardens in this historic Oklahoma City neighborhood.
Mature trees formed a canopy blocking the sun's glare,
while vibrant purple iris, red and yellow tulips and a sea

of white pansies illuminated the yard at Dorothy's home. What a contrast to my new house in the suburbs, where the front flower bed was filled with nothing but pine bark.

Though I was a few minutes late for the meeting, only three others had arrived. The dining-room table was set for a full breakfast of quiche, fruit, sausage balls, and poppy seed and banana-nut muffins. Members slowly trickled in. I was on my third cup of coffee, yet the meeting had not begun. I was a little edgy from the caffeine rush and the thought of all I needed to do at work. Then I learned that the meeting ended at noon and the ladies usually went out to lunch together afterward. I greeted that news with a smile and clenched teeth, and tried to keep from drumming my fingers impatiently.

The members, all past retirement age, introduced themselves. I was the only young person there. But as the meeting began, I found myself relaxing, captivated by the program on native plant species. I was so engrossed in imagining my own bare lawn bursting with plants, that I was caught off guard when President Bonnie announced, "We'd like to hold the meeting at your house next month, Stephanie—if you don't mind."

At the office later that day, I complained to a coworker. "The last thing I want to do is host a dozen women my grandmother's age," I groaned. "The meeting took all morning. And then they wanted me to go out to lunch! I'd been with them two hours already!" But I was stuck.

A month later, on a Wednesday morning, I dashed around my little kitchen. I dumped frozen mini-quiches out of a sack and arranged them on a cookie sheet. I whacked two cans of quick-bake cinnamon rolls on the edge of the counter and slapped the doughy blobs on another pan.

This meeting will not *be like the last,* I thought grimly, looking at my store-bought refreshments. *They probably wanted*

young people in the club just to do all the work!
The doorbell rang.

"I'm a little early, but I thought you could use some help getting ready for your first meeting," announced Dorothy as she entered. "I know you're a busy career gal, so I prepared a casserole and a fruit plate."

Entering the kitchen, she offered to make coffee as I tried to hide evidence of the Pillsbury Doughboy.

"Oh, good! Those cinnamon rolls are my favorites," she confided.

The doorbell rang again. Dorothy suggested she greet members so I could concentrate on being the hostess.

Soon, more than a dozen ladies were assembled. The meeting ran smoothly, and everyone seemed to enjoy the refreshments—even the ones from the frozen-food section.

"Now, since you've been our hostess today, we have a gift for you," said Bonnie. "Open your front door."

When I did, my jaw dropped in surprise. A dozen sacks filled with homegrown plants, potted shrubs and a flat of pansies welcomed me.

"It's your initiation," said Bonnie, laughing heartily. "We brought you something from our own gardens with a note on where to plant it and how to care for it."

"I brought the pansies," whispered Dorothy. "I noticed you admired them at our meeting last month."

Tears blurred my eyes as I thanked them. "I was embarrassed for you all to come out here. My yard is so bare."

"Oh my, no!" exclaimed Bonnie. "It's just a blank canvas waiting for an artist's brush."

Most everyone stayed to help me wash dishes and rearrange chairs.

Two days later, I got a call from Bonnie. "I've separated some coreopsis to plant around your fence," she said. "Say, if you haven't put the plants from Wednesday in the ground, I'll come Saturday morning and help if you want me to. You have been watering them daily, right?"

"Of course," I lied.

That evening I went home and tended the wilting plants, hoping they would revive overnight before Bonnie's arrival.

At seven in the morning, shovels in hand, three members of the Carefree Rose Garden Club arrived. They taught me how to arrange my landscape, and we dug a new twenty-foot flower bed around my front yard. The ladies brought more irises, amaryllis, tulips, hyacinths, coreopsis, pansies, peonies, redbud trees, wisteria, daisies and crepe myrtle bushes. We finished before noon, exhausted.

"It's beautiful," I whooped, as we brushed clumps of dirt and leaves off one another. "I could never have done it without you."

"That's garden club," said Bonnie.

We all staggered over to wash up at the garden hose. Then Dorothy asked me to get a picnic basket and ice chest out of her car.

"I thought we'd be too tired to fix lunch, so I made us sandwiches before I came," she said.

Sitting cross-legged on the sidewalk with my new-found elderly friends, I realized I had never been muddier in my adult life. And, I giggled to myself, I couldn't remember having this much fun.

Me? Join a garden club? Where do I sign up?

Stephanie Welcher Buckley

I'll Plant Anything

You cannot hold back a good laugh any more than you can the tide. Both are forces of nature.

William Rotsier

A good friend of mine was going away on a long trip during the fall. Miriam thought she had given herself plenty of time to do all the things that are required when one goes out of town.

I called her the day before her departure to wish her bon voyage. She was a wreck. She was completely behind on everything she needed to do. "And to top it all off," she lamented, "I bought some wonderful corms to plant for next spring. I'll never get them into the ground now!"

Well, I'll tell you, I can't bear the thought of an unplanted corm, bulb, seed plug, you name it. I always start too many seeds in March and by June I'm tucking them everywhere I can. I just can't bear the thought of a plant not getting a chance to grow. In other words, she was in luck.

"I'll plant them for you," I said.

"Oh, would you? You would do that?" Miriam was elated. She promised to set them out on the porch for me.

I knew her garden well, as we have spent many hours together, toiling in each other's gardens. We quickly brainstormed some nice places for them to go. But then she said, "Oh, just put them wherever you think they'll look nice."

I arrived a couple of days later on a chilly autumn morning and spied a frost-covered paper bag on the back steps. With my trowel and bone meal in hand, I set off in search of just the right place to plant.

The corms were weird-looking—not the usual miniature, rootlike bulbs. I hadn't asked what kind they were when Miriam and I had last talked, but the two of us were always trying out new varieties of anything we could get our hands on. Being a consummate experimental gardener, there isn't a lot I won't try to plant and coax through our seemingly endless Minnesota winters. So I shrugged my shoulders and went to work. After a lot of digging, arranging, changing my mind, digging some more and rearranging, I finally stood back from the patch of disturbed earth and nodded to myself in satisfaction. They were all planted in the perfect spot.

When Miriam got back a few months later, she and I went out to dinner to celebrate her return. At the restaurant we laughed about what a wreck she had been when she was trying to get out of town. And then she said, "You know, I still can't believe I forgot to put those corms out! What a ditz brain I am!"

I looked at her quizzically. "What do you mean? Of course you put them out. They were sitting on the porch in a paper bag, right where you said they'd be."

"No," she said, "they're still sitting on the counter where I left them."

Then an expression of dawning realization spread across her face. It held an odd combination of amusement and alarm.

"Valerie, I'm so sorry. . . ."

"What?"

"I'm truly sorry. . . ."

"What?!"

She paused as if to prepare me for her news. Then she slowly said, "That was cat poop."

"What?!"

"Cat poop," she repeated. "I'm afraid I cleaned the litter box out before I left and forgot to put it in the garbage. I guess I must have left it on the back steps. You planted cat poop."

News like this doesn't sink in immediately. It sort of bounces around in your head and all you can hear are the echoes. Cat poop . . . cat poop . . .

Miriam looked at my face—and did the best she could to keep from laughing. Tears welled up in her eyes, and she pressed her lips tightly together. I usually have a good sense of humor. But I was too busy replaying the images of me picking these hard little cormlike kernels out of a brown paper bag and lovingly planting them in Mother Earth's bosom. I took a long drink of my wine. I wasn't sure I could laugh about this.

Miriam managed to pull herself together. She cleared her throat and, sensing my state of shock, politely asked, "So, where did you plant them?"

"Uh, next to the catnip," I replied. The next thing I knew we both had collapsed into a fit of laughter. Much to my surprise, I was laughing. And it felt good. Very good.

Years have passed since then, and both our gardens and our friendship have continued to grow. That story has grown, too—to become one of our dearest bonds. I guess, true to form, I really will try to plant just about anything.

Valerie Wilcox

The Rose Babies

The fragrance always remains in the hand that gives the rose.

Heda Bejar

Most people press a flower in a book when they wish to keep it as a memento. My mother doesn't believe in preserving a memory by hiding it. Her motto is, "Don't press it! When will you look at it again tucked away in a book? Make it grow! Enjoy its beauty as a living flower, not as a withered keepsake."

That's my mother. She can make anything grow.

Recently, Mom received a mixed bouquet of flowers from her sister for her birthday. She is especially fond of roses and was delighted to find two roses in the bouquet. "Oh, look at the lovely roses. I've never seen such a beautiful shade of peach in a rose. I must save it as a souvenir."

I have seen this process many times, but I watch in awe each time. She takes one of the roses and cuts the bottom at an angle with a pair of scissors, wraps the bottom in a dampened paper towel and places the rose in a plastic bag to keep it moist.

Now I know it's my turn. The magic is about to begin. I run to the pantry to get a quart jar, once used for canning peaches.

"Here's the enchanted glass jar," I announce, as I return with it.

We head for her lilac bush. I carry the jar and the plastic bag that contains the rose. She carries warm water in an old coffee can, bent so that it has a spout on each side of it. My mother deliberately keeps her lilac bush overgrown. She trims it in such a way that it becomes fat and dense. The soil beneath it is damp and warm. She easily digs a hole with her hands and places the rose cutting in the hole. I help her carefully pack the dirt around the rose. She places the glass jar over the rose, and firmly twists it into the ground.

Finally, she gives the rose a drink, pointing the spout of the coffee can to the bottom of the glass jar. She whispers, "Oh, little rose, let me warm your toes, this'll keep you safe when the cold wind blows. See you in the spring, little rose."

"Little rose is all ready for her long winter's nap," she explains to me as we walk back to the house.

My mother is shameless when it comes to asking for a rose from someone's front yard or their garden. But no one ever refuses her request. And one time, the giver was especially glad she had shared her bounty.

It was a lovely summer day. My mother and I were walking past our neighbor Dorothy working in her garden. My mother stopped to admire one of Dorothy's roses.

"I've never seen such a beautiful lavender rose, blending into silver at the edge of the petals. Would you mind if I choose one to enjoy?" she asked Dorothy. Proud of her special lavender rosebush, Dorothy was delighted to cut the rose and graciously hand it to my mother. But the lavender rose did not go into a vase, as Dorothy probably assumed. It joined the others under the lilac bush, protected under its very own glass jar.

That Christmas Dorothy told us that the beautiful lavender rosebush had been stricken by disease in the fall, and it couldn't be saved. "It was my favorite," she said sadly, "and I haven't been able to find another to replace it."

Spring was delayed that year, but finally the fear of frost was gone. My mother was eager to uncover her rose cuttings, each protected under its miniature greenhouse.

"I wonder how many of my rose babies will be ready to begin their new lives?" she mused.

As always, I watched in amazement as my mother uncovered her rose babies. Carefully, she twisted the first glass jar from the warm earth: It was the lavender rose clipping. Would that beautiful rose be reborn? She spied a baby shoot, a tiny leaf peeking its way through the stem. Indeed, the lavender rose was alive.

Mom whispered to me, "Wait until late summer, and I'll have a surprise for Dorothy. I'll nourish our baby, and it'll thrive into a beautiful bush. She'll have her lavender rosebush again. It'll be our secret until then."

And sure enough, late that summer, Dorothy cried for joy as she received her surprise—a healthy new lavender rosebush.

On the card was the following:

> *Here's a small gift from my garden to you.*
> *It began the day someone gave me a rose, too.*
> *I planted that rose in the good, warm earth,*
> *And I nurtured it—hence its happy rebirth.*
> *After you've planted this gift and it grows,*
> *To keep up the cycle, may I impose?*
> *If I may be bold, do you suppose,*
> *That I might request its very first rose?*

> *Georgia A. Hubley*

Of Moose and Men

*You may go into the field or down the lane, but
don't go into Mr. McGregor's garden.*

Beatrix Potter

Gardening in the mountains of northwestern Maine
has its own peculiarities. Our planting-and-growing season is tucked in between the final thaw and the first
killing frost; you may miss it entirely if you have to go out
of state for the weekend or take a long nap.

The wildlife is another challenge, but we have learned
to manage it. Our dinner guests have gotten used to the
delicate scent of insect repellent wafting from the just-
picked salad. We've built a chest-high chicken-wire fence
to keep out lettuce-happy rabbits. The deer seem to be
scared off by our barking dogs, two elderly golden retriev-
ers who wouldn't know what to do with a deer if it lay
down for them and poured gravy over its neck. All was
well . . . until the moose came to the buffet table.

There is something about a bull moose. With its way-
too-long legs, its huge, nose-heavy head and drooping
turkey wattle, its massive rack and hairy body, the moose

comes as close to qualifying for *Jurassic Park* as anything you're likely to see on this continent. Out of season for hunters in the summer, the adult male moose is king. And a king eats when and where he wants.

It was an early August morning that I found the lettuce trampled, several rows of corn nibbled, and those unmistakable hoof prints in the soft soil of our little patch. It appeared that the moose had simply stepped over the fence, chowed down and stepped back into the woods.

We were a little tired of washing lettuce anyway, but we had been looking forward to our corn. I sprang into action. Up went a scarecrow in old overalls, plaid shirt and a felt fishing hat. A rusted BB gun resting against his hip completed the vigilant picture. I went to sleep that night sure that no moose in his right mind would have the nerve to walk into so guarded a garden.

The next morning, of course, proved me dead wrong. New hoof prints circled the scarecrow and wandered away from the corn down to the sugar snaps. As I picked the remaining peas, I racked my brain for another course of action.

I had read somewhere that moose and deer dislike the smell of soap. I ran into the house, grabbed every cake of it, and returned with my trusty pocket knife. Bits of soap were soon sprinkled around the entire perimeter of the garden, giving the area a strangely refined and indoor smell.

But looking more closely, I decided that I had spread my moose repellent too thin. Since we were now out of soap, I came up with what I thought was a wily addition—dog hair. If my dogs weren't man enough to actually attack a marauding moose, maybe their scent would do the trick. I scoured the yard for fallen fur and sprinkled the smelly stuff around the already soapy garden.

Sweet or stinky, I had my bases covered. Or did I? In what I can only attribute to some insane, primal urge, I added my final touch under cover of darkness. After several beers with dinner and two sizeable cups of coffee, I patrolled the garden perimeter before bed, making my mark on every fence post with bladder control my dogs might have envied.

Relieved, I went to bed, satisfied with my personal contribution to protecting what was mine.

Perhaps it was the fact that the soap was Yardley lavender. Maybe the lake had washed the carnivorous smell out of my dogs' coats. Or it could have been that hops are more enticing the second time around. Whatever, the next morning revealed fresh tracks, newly gnawed corn and beans, and distinctly fewer soap flakes. Somewhere out there was a very full, very clean moose.

That day was a gloomy one, with little hope of bathing. By midafternoon, however, I was barreling back from town with post extensions, a bale of wire, porcelain insulators and a 6,000-volt battery. It was time to show my foe some of the benefits of evolution. I strung two rows of conductive wire above the existing garden fence, topping off at a height of more than six feet. Switching on the current as the sun went down, I felt a little like the warden at Alcatraz going home for the night.

I slept the sleep of the innocent and the deluded. Apparently the crashing, wrenching sounds didn't wake me from my dreams of triumph. The next morning, as I walked out back to the produce penitentiary, I stopped in frozen disbelief at the gate. The entire northwest corner of the fence had been caved in and dragged across a full third of the garden, mowing down every vegetable over three inches tall. The moose, it seemed, had stumbled into my high-tech barricade and only been startled enough by the zap it got to take off posthaste in the direction it was heading anyway. Once the beast had trampled the fence and disconnected the current, it apparently remembered why it had got into such a tangle and stopped to graze in the bottom half of the garden.

Looking back, that final day was an oddly peaceful one. For I discovered that aside from our towering intellect, the other quality which makes us human is our ability to admit defeat.

After a breakfast of half of the remaining strawberries (leaving the other half for my garden's new co-owner), I set to work straightening out what was left of my fence. I hosed the remaining soap shavings into suds. The wind blew the dog hair into the surrounding woods. Finally, I took one more ride into town. I returned the battery to the hardware store as unsatisfactory—they didn't have to know why. Needless to say, when I returned to camp that afternoon, I pulled down the scarecrow.

In its place, I put up something more appropriate . . . a small statue of Saint Francis of Assisi.

Peter Guttmacher

A Garden Is to Grow

A garden is a grand teacher. It teaches patience and careful watchfulness; it teaches industry and thrift; above all it teaches entire trust.

Gertrude Jekyll

When I walk out into the schoolyard, lugging a shovel and a big bucket, a jostling crowd of children gathers around me and stares. Some look me up and down with narrowed eyes, inspecting me for flaws. It's my first day as a volunteer at a local elementary school. I'm not sure I'll pass inspection, and I regret the impulse that led me here.

"What's this for, anyway?" a boy in a red baseball cap asks.

For? I think. *What is the garden for? Gardens are for beauty. Gardens are an expression of what is peaceful, noble and good about humanity. In this corner of the schoolyard I want to help you create something lovely and lasting: a children's community garden.*

"Well," I say, "it's to grow things. We could have radishes or flowers, anything you want."

But he is already off, dancing in mock battle with a boy in a crew cut.

I slump with relief when the bell rings. Now the ones who want to garden will stay. Recesses and after lunch, the ones who really want to be here will garden beside me, building something beautiful from soil and seeds.

No one stays, except one: Scott Johnson.

I already know his name, know about him. While I waited to ask the principal for permission to start my garden, Scott put in time on the bench across from me. Another day, after all the other kids bubbled out of the classroom and down the halls, Scott remained, sullen, for an involuntary talk with his teacher. He sat alone at recess the day I removed the sod.

I'd never seen him with a friend. Now here he is.

A shaggy black dog pads in from the neighborhood and stops to sniff at my feet.

"Go away!" I say, frowning.

Scott, wild, wiry hair and untied shoelaces, is perched on a bale of straw, spitting on a sow bug, poking it with a twig. I give him a disapproving frown on behalf of the sow bug, and move out of spit range. That first day I dig by myself.

The second day, as I bend to place a stake at the end of the radish row, Scott swaggers up, hands in the pockets of his faded jacket, squinting.

"Hey, this'll never grow," he says. But when I next glance in his direction, Scott is digging with a trowel. Occasionally he finds a worm and tosses it to the black dog sitting in the grass nearby.

The third day, Scott brings a cactus, possibly stolen from someone's yard, roots ripped and dripping dirt. I watch him plant it where I'd thought to put strawberries.

"Nice cactus," I say, doubtfully.

"It's really sharp. You'd better stay away," Scott says, making a fierce grimace. He pushes the cactus into the hole he'd dug, kicks the soil around it, and runs off, leaving heavy footprints through the soft soil of freshly seeded radish rows.

After that, Scott brings something to plant nearly every day: a succulent with small, bright-pink flowers; cactuses with long, sharp spines; a cherry tomato seedling; a wild rose.

"That's a weed," I say, when he brings a thistle.

"So? I like it." Scott plants the thistle gently, but winces as he is pricked by a spine. "You said this was a garden for kids; I'll plant it if I want."

Scott does not welcome others, kids or not, in the garden. The dog is allowed to lounge in the grass and watch, but if kids come too close, they might have to dodge a flung worm or a dirt clod.

I chide him: "The garden is for all the kids." Scott turns a dull face to me, his body held stiffly. He is hurt, I realize. He wants to be special to me.

One day, while stringing a trellis for peas, I watch Scott fuss with a trowel around a small daisy. He stands abruptly and looks at me. "See there?" he says, gesturing with the trowel. "Over there is going to be a whole row of giant sunflowers. Taller than the fence." He turns and points the trowel at me. "Bigger than you! Ha!"

I smile. "That'll be wonderful. I can't wait to see them." Scott drops to his knees and attacks the earth with his trowel. I turn back to my trellis, but in a minute Scott stands before me. "I like you okay," he says and runs off, throwing his trowel at the pile of tools.

The garden grows beautifully, cactuses mingling with strawberries, daisies surrounding a rose, thistles among marigolds. A newspaper promises to take pictures and write a story. Scott raises his eyebrows when I tell him about the photographer. "They can't come in and touch nothing. Just take the picture." A couple minutes later, he glances my way with a half-smile.

"It'll be in the paper?"

I arrive early the day the photographer is to come. I see Scott standing in the garden, fists by his sides, his face knotted, white-hot with rage. All around him, the garden is torn up. Most of the cactuses are kicked to pieces, their moist insides exposed. Roots of marigolds, daisies and strawberries are spread-eagled to the sky. Through the middle of the garden are motorcycle tracks. Anger burns in me and blurs my vision. I can see the scene in my imagination: The vandals must have dropped their bikes in a heap, wheels still spinning. They ripped the plants, roots snapping, from the earth, threw them at the moon, then took off again.

Children begin to assemble around the garden, curious to see what Scott will do. But time passes and Scott just sits in the dirt, quivering and shaking with tears. The angry monster is just a sad little boy.

Scott begins to dig with his hands, gently placing the plants back into the loam. I am jittery with the urge to help, to jump in and fix it for him. But I hold myself back and watch.

A little girl, Amy Brown, squats down and picks up a daisy. Scott snatches the daisy away. He sits there a moment, the daisy limp in his hand. So many plants lie before him on the dirt. Slowly, Scott hands the daisy back. He digs a hole. Together they arrange the daisy in the hole and pat the soil around the roots.

Amy gingerly picks up a thistle. Another child sits down cross-legged in the dirt to dig a hole, and then another. Soon most of the children hunch over in the garden, digging and patting and chattering. Scott gives occasional direction and advice: "Careful with that one, it has spines," and "Make the hole bigger, I think."

Watching a pair of boys work an especially large strawberry into the soil, I feel Scott's eyes on me. His face is a beacon over the many-colored backs of his classmates.

He smiles slowly at me, and I feel a pang in my heart as I nod back.

In a half hour, a child pats the last marigold into the earth. Dirty, with soiled knees and dresses, the children stand around their garden. They are proud. A hand pounds a back, dirty fingers poke here and tickle there.

Scott gives me a slapping handshake. I clasp him to me in a hug, which he accepts for a moment before wriggling away to join his classmates.

Surrounded by friends, Scott inspects his hands. A boy near Scott pats him on the back, a little too hard. Scott looks up. The boy meant no harm; he meant friendship. Awkwardly, Scott tries his arm over the boy's shoulders. Finding his arm accepted, he grins.

A few minutes later their teachers come for them. I am left staring at the garden. It is tattered, limp, ruined for the photographer. I don't care. Today it is the most beautiful garden in the world.

The black dog wanders over and pees on the rose.

"Hello, dog," I say. I kneel and put my arms around him, his fur rough against my cheek. "You know what? A garden is to grow people."

Erica Sanders

The $100,000 Stray Cat

Plants teach us about the human condition, what it means to be fully human. Pets do the same thing.

Judith Handelsman

One orphan kitty with golden eyes—it's hard to believe all he has inspired.

I've always loved cats. But until nine years ago, my pet cats suffered a high mortality rate. I decided that my next cat was going to live indoors only. Besides, I love wild birds, and this way I could be sure my cat wouldn't hunt birds or little woodland creatures.

But then came Oliver. My sister works at a veterinarian's office. One day she called up and pleaded with me to come see a six-month-old kitten that had been abandoned there. They were having trouble finding him a home. The other staff found him ordinary. They only kept him because he was a willing blood donor. It broke my sister's heart to see the little kitten offer his paw for the needle and then purr while his blood was being withdrawn.

I went to the office and within thirty seconds had fallen

in love. The kitten had short but soft black fur with a white undercoat, a round, pudgy face and luminous golden eyes. He was dignified but affectionate. I instantly thought of the name Oliver, after the Charles Dickens orphan. Home we went—together.

But Oliver didn't want to be an indoors-only cat. He cried at the door, paced around the house, and tried to run outside whenever we opened a door. After much family discussion, we decided to build an outdoor cat run, an enclosed area where Oliver could safely spend time during the day. With the help of my dad, a retired carpenter, we built a thirty-by-fifteen-foot structure that had chicken-wire fencing on its sides and top.

Inside the cat run was a long strip of grass, food, water, litter pan, toys, scratching posts, a planter with catnip, and plenty of perches and high shelves. Oliver adored it. He loved lying in the grass, basking in the sun, chasing bugs and watching birds fly by.

But that wasn't the end of it. Oh, no. The cat run overlooked our vacant, one-acre lot. Wouldn't it be wonderful, I decided, if we could grow a wildlife garden there to attract more creatures for Oliver to watch? So I read books and magazines, visited nurseries and went on garden tours to educate myself. I was a little nervous about tackling such an ambitious project—I'm rather shy, really—but, I reasoned, no one would ever see the garden but us.

I recruited my dad to help. He quickly became so enthusiastic that he began adding his own ideas. His contagious spirit spread to my other family members, and before I knew it, we were all out there clearing the field, preparing the soil, marking out paths and starting to plant. We put in trees, shrubs, perennials, annuals, bulbs—thousands of plants over a two-year period. Dad built arbors, trellises, pergolas, benches, a pond with waterfalls and a bridge. We started collecting all sorts of garden décor—statues, stepping stones, fountains, planters, wind chimes, flags, birdhouses and wind vanes—all with cat designs. A friend even made me wooden signs saying "Meow Meadows," "Cat Country" and "Kitty Grazing Area." Everything was purr-fect!

And even that wasn't the end of it. A friend recommended our garden for Spokane's big annual garden tour. So on a hot August Sunday afternoon, I had five thousand people tour our garden. People went nuts over it! They didn't respond as much to the planting scheme as to the heartfelt emotion that went into it all. For weeks afterward, I was in the newspaper and being interviewed on TV. People called constantly.

Since that day, the Meyer Cat Garden is no longer our "little family secret." Over 10,000 people have visited it—everyone from nursing home residents to a tour group from a national garden convention. During my now well-practiced speech, I emphasize the importance of caring for your pets properly so they don't harm wildlife.

And wildlife we've got. As the garden has grown, it's attracted birds, frogs, squirrels, chipmunks, even raccoons, skunks and deer. I've grown, too. I'm now a master gardener and president of our local garden club, and I'm comfortable with both writing and public speaking. And our whole family has grown: Working on such a tremendous project has drawn us all closer together.

And what about Oliver? He watches it all contentedly through his cat run—his window to the world. Our family joke is that if we added up the cost of all the thousands of plants, cat decorations and hours of labor that went into the Meyer Cat Garden, we have easily spent over $100,000.

That's why we call Oliver our $100,000 stray cat.

But you know what? He was a bargain.

ViAnn Meyer

2

BLOSSOMING FRIENDSHIPS

Wishing to be friends is quick work, but friendship is a slow-ripening fruit.

Aristotle

For Better or For Worse®

As Thyself

A good friend is my nearest relation.

Thomas Fuller, M.D.

In the peaceful years before the Second World War, two rose farmers lived across the street from each other in the town of Richmond in northern California. Francis Aebi was of Swiss descent, and Tamaki Ninomiya was Japanese. The two men's fathers had settled in Richmond at the turn of the century. They had built the neat homes that faced each other, and they had started growing roses and selling them in San Francisco. Although they were competitors, they also became friends, and their young sons played together after school.

By the start of World War II, Francis and Tamaki had taken over their fathers' businesses and both had become modestly successful. Roses from the two farms had earned well-deserved reputations for their long vase-life. The families worked too hard to socialize much, but they enjoyed visiting each other on occasion, and the children played together as their fathers once had.

Then December 7, 1941, arrived. With the bombing of

Pearl Harbor, life changed for most Americans, but especially for those of Japanese descent. In Richmond, rumors circulated that a car owned by a Japanese family had been overturned and that a greenhouse owned by a Japanese farmer had been vandalized. There was frightening talk of people being sent to something called "internment camp."

One day Francis walked over to Tamaki's house with his wife Carrie and two children. When Tamaki greeted them at the door, Francis said, "We've lived across the street from each other for a long time."

"Three generations," Tamaki said, nodding to the five children around him.

Francis made it clear that, if the need arose, Tamaki could count on him to look after his property. It was something they had both learned as boys in church: *Love thy neighbor as thyself.* "You would do the same for us," he said.

Soon after that visit, President Franklin Roosevelt signed an executive order that identified "military areas" from which certain people could be excluded. Much of the entire state of California was designated such an area. This was the first sign that the relocation of Japanese-Americans to camps was about to become a reality.

Now it was Tamaki's turn to visit Francis. He arrived carrying the family's most valuable possession, an ornamental Japanese doll dressed in an elaborate costume of black and white silk, housed in a glass case. Tamaki offered it to Francis as a gift.

Francis told Tamaki that he couldn't accept the doll as a gift. But he did agree to hold it for the Ninomiyas "until things get back to normal."

A month later, Tamaki arrived again. This time, he handed Francis his bankbook.

On a cold February day less than a month later, a black sedan pulled up to the Ninomiyas' home. The Aebis watched as four men dressed in business suits escorted Tamaki to the car and took him away with only the work clothes on his back.

That same day, Tamaki's pregnant wife Hayane and their five children went to stay with friends in Livingston, in central California, hoping to avoid the same fate as Tamaki. They loaded their pickup truck with clothes, a few pots and pans and some favorite toys. With tears in her eyes, Hayane drove away from the home that Tamaki's father had built with his own hands.

But they found no protection in Livingston. Soon after they arrived they were sent to Granada, Colorado, along with hundreds of other Japanese families. They were assigned to wooden barracks covered with tar paper and surrounded by barbed wire. Armed guards watched over their every move. But the worst discovery was that Tamaki was at another camp, and no one could tell them where.

Back in Richmond, Francis Aebi was determined to keep both his own and his neighbor's nursery running. This required many long hours of grueling labor. In order to qualify for a farmer's ration of fuel, Francis had to clear out many of the lovely rosebushes in both greenhouses and plant tomatoes and cucumbers instead. He did manage to save a few choice rosebushes in each.

"For tomorrow," he told his children.

Months turned into years. The whole Aebi family now had to labor with Francis to keep the nurseries operating. The children worked in the greenhouses before school and on weekends. Still, Francis routinely worked sixteen and seventeen hours a day.

During the next three years, a letter occasionally arrived from the internment camp. The Aebis celebrated when Hayane's child was delivered safely. But the happiest news came a year later when Tamaki was allowed to join his family in Granada and to meet, for the first time, his new son.

At long last the war ended. Sitting in the cafeteria in the camp, the Ninomiyas heard the announcement over the public address system that they were going home. As the family packed up their few belongings and boarded a train, Tamaki's relief was mingled with apprehension about what they were returning to.

In his letters, Francis had reported that all was well at the Ninomiya nursery. Yet it was only natural for Tamaki to wonder if this could possibly be true. Many Japanese-Americans returned to find their homes burned down or their property looted. At the very least, they knew their homes would be in terrible disrepair.

When the train pulled into the Richmond station, Francis Aebi was waiting on the platform. Both Francis and Tamaki had grown so thin and drawn they barely recognized each other. As Tamaki stepped onto the platform, they shook hands awkwardly, feeling shy about the emotions that welled up.

As they rode through the familiar streets, the Ninomiyas looked anxiously around at the changes the three years had brought to their hometown. Finally, the car pulled into the driveway of their home. The children spilled out of the car, followed by Tamaki and Hayane. Then they all stood and stared in silence.

The nursery was exactly as they had last seen it, only now there were vegetables growing along with the roses. It was so clean, the panes sparkled in the sunlight, and healthy plants crowded the walkways.

Carrie Aebi and the Aebi children came running across the street, and the two women embraced. Together the families entered the Ninomiyas' home. Everything was spotless and the family's possessions were just where they had left them. The Japanese silk doll was back in its place of honor. The Ninomiyas' bankbook was on the dining-room table, full of deposit slips from the sale of Tamaki's roses and vegetables in San Francisco.

And on the kitchen counter, a single red rose stood in a bud vase—the gift of a man who had learned as a child to love thy neighbor as thyself.

Dick DeVos

Ruby's Roses

*F*air and softly goes far.

Cervantes, *Don Quixote*

The neighborhood kids nicknamed the cranky old couple Crazy Jack and Ruby Rednose. Rumor was that they sat inside and drank whiskey all day. It was true that Jack and Ruby Jones preferred to keep to themselves. About the only words we ever heard from them were "Keep out of our rosebushes!"

The rosebushes were seventy beautiful floribunda shrubs that served as a fence between our house and theirs. The rose fence took quite a bit of abuse, since our house was the neighborhood hangout. I was eleven at the time and the oldest of six active girls. We should have played our softball games elsewhere to avoid hurting the roses, but we secretly enjoyed irritating Crazy Jack and Ruby Rednose.

Jack and Ruby had a son whom we nicknamed Crazy Jack Junior. He was due to come home from Vietnam. We heard he had been discharged because of a nervous breakdown. The neighborhood had thrown a big party for

Jimmy Brown when he came home from the war, but no one offered to have a party for Crazy Jack Junior.

The day Crazy Jack Junior was scheduled to come home, we had a neighborhood softball game in our yard. Johnny McGrath was trying to catch a fly ball. He stumbled over one of Ruby Rednose's thorny rosebushes and fell on top of several more. Boy, did he yell, but the roses were the ones that really suffered. From my vantage point at second base, it looked like about ten of them were damaged pretty badly. Johnny's timing was terrible, because as he lay there swearing at the roses, the Joneses' pickup rolled into the driveway. The truck screeched to a halt and Crazy Jack Junior sprang out. He ran full speed toward Johnny.

"You little punk!" he screamed. "Look what you've done to our family's roses! You've always been trouble. I'm going to fetch my gun and shoot you!"

The next few minutes were a blur. The neighborhood kids ran for their lives. Ruby and Jack tried to restrain their son. He continued to yell threats and profanities. Ruby wasn't my favorite person, but I felt sorry for her when I saw her tearfully pleading with Crazy Jack Junior. Finally, they coaxed him inside.

Meanwhile, my sisters and I tore into our house. Breathlessly, we told Mom what had happened. She put down her sewing and scolded, "Girls, I have told you not to play softball near those bushes. Come outside right now and help me fix them."

"Mom, we thought you didn't like the Joneses," we protested. "They're mean to us. Besides, Crazy Jack Junior might shoot us."

Mom just glared at us. We followed her outside to help mend the rose fence.

While Mom examined the damaged roses, my sisters and I hung back, plotting how to get out of the thorny job.

As we whispered back and forth, the Joneses' garage door opened and Ruby slowly walked out. She looked sad. And it wasn't her nose that was red, it was her eyes.

Ruby walked over to my mother. The two women stood looking at each other through the new gap in the rose fence. We girls held our breath, waiting to see who would shout first and what terrible things would be said. How much trouble would we be in when it was all over?

Suddenly my mother stepped forward and hugged Ruby. "I'm glad your son came back home," she said gently. "It must have been a horrible experience in Vietnam. We're sorry about the flowers. The girls will replace them if we can't fix them. In return for all the bother, they'll help you weed the roses this summer."

My sisters and I looked at each other in horror, but Ruby smiled at my mother through her tears. "I know we're particular about these roses," she said, "but they're very special to us. When my mother came from England, she brought one tiny part of her favorite rosebush. That was her reminder of home."

She paused a minute, then said sadly, "My mother had a magic touch with flowers. Over the years that one plant multiplied into all these bushes. Since she died, I've tried to keep them up, but I just don't have her magic touch."

Her voice was all choked up. "Mom died while Jack Junior was in Vietnam. He just found out about her death today. When he saw her rosebushes damaged, it was the last straw."

Ruby mopped at her tears. "Once we got him inside and calmed down, he admitted he's out of control. Jack just drove him to Clinton Valley to be admitted to a treatment program."

By now I felt really bad for the Jones family—what a sorrowful homecoming! I could tell my mother and sisters felt the same.

"We all enjoy the roses as much as you do. We'll be happy to help you care for them," my mother said. "You know, some people say I have a magic touch with flowers, too."

Soon both women were down on their knees talking and examining the damaged bushes together. A few weeks later, the plants all returned with vigor.

My mother and Ruby worked together on the roses all summer long and many summers to follow. So did my sisters and I. A friendship formed between the families that would include countless birthdays, graduations and weddings—including Jack Junior's.

Years later, when her son left home and her husband died, Ruby became part of our family, spending many happy hours at our house.

She wasn't Ruby Rednose anymore; she was Aunt Ruby. And the rose fence wasn't a fence any longer. My mother had turned it into a bridge.

Donna Gundle-Krieg

Garden Meditations

Friendship is a sheltering tree.

Samuel Taylor Coleridge

Let us give thanks for a bounty of people.

For children who are our second planting, and though they grow like weeds and the wind too soon blows them away, may they forgive us our cultivation and fondly remember where their roots are.

Let us give thanks:

For generous friends, with hearts—and smiles—as bright as their blossoms;

For feisty friends, as tart as apples;

For continuous friends, who, like scallions and cucumbers, keep reminding us that we've had them;

For crotchety friends, sour as rhubarb and as indestructible;

For handsome friends, who are as gorgeous as eggplants and as elegant as a row of corn, and the others, as plain as potatoes and so good for you;

For funny friends, who are as silly as Brussels sprouts and as amusing as Jerusalem artichokes;

And serious friends as unpretentious as cabbages, as subtle as summer squash, as persistent as parsley, as delightful as dill, as endless as zucchini and who, like parsnips, can be counted on to see you through the winter;

For old friends, nodding like sunflowers in the evening-time and young friends coming on as fast as radishes;

For loving friends, who wind around us like tendrils and hold us, despite our blights, wilts and witherings;

And finally, for those friends now gone, like gardens past that have been harvested, but who fed us in their time that we might have life thereafter.

For all these we give thanks.

Reverend Max Coots

"Stop and smell the roses. Stop and smell the roses. That's all we ever do anymore!"

Reprinted by permission of David M. Cooney.

An American Beauty

Have we not all one father? Hath not one God created us?

Malachi 2:10

In the 1930s, after the death of her husband, a middle-aged woman named Marguerite left Germany to make a new life in America, away from Hitler and the Third Reich. Marguerite's younger brother, Wilhelm, stayed behind with his Jewish wife and family to protect their assets, unaware of the horrors to come.

In her adopted country, Marguerite lived on a small pension and supplemented her income by raising a variety of roses, which she sold to local florists and hospitals. She sent some of the earnings from her roses to help support her brother in Germany. And, as the war advanced, she also sent money to help Jews escape from Germany.

Marguerite's neighbors viewed her as a quiet, unassuming woman who spent most days in her garden or greenhouse. Not much was known about her, nor did the community try to befriend the foreign-born woman. But when the United States entered the war against Germany,

Marguerite became suspect. While her neighbors and shopkeepers had never been friendly or particularly kind, they were now openly hostile. There were mutters and whispers about her being a Nazi, always just loud enough for her to hear.

Without fanfare, Marguerite continued to send money to Jewish families and to her brother in Germany. Then, one day, she received a letter from her sister-in-law with devastating news. Her beloved Wilhelm was dying of cancer. He was praying for a miracle: to be able to come to the United States where he could receive better medical care. At first Marguerite was panic-stricken; she didn't have the extra money. But soon, she was overjoyed when a hospital requested an unusually large order of roses. This was the extra income she needed to make the miracle happen!

For weeks she tended her roses, nurturing and fertilizing them with tender care. Each rose meant another dollar to help bring Wilhelm to America.

In August Marguerite entered a local contest for the most beautiful roses grown. If she won, the prize money of $25 would ease her financial burden when Wilhelm and his family arrived.

On the day of the festival, she rose early to cut the flowers before they were wilted by the sun. As she stepped into the garden, she nearly fell to her knees with shock. All one hundred rosebushes, lovingly planted and nurtured over the last seven years, lay in shambles before her. Every plant was slashed and chopped to the ground. They all but bled before her eyes. She could barely take it in: her beloved flowers, and her livelihood, gone, possibly forever. And the worst of it was that Wilhelm would not be able to come to America.

Marguerite was devastated but more determined than ever to show up at the festival. She would not give the hooligans the satisfaction of her absence. She would still enter the contest, even if they had left but a petal. She walked down the garden path to see if she could salvage anything from the debris.

Clinging to life by the back fence, obviously missed by the vandals, was one single red rose. It was an 'American Beauty.' She took the rose into the house, cut the stem on an angle and placed it in the icebox to keep it fresh until the contest. Then, shaking with distress, she cleaned up the ruined rose garden as best she could. When she could do no more, she put on her best hat and took a trolley to the contest, holding the lone rose in her hand.

When Marguerite's turn came to show her entry, she held up her single 'American Beauty.' In her halting English, she proudly described its origin, how she had bred it, and the special fertilizer she had used to enhance the color of its petals. But, when the winners were announced, she wasn't surprised at the absence of her name. Why would they give the prize to a rose from the garden of the enemy? She went home that evening trying to think of some other way she could earn money.

The next day, Marguerite attended church, as was her custom, to pray for strength and guidance. When she arrived home and opened the door, the scent of flowers filled the air. Someone had placed a large vase filled with summer flowers on the entryway table. As she walked toward the kitchen, she saw that every room in her home had more bouquets of flowers in Mason jars and pitchers. It was heavenly!

As she approached the kitchen, she saw a fresh coffee-cake in the middle of the table. Under the cake plate was an envelope addressed to "Marguerite." She opened it to find $300 in single bills and a card that said simply, "Many thanks from your friends in town."

Stunned and happy, Marguerite realized that this was the miracle Wilhelm had been praying for! Now she could bring him to America.

The miracle did come to pass. With the $300 Marguerite bought steamship tickets. Within a few months, Wilhelm and his family arrived. Marguerite and his wife cared for him tenderly, and he received excellent medical attention that added years to his life.

For years Marguerite tried to discover who her benefactors were, but without success. Many years later, a local woman was going through the personal effects of her late grandfather, who had been a cantor in the local synagogue. She found his journal—and in it, an entry of particular interest. The journal stated that while attending the rose festival, the cantor had overheard two men in the audience brag about ripping up "the Nazi's" rosebushes. He knew who they meant. Marguerite had never sought recognition for her charity, but many Jews in the community knew that her roses helped Jewish families escape the nightmare of the Holocaust.

That day the cantor set about calling on members of his synagogue, explaining about the vandalism and the financial loss Marguerite had suffered. The men and women in the synagogue gave with their hearts and pocketbooks to the "rose lady." Several women who shared Marguerite's love of gardening gathered flowers from their own gardens to honor her for all she had done for their people. Rather than have her feel an obligation, they took an oath to remain anonymous until death. They all kept the promise.

With patient love and care, Marguerite's roses bloomed again. And Marguerite bloomed as well. She made many friends in town in the years following the war, never knowing that many of them were her secret benefactors. And she continued to send money to Germany to help Jewish families until her death in 1955.

Arlene West House

The World's Largest Rose Tree

Bloom where you are planted.

Nancy Reader Campion

On a warm spring day in 1885, a young Scotswoman named Mary Gee sat on the porch of the Cochise House, a boardinghouse in Tombstone, Arizona. She and her husband Henry were lodging there while their new home was being built. Just two months before, Mary had married Henry in her village church in Scotland and then, the next day, set sail for America, her husband's home. Henry was a mining engineer, and his work required that he return immediately to the Old Guard Mining Company in Tombstone.

Mary was talking with her new friend Amelia Adamson, owner of the Cochise House. Mary had already told her all about everyone in her family back in Scotland: her younger brothers and her parents, her childhood friends and her beloved grandmother. Today she was talking about the land itself, the smoky heather, the green hills, and the flowers and vegetables she and her mother had tended in their backyard.

As Mary described the bountiful harvests, the lush blossoms and, especially, the delicate beauty of her favorite roses, she gradually fell silent and turned away, her eyes filling with tears. Amelia wanted to comfort her, but what could she say? The view from the porch was a vast expanse of brown desert dotted with cactus, some brush plants and an occasional mesquite tree.

Very little grew in Tombstone. Even people seemed more likely to die than grow here. Gunfights erupted on the town streets almost daily, and if the outlaws weren't killing each other, they were swinging from the gallows in the yard of the County Court House. Mary longed for the peaceful people and the deep green hills and gardens of her home.

When Henry came home that night, his kind face was beaming with happiness. He carefully brought three large packages into their room, one at a time. Mary caught sight of Scottish postage stamps and her mother's handwriting and ran to get a knife to cut the heavy twine. Together they opened the sturdy boxes and removed layer upon layer of padding. Suddenly, a fragrance filled the room, and Mary cried out with joy. Heather!

Pulling away the last tissue, Mary saw the familiar bluish-green foliage of a heather plant. She pressed her cheek against the dry branches and breathed in the scent of her childhood, her loved ones and her home.

Beneath the heather they discovered two purple columbines and a hardy primrose. The second package held dozens of bulbs: tulips, narcissus and daffodils. And in the third, Mary found her favorite: the 'Lady Banksia' rose she had planted as a child. Mary dug her fingers into the crumbling Scottish soil, and her tears fell on the dusty canes.

In the next few days, she and Henry planted most of the flowers on their land. But Mary gave the 'Lady Banksia' rose to her new friend, Amelia Adamson, and they planted it together in the backyard of the Cochise House. It grew— superbly.

* * *

Today, well over one hundred years later, Amelia's rose is not only flourishing, it is officially the World's Largest Rose Tree. *Ripley's Believe It or Not* gave it that title in 1937, and the *Guinness Book of World Records* has confirmed it since. Still growing in its original spot behind the Cochise House (now called the Rose Tree Inn), it covers an area of over 8,000 square feet, an unbelievable spread of branches and blooms supported by many pipes and posts. The trunk of the tree is over twelve feet around!

The Rose Tree blooms just once a year, with delicate and fragrant white blossoms. Usually the buds start opening in the middle of March, and it continues to flower throughout the month of April, raining a carpet of blossoms onto the patio beneath the tree.

Thousands of visitors from around the world visit the Rose Tree every year and can hardly believe their eyes. They marvel at the Tree's amazing size and ancient grandeur. And when they hear the story of its origin, they realize that this rose may never die, its roots are sunk so deep in love—the love of a young bride who gave up her cherished homeland for her husband, the love of a mother who reached out to comfort her distant daughter, and the love of a woman whose joy was not complete until she shared it with her friend.

Cindy Buck

The Man Who Lived in a Box

Treat a person as he is, and he will remain as he is. Treat him as he could be, and he will become what he should be.

Jimmy Johnson

MacDuff was his name. Tom MacDuff, although I never heard him called by his first name.

My mother met him at the day-labor pickup corner down on Third Street near the river. He was the leanest, saddest, hungriest-looking of the men standing there, anxiously watching as she slowed her car and parked.

MacDuff was not the first man to approach Mother's car, where she sat looking over the small crowd. He simply was not able to move that quickly. But when she called out that she needed a man to dig gardens for several mornings only, the others fell back. They wanted full days of work.

MacDuff then came forward. He doffed his weather-stained felt hat and stood holding it nervously in his hands. When he spoke, his voice was low and he coughed between sentences.

"I can dig, ma'am," he told her. "I dug lots of foxholes and trenches in the war."

"Do you know anything about gardening?" Mother asked.

"Not yet, ma'am," he answered, with a slight crinkle at the corners of his eyes.

That hint of humor and willingness to learn touched my mother, along with the sad condition of the old army coat and broken boots MacDuff wore that chilly autumn morning.

"I'm the city landscaper, with a tiny budget. I can pay you only minimum wages," she cautioned him.

He accepted, adding that he had recently been in a veteran's hospital with pneumonia and was not yet able to work a full day. As Mother drove them toward the new park, she wondered if her new worker would be strong enough for even a full morning's work.

When they passed a bakery perfuming the morning air with the smell of freshly baked bread, MacDuff inhaled deeply.

"Have you had any breakfast?" Mother asked.

"No, ma'am," came the shy, quiet response.

Mother pulled abruptly to the curb, got out and went into the bakery, returning with a bag of doughnuts and two containers of coffee.

"I'll have mine later. You eat now," she told her passenger.

"Much obliged, ma'am."

She pretended not to see tears spring to the man's eyes as he tore into a doughnut, almost swallowing it whole.

That was the start of a working partnership and loyal friendship that would last twenty years.

When MacDuff failed to show up for work later that week, my mother went looking for him. Another laborer told her to check down by the river. She was shocked to discover MacDuff and a dozen other homeless men living in boxes under a bridge over the Arkansas River! Adrift since separation from the army at the end of World War II, they were in poor health and untrained for available work. Local police tolerated the shack community as long as there was no trouble. Few knew of its hidden existence. When the weather grew cold, some of the men would "disturb the peace" enough to get themselves thrown into a warm jail. There was no town shelter for such unfortunate people.

Mother didn't have a big budget, but she had a big heart. She scrounged up more funds, and MacDuff's first days planting bulbs were soon extended to full-time employment. Many long days, he and my mother worked side by side.

It was not easy for either. Mother was a small woman with back problems that were a forerunner to osteoporosis, but she had a mental backbone second to none!

For a long time, MacDuff did not really have the strength for a full day of arduous work, and he suffered from frequent colds. He missed quite a few days of work. And several times Mother saved his life by rushing him to the hospital when pneumonia struck again. She was patient with MacDuff's absences, and his progress was steady.

The day Mother hired him marked a new beginning for MacDuff. He assured her that the piano crate under the bridge was better than what many homeless folks could call home. But it was with immense gratitude that he accepted a loan to pay rent for a real room in December. It was a tiny room in a boarding house next to the railroad tracks, but a giant step for a man who had been driven almost to despair. He repaid my mother gradually by working in her own yard in his spare time. She gave him the bicycle I no longer rode, and that was his transportation to work for several years.

Day by day, chore by chore, she taught him horticulture. MacDuff was an eager student. Day by day, too, as his life stabilized, his strength improved. When spring came and those daffodils bloomed and were admired by visitors, MacDuff was as proud of them as Mother was.

The city provided mowing crews and equipment operators to clear more garden areas. With MacDuff's help, Mother established great sweeps of iris and daylily beds. A fountain was added with formal flower beds around it. MacDuff learned the Latin names of all the flowers, shrubs and trees in the park.

Over the years Mother often wrote to me of improvements in MacDuff's life. He moved into a tiny apartment, and he managed to buy a truck. He joined a church and married a widow with children. Almost the day after the wedding, Mother learned, he began planting a garden in their yard and teaching his stepchildren the proper names of flowers.

His happiest moments were when visitors from out of town came to the park to see the gardens with their fine beds of flowers, some of which Mother and MacDuff had hybridized. MacDuff would stop work, lean on his hoe or rake, and listen to the strangers' compliments. He was delighted if someone asked him a question about the plantings, proud that he could answer.

Mother felt a deep affection for MacDuff. "We were a blessing to each other," she told me, "because I had so little to work with and yet was expected to make a park."

And MacDuff, though a man of few words, was devoted to Mother. Theirs was a friendship born of flowers and the gift of dignity.

Marcia E. Brown

The Tulip Tradition

You can make your world so much larger simply by acknowledging everyone else's.

Marie Laskas

It's very difficult to grow tulips in Southern California. But each year for nineteen years, Rae Viney planted 800 bulbs in her front yard. As children, we'd go by the house, and Mrs. Viney would hobble out and wave her cane at us.

"Come see the tulips!" she'd call cheerfully, and we'd find ourselves standing in a sea of colors, gaping at wave on wave of those rare blooms.

Then, just before my husband and I moved in across the street, Mrs. Viney died. So did all her tulips. Although they are technically perennials, tulips rot quickly in our warm climate. It was only Mrs. Viney's persistence that had kept her colorful spring tradition alive year after year.

Fortunately, the house was bought by Helen and Jack Crawford. Helen, an avid gardener, decided to continue the tradition, but on an even grander scale.

On the day after Thanksgiving, 1973, we looked out our dining-room windows and saw Helen, Jack and their two children digging in the garden. With no idea of what to expect, our family trooped across to help.

My husband and I were shown how to "double-dig," removing the topsoil before turning over and fertilizing the ground underneath. Our young son Greg learned to set the bulbs point-up, four inches apart, and how to step without treading on them. Only someone with small feet could plant in the corners between the hedges, so Greg was made to feel his contribution was essential. When we began to tire, Helen brought out tea and cookies for everyone, and we went back to work willingly.

After four hours, 2,400 tulip bulbs were in the ground. Invigorated by the good company and a task well done, we promised we'd be back to plant the next year.

In the spring, we were stunned by the overwhelming beauty of our labors. Those 2,400 tall, fat tulips blossomed in every color imaginable.

They filled the large front garden, framed by flowering dogwood and other spring flowers. Cars came from miles around to drive slowly past the incredible sight. Adults roamed up and down the brick path in awe, and children in their Easter best came to pose for photos among the blooms.

At the 1974 planting, our new daughter Paula joined us in her baby stroller. Eight years later, baby Matt attended his first planting, watching everything from his jump chair. We've participated every year since.

We bring our friends, our children bring their friends, and many neighbors turn out. The Friday after Thanksgiving has become a neighborhood tradition, with plenty of work for adults and children of all ages.

A few autumns ago, Greg was out of college and working in London. He called long-distance from England to apologize for missing planting day. After all, he'd been part of it from the start. With that one exception, no one in our family has missed a planting day in twenty-six years. Through babies, college, marriage, travel and life, no matter how widely we are scattered, we have a bond with that November Friday.

Yes, it's about tulips and the community, but it's really about establishing family traditions. Life moves so fast. Often, we get cut off from the rituals that were meaningful to our ancestors, so we must invent our own. Years ago, we went across the street just to lend a hand.

We returned home far richer than we ever realized.

Doris Meyer

The Golden Girls

There is no security quite as comfortable and undemanding as the kind you feel among old friends.

Peter Bodo

Rose and I met when we were in our mid-twenties. I had invited her daughter to my daughter's third birthday party, and Rose came along. We scrutinized each other and assessed the obvious differences. She was a smoker; I wasn't. I dressed conservatively; she didn't. She wore a long, black flowing wig whenever she tired of her short frosted hair; I wore the same "flip" hairstyle for years. But we became best friends.

Despite our differences, we wore a path from my house to hers (sometimes in our fuzzy robes), borrowing sugar, guzzling coffee, sharing baked goods and details of our lives. For twelve years, we went to yard sales, fast-food restaurants, playgrounds and school events together.

Rose and I stayed best friends during tough times, as well. Both of us had turbulent marriages. One summer, both marriages finally fell apart. Coincidentally, Rose's sister Millie ended her marriage about the same time, and so did Rose's childhood friend, Judy.

The four of us became known as The Golden Girls. We discovered a neighborhood club with an outdoor patio, and we spent that summer sipping soda and dancing together to old-time rock and roll.

After that summer, we calmed down a bit. As we created new lives for ourselves, we saw less of each other. Eventually, Rose and I attended each other's weddings, and we visited together at family gatherings and holiday celebrations. Each time, it was as if we'd never been apart.

At my daughter's baby shower, I noticed that Rose's one-of-a-kind laugh seemed hoarse. She told me she'd had a persistent cough for weeks. Soon, diagnostic tests indicated a mass in her lung. Exploratory surgery revealed a large inoperable malignancy. I visited Rose in the intensive care unit afterward.

"I love you," I told my friend, realizing it was the first time I had said the words aloud.

"I love you, too," she said groggily, sealing our bond.

After Rose recovered from surgery, I took her for radiation treatment. We held hands in the waiting room. When our eyes met, they brimmed with tears. On the drive home, we talked about this life and the afterlife. And we talked about a story we'd both read many, many years before, about two friends, one of whom was terminally ill.

"You'll remember that story, won't you?" Rose asked.

"I will," I promised.

The Golden Girls reunited. Millie, Judy and I spent countless hours with Rose. We took her shopping and dining. We humored her when her medication gave her hallucinations. When she became incapacitated, we visited her at home in shifts. I fluffed her pillows, brought her doughnuts, massaged her feet and colored in coloring books with her.

Rose spent the last week of her life in the hospital, heavily sedated, surrounded by loved ones. At fifty-one, her breathing ceased and our mourning began.

A year followed, and I thought of Rose often. One cold November morning, as I left for work, I saw something pink protruding from a drift of decaying leaves. I cleared the debris and gasped in disbelief at a flower bud. During the summer I had planted a tiny, three-inch potted azalea, hoping it would grow into a bush. It hadn't grown at all and had never flowered. But here on this frosty Missouri morning, with the rest of the garden killed by a hard frost, the azalea bloomed.

I thought about Rose all day, and that afternoon, I called her daughter.

"Denise, can you come by after work?" I asked. "I have a surprise from your mom."

When I got home, I checked the azalea again. The tiny pink bud had opened completely and blossomed to the size of a carnation.

That evening, Denise came to my door. She looked just like Rose.

"You're not going to believe this," I said. I told Denise about the conversation Rose and I had had after her radiation therapy.

"Twenty years ago, your mom and I read a story about two best friends. One was terminally ill. She vowed to make a flower bloom in winter to prove there was an afterlife. Your mom and I discussed that story and made a pact that day."

I led Denise to the backyard and showed her my azalea, blooming in winter. Denise and I laughed, embraced, stared in disbelief and cried tears of joy.

"This couldn't have come at a better time," Denise said, wiping her eyes. "It's been almost a year since Mom passed away. You've taken away so much of my sadness. Thank you."

During the next week I watched in amazement as three more flowers bloomed fully. I called Millie and Judy and told them about the plant I nicknamed The Golden Girls, with one blossom for each of us. We rejoiced at the message from our friend. Incredibly, the plant thrived for two weeks, surviving snow, wind and chill. Then, the flowers gradually withered and died, completing the cycle of life. But they left behind a vivid memory and a message for all us Golden Girls that true friendship never dies.

Linda O'Connell

Madeleine's Wheelbarrow

What is a friend? A single soul dwelling in two bodies.

Aristotle

I've always known Madeleine.

We were both born and raised in the same small Alaska town. But it wasn't until we both found ourselves married with small children and living in the same city that we became best friends.

Every morning as soon as the older children were off to school, we'd call each other and talk over the day's plans. In the summer, we spent many days in our gardens together while the children played. At Madeleine's, we picked countless weeds off the bank in her backyard. We'd load them in her big green wheelbarrow—along with a child or two. Then we'd wheel the pile over to the other side of the bank and dump out the wheelbarrow load—taking the kids out first!

In 1996, we had just finished putting in our spring gardens. Suddenly, we weren't thinking about gardens anymore, but survival. I had been diagnosed with a rare form of cancer. Immediate surgery was my only option. I was only thirty-four, with two young children. My husband Pat and I were numb with shock.

It was Madeleine who stepped in and steadied us. While Pat, my mother and my sisters concentrated on me, Madeleine made sure the everyday tasks were taken care of. Efficient and organized, she handled everything from meals to play dates for the children.

She even thought of the garden. Already it was weedy and overgrown. She knew how frustrated I'd be, trying to recover from major surgery, staring out at a tangled jungle and too weak to do anything about it. Madeleine gathered a team of friends, and together they snipped and mowed, pruned and planted. I came home to a shining house, a full refrigerator and a beautiful garden.

Madeleine and I adjusted our routine of friendship around my slow recovery and a steady stream of doctor's appointments. The surgery appeared to be working. Life went on.

Then a year later, it stopped.

Madeleine was dead. On a bright, sunny summer afternoon, my best friend was killed in a tragic boating accident. She left a bewildered husband and three little boys, the youngest only three. The sudden, brutal loss shredded everyone who knew her—her family, her church, her friends. Our lives were dazed.

A month later, the doctors found my cancer again.

The double blow of Madeleine's death and the recurring cancer shook my faith in nearly everything. I felt sick in mind, in body, in heart.

In the gray days of October, my family and friends gathered to help me. They were as loving and supportive as anyone could wish, but I was painfully aware of who was missing.

"Try to relax," the nurses said. "Think of something happy." But the chemotherapy was agonizing. I spent days hunched over like an old woman, my muscles too cramped from vomiting to let me sit up.

When the chemotherapy treatments finally ended five months later, I told myself I would never be so weak again—spiritually or physically. I began working out, reviving my battered body. With the help of time and friends, I began to revive my battered faith. And I began to see Madeleine, not as the friend I no longer had, but as a friend who would be with me always. I pictured her watching us all from heaven. I pictured her wheeling her green wheelbarrow around and making a beautiful garden even more beautiful. *God must really be organized now*, I thought.

Gray autumn came again. The cancer was back. But this time was different. This time, I was ready. Madeleine was with me again.

Once a week for twelve weeks, I lay in the hospital, watching the chemo move through the IV tube. "Try to relax," the nurses said again. "Think of something happy."

So this time, I pictured Madeleine walking through heaven with her big green wheelbarrow. I pictured all the prayers my family and friends had for me, floating around like bits of light. Madeleine gathered up each prayer, one by one, and put them in her wheelbarrow. Then, as the chemo started dripping in, I imagined her tipping the wheelbarrow over me. The white lights of love and prayer floated down and into my body. I became filled with a white, starry light that protected me from harm and cleansed the "bad" spots.

Every time I envisioned the wheelbarrow and its load of prayers flooding my body, I knew I was not alone. I had my husband, my children, my parents and sisters and cousins. And an angel for a best friend.

It's autumn again. This year, I have no cancer.

Jenny Gore Dwyer

3

LOVE IN BLOOM

Love is a fruit in season at all times and within reach of every hand.

Mother Teresa

Twins Entwined

"Diane! Marsha! You girls get on in here. Supper's on the table!"

My sister and I glanced up, quickly and silently signaling each other for a race to the back door. My grandmother stood there, one hand on her hip and the other shielding her eyes from the summer sun. She was heaven in a housedress. She smelled of Jergen's Lotion, chocolate-covered cherries and TubeRose snuff. We worshipped her.

I won the race, almost tackling Nannie in the doorway.

"My Lord, hon, look at you!" she scolded as she pulled me back for inspection. Then her gaze turned to Marsha, who had finally reached the steps. "Now look at your sister. How come she looks like a little lady?"

As we sat down at the dinner table, I shot a look at Marsha. We were twins, joined at the soul from the moment we took our first breaths. We were supposed to be the same, but we weren't—not by a long shot. Marsha loved lace, velvet, patent leather shoes and all of the things girls were supposed to like. She could sit for hours drawing paper dolls, designing their elaborate wardrobes and cutting out all of the patterns with precision.

I was a tomboy. I had a passion for trees and had conquered each and every one in our neighborhood. No boy could climb higher or faster.

I closed my eyes and started to pray that Marsha might be more like me. But then it occurred to me that we were okay with who we each were. I made the mud pies, and she decorated them with pebbles and rose petals. We found ways to work around our differences.

Years passed. We both grew up, married and took on the trappings of responsibility. No more climbed trees or paper dolls.

Somehow during those years, my sweet, prim, spotless sister became a gardener. The child who would never jump into a rain puddle or pat out a mud pie now reveled in the earth. But I, the one who had practically eaten the outdoors every day, shunned it. I was an adult now, after all.

I would shake my head in disbelief when I saw her bury her hands in the soil. When she rattled off the names of her roses, I'd roll my eyes. "I'll never relate to this, Marsha. A rose is a rose!"

So many other things taxed our childhood connection. Finally a time came when it seemed as though our special bond could never be repaired or regained. I had been divorced for years, struggling to raise my son on my own and bouncing from one relationship to the next. My sister was a counselor on a community hotline for battered women. She saw the signs in my life way before I did. She told me—but I didn't want to hear. By the time I realized that she spoke the truth, I had made her the enemy. I ignored the fact that the man that I was living with was methodically and systematically chipping away at my self, at my own identity.

Things got worse. Each day, my only goal was survival. My soul went underground. Finally, one morning while I was getting ready for work, I looked into the mirror and didn't recognize the person staring back at me. Something inside of me snapped. I had to find a way out or die. I called my sister. Although we only lived a few blocks from one another, it had been four years since we had last spoken.

Marsha came to me without hesitation. We agreed that I had to move out, yet I was nearly penniless. I started spending every spare moment looking for a place to live, all the while worrying how I could afford it.

One particular night, after I'd just finished another disappointing search through the real estate ads, my sister called.

"Get dressed, kiddo. I'm coming to get you."

As we drove off in the darkness, I asked Tony, her husband, "What gives? Where are we going?"

All he said was, "Just wait, Diane, you'll see."

We turned down a street and pulled up in front of a house that looked just like the house my grandmother had once owned. It was in disrepair and looked as if it had been vacant for years. The yard was barren—just like my life, I thought. But the place called to me. I knew it was meant to be mine.

Tony worked with someone who knew the owner and persuaded him to rent the property to me, cheap. Marsha's only request was that I let the garden be hers. No problem. I had no interest in it.

On the move-in day, Marsha arrived with a plan showing the beds of the garden, but she said that the choice of plants would be mine.

"I don't know a daffodil from a clump of crab grass," I told her. "You figure it out."

"No," she replied. "This is your playground. The plants have to suit you, not me." I thought she was nuts, but I went along.

We started the garden just days after I moved in. I went to the nursery with her and tried picking by color. I'd point to something and Marsha would shake her head and pass it by, or smile and put it in the cart. It amazed me that you had to buy soil! I was totally ignorant of the process. I thought that things just grew!

Together, we loaded everything in the car and headed for home. We chatted about our purchases and joked about my gardening ignorance. As we pulled into the driveway of my "new" home, I suddenly realized I had not been frightened or unhappy that day—not once.

And then something more happened. There is a moment for each of us that transforms us—a moment just as mundane as any other, but a moment that will forever be etched in your mind just the same. Mine came as I tugged the huge bag of soil over to Marsha. She was on her knees, weeding out a bed we were planting.

"Open it and dump it right here," she demanded.

"The whole thing?" I asked.

"Yep," she said. "The whole darn thing."

I took off my shoes and stood in the midst of the flower bed we were constructing. Then I slit the bag and let the soil cascade down my legs and bury my feet. As the sensation of the warm dirt traveled across my skin, something clicked in my memory: all of those days when I had gone barefoot as a child, and how much I had loved to feel mud squish between my toes. Suddenly I plopped down in the middle of all that dirt and looked directly at my sister.

She knew something had happened. As our eyes held, I reached down and picked up a handful of earth and made a perfect little pie. With tears in her eyes, she looked down beside her, picked up a small pebble and placed it right in the middle of my creation.

We sat there in the warm earth, two grown women streaked with dirt and tears, awed by the love that had never really left us. At that moment, we knew without words that we had come full circle. Nothing on this earth would ever separate us again.

Now as I weed in the fragrant peace of my garden, I realize that there is still a lot of work to be done—in my garden and in my life. But thanks to a sister who wouldn't let go, we're growing just fine, both my garden and I.

Diane C. Daniels

"I don't get it—what's in it for her?"

Accidental Blessings

Challenges make you discover things about yourself that you never really knew.

Cicely Tyson

I was in the hospital mending from a bad car accident when I met Joe. We hit it off right away. It was a cold March in Georgia, but my heart was warmed by this handsome, loving man. He was recovering from the loss of his left hand in an accident a month earlier.

A couple of weeks after we met, I became anxious about being away from home. I had ordered all sorts of fruit trees, shrubs and flowers from various catalogs. They'd be arriving in the mail any day, and I knew they wouldn't be safe just sitting outside. I had to get them planted!

"I've got to get out of this hospital and back home to put in my garden," I told Joe. "I've got so much to do!"

"I'll help," he offered immediately. Neither of us stopped to think that Joe no longer had his left hand.

Two weeks later I was discharged from the hospital. Sure enough, I was greeted by box after box of plants. Joe called that evening to say hello. I told him what had been waiting for me.

The next morning Joe called again. He had spoken with his doctor and been granted a day pass away from the hospital.

"If you still want help with the garden, I'll be glad to come over," Joe said.

"I'd love some help," I answered with relief. "It'll be a big job!"

Saturday morning I was in the yard getting organized when Joe arrived with a big smile on his face. I showed him where the shovel was, and I grabbed an armful of fruit trees.

When I got to the section of property where the trees were to be planted, my eager helper was all ready to get to work. All of a sudden, I stopped and focused on Joe's left arm. It was at that moment that it struck me what a challenge this was going to be for Joe.

"Don't worry," said Joe, as if reading my mind. "I had my therapist bandage my arm extra well so I won't get dirt on it. Now, where do you want these trees planted?"

After I showed him the layout, Joe wrapped his left arm around the shovel handle, grabbed the handle end with his right hand and started digging.

By sunset, Joe and I were planting the last shrub. Both of us were exhausted and hungry. We cleaned up and headed out to a nice restaurant.

Over dinner, we talked and laughed and had a wonderful time. Then Joe got really quiet. "I didn't think I could do it," he said softly.

I looked at him, puzzled.

Joe raised his left arm. "I didn't think I could do it," he said, as a beautiful smile spread across his face. "The end of my arm is really throbbing now, but I feel great! In fact, I've never felt better in my life!"

There is truth in the saying that "gardening is the best medicine." After that day, Joe often came to work in the garden with me. The exercise strengthened his arm, and he was out of the hospital much sooner than the doctors expected. Not only that, Joe fell in love with gardening. He was hooked for life. And best of all, we fell in love with each other. We were married six months later.

Today, Joe's even more passionate about gardening than I am. Sometimes I catch him pulling weeds in public flower beds! Our marriage, too, grows stronger every day.

I often think about how much we might have missed if we hadn't both been in the hospital and I hadn't been so eager to get my plants in the ground. Joe and I met by accident—or by *accidents.* But life's funny, isn't it? Those accidents brought us the best blessings of our lives.

Joanne Bryan

First Penny

*To love and be loved is to feel the sun from both
sides.*

David Viscott, M.D.

My husband and I had birthdays six days apart. We
always celebrated on a day in between by giving ourselves a joint present. One year we decided to buy a rosebush. So, on a cold, blustery January day, we set off
eagerly for the nursery to make our selection. After much
thought, we chose a gorgeous, velvety, deep burgundy
rose named 'Mr. Lincoln.' With tall, straight stems, it's as
stately as our sixteenth president. It was sure to do well in
our Northern California climate. And since my husband's
name was Abe, we thought it a good match.

We followed the planting directions and by early July, the
'Mr. Lincoln' bush was loaded with lush burgundy blooms.
I cut bouquets for most of July and well into August.

Years earlier, my husband and I had started a tradition.
We loved to take early morning walks together. On our
walks, the first one to spot a penny could keep the coin for
the day's good luck. At the end of the day, the "First

Penny" was deposited in a small crystal dish. When there were enough pennies in the dish, we'd go out for an ice cream treat for two.

Years passed, happy years when the roses bloomed and the copper coffer grew.

Then, it was over. On a July second, when 'Mr. Lincoln' was in full bloom, my own Abe died. There would be no more walks, no more talks and no more First Penny contests. I went to the garden that day, cut a bountiful bouquet of the roses and tearfully closed a chapter of my life.

Or so I thought.

A decade passed and on another July second, I set out on my solitary walk. As I passed our rose garden, I thrilled to the bounty of blossoms on the 'Mr. Lincoln' bush. My walk took to me to a nearby park, and, as I came up behind the bandstand, there on the path, shining in the morning sunlight, was a bright copper penny! When I got home, I took the long-unused crystal dish out of the cupboard and put my First Penny in it.

Each morning in July after that day, I took a walk and found a First Penny—sometimes shiny bright and sometimes tarnished—but always there. I began to look for it eagerly. I sensed that a countdown was underway, though I didn't know to what. One penny, two pennies, three pennies—more. At the end of July, thirty copper coins were in the crystal dish.

August first brought me the shining realization that the pennies were counting the days till our wedding anniversary on the eighteenth. If I found one every day between the anniversary of Abe's passing on July second and our wedding anniversary on August eighteenth, I would have forty-eight pennies.

Suddenly, I had a thought. Could it be? I counted out the years. Yes, it was true: This would be our forty-eighth wedding anniversary!

I'm not a superstitious person, but I got hooked. The small ritual became a consuming passion. Eighteen days until our anniversary! I scarcely slept at night waiting for the dawn and First Penny. I found the penny on the path in the park, in front of the convenience store, in the parking lot at the mall, and in front of the grocery store. Not a day was missed.

August eighteenth arrived. There were forty-seven pennies in the crystal dish. Would there be that last forty-eighth coin?

On the afternoon of our anniversary, I drove to the supermarket to pick up some groceries. On the way back to my car, I looked down and there it was: First Penny, shimmering brightly in the late-morning sun!

But there was more. When I returned to my car, there, on the hood, lay a single, long-stemmed 'Mr. Lincoln' rose!

I picked it up reverently and pressed it to my lips, allowing the tears to flow unashamedly. How could this be? How had he done this? As I stared at the lovely flower in amazement, a young man closed the trunk of the neighboring car and walked up to me. "Oh," he said. "Sorry! That's for my wife. It's our anniversary."

"That's quite all right," I said, smiling at him through my tears. "Thank you. Thank you so very much." I handed him the rose, and he smiled at me.

"You must be thinking of someone special," he said gently.

"Yes," I replied, "and he's thinking of me."

Bernice Bywater

Keeping the Harvest

Never lose sight of the fact that old age needs so little but needs that little so much.

Margaret Willour

He rounded the corner where cornstalks still stood, tattered heroes of the garden patch. Late-afternoon sunlight filtered through a canopy of bare branches, laying down a grid of shadows. Underfoot, the crunch of dry, caramel-colored leaves sounded the music of a Colorado autumn.

It was the season for "after harvest." Or, what Emma called their "time of plenty." A time to count their many blessings. Long after the last sun-ripened tomato was picked, the last of the autumn raspberries eaten and the garden put to bed for the winter, his wife always insisted on seeking out the later gifts of nature.

Fred knew the best places to start. Hadn't he searched and gathered on every square foot of this property for forty-four years now? Planted it? Tended it? If Emma were here, she'd be out here with him.

But Emma wasn't here. So he would do alone what they had always rejoiced in doing together.

At the grape arbor, Fred took out his pocketknife and cut away aged vines, careful to take only the overgrowth. When he had enough, he tucked and plaited, wove and wrapped, shaping the supple lengths to form a wreath.

At the lip of their hand-dug pond, Fred pawed through the disheveled heads of cattails. Finding two still nappy and whole, he snapped them from their stalks and laced them through one side of the circle.

At the fence line, Fred clipped a few twigs of juniper berries and harvested two feathery plumes from the towering pampas grass. Thick fingers knew automatically where to put them, how to secure them.

He paused beneath a flaming mountain ash. Its clumps of jack-o'-lantern orange berries added a festive touch. Satisfied, he studied the wreath, inspecting it for soundness. For balance. For beauty.

The drive to the Alzheimer's unit was short and pleasant. Humming under his breath, Fred nodded a greeting at the nurses' station and walked into the day room.

Emma stared unseeingly out the bank of windows while her veined hand plucked rhythmically at her blouse. Fred laid his offering on a round table and leaned to kiss her.

"Look what I made today, sweetheart. It's 'after harvest,' and the property is brimming with all your favorite things." Fred pointed to the circle. Emma's bleached blue eyes focused on the wreath.

"Just see how thick and sound the grapevines are now, Emma. Remember how you insisted we plant those spindly things the very first year we moved to the farm?" Stilling her hand with his own, he guided her fingers around the broad circle.

"Why, looky here. Pampas grass. And cattails, two of them. One for you and one for me." Her tentative finger traced the velvety lengths.

"And, oh, sweetie, these beauties are clustered thick on the mountain ash. Nearly had to fight off the grackles to get to them this year!"

Emma was smiling. Fred squeezed her hand and grinned back. If she couldn't tromp through the seasons herself, then he would bring those blessings to her. After all, it *was* a "time of plenty"—plenty of memories.

And Fred had gathered enough for both of them.

Carol McAdoo Rehme

Say It with . . . a Rhododendron

All married couples should learn the art of battle as they should learn the art of making love.

Ann Landers

I read somewhere that starting a new job is one of life's most stressful events. So when my husband began behaving in a less-than-charming manner after he'd moved to a new workplace, I tried to remember that the source of his tension was probably elsewhere. I tried to hunker down and weather the unpleasantness until it ran its course.

I failed.

Eventually, one night at bedtime, he asked me if I was angry. We began to hash it out.

"Tell me, would you behave toward the people at work the way you've been acting toward me lately?" I asked.

"It's funny you say that," he answered. "Lately I've been thinking that they're a lot easier to deal with than you are."

"Maybe that's because your biggest criticism at work is only 'I think this paragraph needs revision' instead of 'I'm completely disappointed in everything about you.'" My voice broke. We continued trading accusations the way tired people at night should never do. Finally we went to bed, saddened and exhausted, with nothing resolved.

The next morning, we both acted carefully cordial. Our argument had succeeded in airing our tensions—only to have them hover oppressively all around us. It was a relief when the afternoon came and I got a chance to be alone; my husband was driving our daughter to a birthday party. It was far enough away that he was planning to wait there until it was over.

I gloomed around by myself for the next few hours. If being angry was bad, this uneasy peace was even worse. I dreaded his return and the resumption of our polite détente. Finally came the sound of the car in the driveway. Then my daughter stuck her head in the door and announced gleefully, "Daddy's got something for you!"

It is a historical element of our relationship, harking back to our courtship days: My husband will bring me flowers after his most dire offenses, even if he's not clear just what his offenses were. Yes, maybe it's a little trite, the typical way a male seeks forgiveness, but there it is. In times of romantic uncertainty, he is a man with a bouquet.

But this time he didn't bring just flowers. No, he struggled through the doorway with a large, balled-and-burlapped rhododendron, in full bloom. I couldn't help feeling a growing sense of amusement.

"I went with a shrub," he said with twinkling eyes. "I thought repeated flowering might be wise in the long run, considering how difficult I can be to live with." Then he added, "I hope you know I love you."

The hug that followed was warm and healing. I felt his embrace and, more important, felt the ease between us return.

The next day, we gave the rhododendron a careful planting out in the garden, tucking it into peat moss and compost. It has thrived, and when in bloom inspires many a knowing smile between my husband and myself. It is our special rhododendron, a fitting symbol of the romance between a gardener and her mate. Both the flowers and our love grow more beautiful as each year passes.

Did I say that flowers are trite? Well, maybe it's my turn to be wrong.

Martine Caselli

Girls Like Roses

Like people, plants respond to extra attention.

H. Peter Loewer

Girls like roses. Todd liked girls. Therefore, to get girls, Todd must have roses. This logic launched my thirteen-year-old son into the world of gardening.

"Dad, how much do roses cost?" Todd asked one day.

"That depends, son," his father said, lowering his newspaper. "Do you want a plant, or do you just want a rose to give to someone special—like your mom?"

"I dunno," Todd said, giving nothing away. "What do both of them cost?"

"Well, you can go to a florist and pay anywhere from two dollars on up, if that's what you want."

Todd did the math. Two dollars a rose! If you gave a girl a dozen roses, that'd be twenty-four bucks! That's a lot of money for a girl. Even for a girl named Michelle.

"But if you planted a rosebush," his dad continued, "you could get roses all season."

"How much does a rosebush cost?" Todd asked.

"They can be pretty expensive, but I'll tell you what: If you want to grow roses, I'll help with the cost and teach you how to care for them. But you'll have to do the work."

Todd thought about it. How much work was a girl worth, even Michelle, who rode her bike by his house every day? He thought again of how she always waved and said, "Hi, Todd," and how her laughter made his throat tighten. "All right, I guess," he said, but he didn't look his dad directly in the eye.

So Todd and his dad went rose shopping. They picked out three rosebushes and his dad taught him how to plant and care for them. Todd fertilized, powdered and fussed over them. They grew and grew. One day he noticed rosebuds forming. "Hey, Dad! Come look what I've got! I've got roses starting! I'm going to have tons of roses!"

His dad laughed at his enthusiasm. "That's great, Todd. Now, you won't really have tons of roses, not the first year anyway. But if you keep taking such good care of your plants, you'll be sure to have some."

One day soon after, Michelle and her friend rode by. "Hi, Todd!" Michelle called out. "What are you doing?"

The perfect opportunity! "Oh, I'm just going to check on my roses," Todd said.

"What do you mean 'your roses'?" Michelle asked, smiling. Gee, she was pretty.

"Can we see them?" Michelle's friend asked.

"Sure, if you want to," Todd said, and they walked to the rosebushes in the backyard.

"Oh, come on!" Michelle teased. "You didn't grow these by yourself!"

"Yes, I did," Todd replied.

Michelle's friend looked at Todd with respect. She was quiet and didn't say much. She left that up to Michelle. Michelle kept teasing Todd, though.

"What are you going to do with them? I bet you're saving them for someone, aren't you? Who you going to give them to, Todd?"

Todd felt himself starting to blush. "Nobody, really. I just like to grow them. Do you want one?"

"Sure," she said, "why not? Don't you want one, too?" Michelle asked her friend.

Todd wasn't sure he liked Michelle offering her friend one of his flowers, but what could he say? He took out his pocketknife and selected a big, beautiful red rose for Michelle and a yellow rose for her friend. The friend smiled and carefully wrapped her rose in a napkin she had in her pocket. Michelle laughed. She took her rose, pointed it at Todd's nose and waved it about. "Who were you really saving them for, Todd?" she asked.

The large, special rose flopped up and down in front of Todd. Michelle was still talking, but he didn't see her. All he could see was his rose bobbing up and down one inch in front of his nose. Didn't she have any respect for his rose? Those roses were a lot of work!

Michelle's face seemed distorted to Todd. Horrid sounds were coming out of it—her laughter. His chest felt tight. A petal fell off the rose. It continued to wave up and down in front of him.

Michelle's friend spoke. "Thank you for the beautiful rose, Todd," she said. "I better hurry home now so I can put it in some water."

Michelle and her friend started to leave. Michelle was still talking and flapping her rose around. Todd looked at her friend as she gently held the wrapped rose in her hand, carefully got on her bike and turned to go.

"Hey," Todd called, "what's your name?"

Janice Hasselius

"Nice tattoo!"

Romeo Sets the Stage

Flowers are love's truest language.

Park Benjamin

As a flight attendant for a major airline, I've had many memorable moments attending to passengers' special needs. Most of the memories bring a smile to my lips. Some make me grin from ear to ear.

My all-time favorite occurred a few years ago on a Friday-night flight to Denver. A passenger asked the flight attendants if we could do him a favor. The young man's girlfriend was meeting him at the airport in Denver, and he was planning to propose. He had brought with him ninety-nine long-stemmed red roses and one long-stemmed white rose. Nestled between the petals of the single white rose was an engagement ring. Our Romeo wanted ninety-nine passengers to deplane before him, each handing his girlfriend a red rose. He would come out last, carrying the white rose with the ring, and propose to her.

We made an announcement explaining the gentleman's plan and asked for volunteers. Immediately, hands waved and people called out. Everyone wanted to be a part of the romantic event! The lucky ninety-nine were thrilled to be entrusted with a rose. Throughout the flight, the young man went through the cabin showing the engagement ring and receiving congratulations. Many passengers shared stories of their own engagement, wedding or honeymoon, and waves of laughter rang through the cabin. The warm wishes and feelings of joy were overwhelming.

When we arrived in Denver, the passengers deplaned in a buzz of excitement, and the crew followed our Romeo out of the jetbridge. There, under a mountain of roses, we found Juliet—and a planeful of passengers patiently waiting to spy on this special moment. Romeo took the roses from his sweetheart's arms, laid them on a chair, dropped to one knee and professed his love. Then he handed her his single white rose. Through her tears, she said "Yes!" and the audience broke into cheers. Cameras flashed and best wishes were given.

Truly, all the world loves a lover!

Jill LaBoy
Submitted by Dianne Janis Wight

Unspoken Love

Saying "I love you" is a conversation, not a message.

Douglas Stone

When it comes to flowery speech or emotional expression, my husband, Dave, is a man of few words. That was one of the first things I learned about him when we married thirty-one years ago.

One of the next things I discovered is that Dave has little use for rosebushes. He had no second thoughts about yanking out mature plants to widen the driveway when we purchased our home. To him, roses represent hours of pruning and spraying, mulching and fertilizing. As far as he's concerned, a lawn mower and hedge trimmers are all you need for the perfect garden.

On the other hand, I treasure my roses. I consider every minute of their care well worth the beautiful, fragrant results.

One winter, I spent several evenings drooling over rose catalogs and planning a small garden. In the spring, I ordered several English varieties of self-rooted plants. I removed an area of sod, worked and reworked the ground, and planted the foot-long starts. During the heat of summer, I watered them daily. In my mind, I saw the fruits of my labor: masses of color and fragrance perfuming the air just outside my kitchen window.

But as it sometimes does, life spun us around and redirected our attention. In the fall, I began to have pain in my lower abdomen. At first I passed it off as nothing serious. But instead of getting better, the pain intensified. I went to see my doctor. He ordered tests; when the results came back, he asked to see me in his office right away. He also requested that Dave come with me.

Our worst fears became reality: colon cancer. I'd need surgery immediately. After a short recovery period, I'd undergo a six-month course of chemotherapy.

We cried . . . and prayed . . . and cried some more. We had one week to inform our family and friends. Then, trusting God and my doctors, I entered the hospital.

One month later, as I lay on the sofa still recuperating from surgery, Dave and I watched the TV weather forecast. It promised bitter cold temperatures and possible snow.

"Oh," I moaned to myself, "I never did get the roses mulched."

Dave just sat and watched the end of the forecast. Then, always the practical, on-top-of-things handyman, he said, "I'd better go winterize the outside faucets." He bundled up and headed toward the garage.

Fifteen minutes later, I hobbled to the kitchen for a glass of water. What I saw from the window brought tears to my eyes. There was Dave, bending over the roses, carefully heaping mulch around every plant.

I smiled and watched as my quiet husband "said" *I love you.* You know, sometimes words aren't needed at all.

Emily King

Tall Corn

Keep your face to the sunshine and you cannot see the shadows.

Helen Keller

Jim Carlton sat by his kitchen window. He gazed across the hot afternoon at the corn that grew like a rising hedge around his single-story Iowa farmhouse. This year's crop had jumped up tall and early. Now, only the corn that crowded around the edge of the home site was visible from the house.

His wife, Sue, stood at the sink washing fresh-picked carrots with a dribble of cold water. She eyed the sky uneasily as she worked, willing a cloud to appear. It had been twenty-seven days since the last rainfall, and that, to use Jim's words, had been hardly enough to knock the fuzz off a dandelion.

Jim sighed, looking at the blank, blue sky. "It's been too long. We're going to start losing corn pretty soon. And there's not a dang thing anyone can do about it except look for clouds and watch the leaves go soft. . . ." He paused. "But then, I guess worrying doesn't help any. Just makes you see things worse than they really are."

Sue Carlton, a strong-looking woman in her early forties, set the carrots in the sink and dried her hands. She walked over to her husband who sat in a wheelchair, one leg extended forward. A month ago, Jim had been repairing the roof of the barn when a board gave way. Along with shattered bones, the X rays had shown damage to his spine. Just how much damage, and whether Jim would ever walk again, the doctors couldn't yet say.

Sue perched on the arm of a chair and stroked the side of Jim's neck. "I reckon you're right about worrying," she said. She looked down at him. "Sometimes I think the drought's harder on the farmers than it is on the crops."

She looked out the window at her garden. They had talked about letting part of the vegetable garden go dry, or selling some of the animals, but so far there seemed to be enough well water for their own use. There just wasn't enough for three hundred acres of corn.

She bent down and kissed his head. "We'll be okay," she said quietly.

The days rolled on and on, same after same like crystal-clear beads on a string; early heat, dry winds and spotless skies of beautiful heartbreaking blue. Leaf edges began to brown and curl on the corn that hedged the Carltons' yard.

One day in mid-July, Jim called to his wife as she came in from the garden. He told her he had just been on the phone with their neighbor Pappy Dickson. Pappy's crop was failing; he couldn't see any ears at all and even the stalks were turning brown.

"Pappy says he's going to start plowing his corn under if it doesn't rain by the end of the week," Jim said in a worried voice.

"Plowing it in?" Sue stared at Jim.

"Sounds like it. I think the worry must be getting to him. What he says is impossible. We all planted the same seed at about the same time, and it looks to me like the corn's holding up pretty good."

A few days later, Sue returned from a trip to town. Jim heard the screen door slap behind her but didn't call a greeting. She came into the room, her eyes questioning. Jim was sitting there as cool as a handful of rose petals, a big smile on his face. She set down her packages.

"Don't tell me," she said. "There's a rainstorm coming!"

"Better than that! Doc Henderson called, says the new X rays look good, real good—a lot better than he expected." Jim paused and his smile grew wider. "He figures I could be walking by September."

"Walking . . . ?" She looked straight into her husband's eyes. "He figures you'll be able to walk?" She reached down and held his face in both hands. "That's the best news you could have given me!" she said, laughing. She jumped up and twirled a few times around the room, hugging herself with happiness.

"Better than a rainstorm?"

"Oh, honey! A hundred times better," she laughed and fell into a chair beside him.

"You know," he said, reaching out and touching her arm, "a month ago I couldn't believe how our life was going. I figured maybe we were praying in the wrong direction or something. Then along comes the good news, and suddenly the drought hardly seems worth worrying about."

"Well, that's good. Then I don't need to keep sneaking out at night to water." Sue lifted her head and looked in Jim's eyes.

"The garden?"

"The garden and all the corn you can see from this house."

"Corn?" Jim stared at her.

"What else could I do?" Sue smiled. "You said it yourself, worrying doesn't help any. It just makes you see things worse than they really are."

Gary Carter

The Best of Wives

Whoso findeth a wife findeth a good thing.

Proverbs 18:22

I'll always remember May 4, 1959. It was a warm, breezy day, and all the trees were bursting into bud and leaf. I ran home from school, lighthearted as spring—only to learn that my mother, Rose Flynn, had just died of a heart attack.

My mother and father had many friends. At the wake, they all talked in hushed tones about her life, her family, her smile and the rose garden that she tended religiously in her backyard.

"I never saw such gorgeous roses," one lady with red hair exclaimed to a woman from down the road.

"I once asked what her secret was," the neighbor replied. "And you know what she told me? 'It's all in the name.'"

The day of the funeral, it rained. Heavy spring showers. I remember placing a crimson rose on my mother's oak coffin. She would have liked that. Red roses were her favorite.

Old Aunt Jennie came to live with us temporarily. She cooked, did laundry and straightened up. She convinced my dad to hire a housekeeper, a nice Irish girl in her twenties who had just arrived from Dublin. Her name was Mary. Mary moved into the spare bedroom—and into our lives. I got along famously with her. Half the time I didn't know what she was saying—her brogue was so thick—but she smiled a lot and her sky-blue eyes twinkled so brightly. She'd tell us stories about herself and Dublin and would make us all laugh.

It was good to see my father laugh again.

One of Mary's favorite stories was about the time she played the villainess in a high school play. She excelled so at acting wicked that her father sent a box of twelve long-stemmed roses backstage. When she opened the box, all it contained were twelve long, thorny canes—the perfect gift for such an evil character. (He did give her a dozen roses with flowers that night at home.)

One day in late June, Mary discovered my mother's rose garden out back. Weeds had almost overtaken it, and Japanese beetles were making skeletons of the leaves and buds. She spent the afternoon picking Japanese beetles and dropping them into a coffee can filled with water and gasoline.

"I drowned one hundred thirty-four of them," she boasted at dinner. "Only six of those bloody beetles got away."

During the summer, my father started going for long strolls along the road in the evenings. Sometimes he asked Mary to walk with him. They'd talk of good times and bad times, of Ireland and America, of red and yellow roses. Sometimes they'd be gone for hours.

As time passed, the shock of my mother's death began to lessen. Still, sometimes, little things that Mary did reminded us of Mother. Like the way Mary would spread jam (but never butter) right to the edge of her toast. Or how, when we went to my father's favorite Chinese restaurant, she'd always ask to speak to the owner afterward— just like my mother had—to thank him for the meal.

The following August, my father and Mary were married. I knew it was coming, and I was happy for them. It was a small ceremony. The priest came and married them in the rose garden, my mother Rose's rose garden, now Mary's rose garden. Aunt Jennie came, and Mary's father flew in from Dublin. He was just like Mary: I could barely understand a word he said, but he smiled a lot. We were starting to feel like a family again.

A week after the wedding, my father surprised Mary by sending her a box of twelve long-stemmed red roses. She peeked inside before she opened it and, yes, there *were* roses on the stems. Next to them was a handwritten copy of an old Chinese poem. The restaurant owner—the same gentleman Mary always took time to thank—had translated it and given it to my father. Mary had trouble deciphering the writing, so she handed it to me. With difficulty, I read:

I married a second time the other day,
Happy about the present, still grieving for the past.
Once more there is someone to take care of the
    household;
My shadow is no longer alone in the moonlight.
Yet sometimes when my heart is troubled,
I still call my old wife's name.
Luckily both women are kind and gentle
And I have married again the best of wives.

George M. Flynn

4

MAKING A
DIFFERENCE

The purpose of human life is to serve, and to show compassion and the will to help others.

Albert Schweitzer

Pop's Farm

The best things that can come out of the garden are gifts for other people.

Jamie Jobb

My grandfather, "Pop," was born to a family with thirteen children in 1879. By the time he was nine years old, both parents had died and the family was split up. Children were parceled out amongst various relatives. Pop went to a bachelor uncle who put him to work in the fields to earn his keep. He never went to school again. From then on, he did a man's work, putting in twelve- to fourteen-hour days.

It was hard work, but Pop was good at it. He liked farming. He liked the feel and the smell of the earth. And he loved the plants. Nothing made him happier than putting in seeds, tending them and harvesting the crops. It gave him a sense of accomplishment, and it made him feel close to God.

After his uncle died, Pop began looking for a farm of his own. He was in his early twenties and engaged to my grandmother, and he desperately wanted to farm. For a few years he worked at jobs and tried to save the money to buy his own farm. But progress was slow, and my grandmother's patience was wearing thin. Finally, he gave up his dream. He went to Chicago and took a job at Pullman making railroad cars. He rented an apartment and married my grandmother.

I was born in 1944. By then Pop was retired; he'd worked at Pullman for thirty years. He'd supported two children, my mother and my aunt, and he'd built and paid for his own house. World War II was dragging on. My father was overseas, so my mother and I had moved in with my grandparents. Times were hard. Food was still rationed, and a lot of people were just getting by.

Pop mulled it over and decided what to do. There was no land to farm on the South Side of Chicago, but there were plenty of vacant lots. So, without bothering to ask anybody's permission, he started planting. From the time I was two, I went with him. We were a strange pair, the toddler and the old man, bearing our hoes and shovels. Every day we went from one vacant-lot garden to the next until all four or five had been tended. I played in the dirt while Pop planted potatoes, corn, cabbage, squash and carrots: food to eat fresh and for my grandmother to can.

Every day, as we worked and played in the gardens, people came by. Food was scarce for everyone, and people with small children often had a hard time feeding them. Pop shared with them all. Anyone who needed food got some: families of all sizes and backgrounds, men who didn't speak English, old people. They all got fed from those vacant lots. It became a tradition that lasted into the 1950s.

Pop passed away in 1972. He was ninety-three years old. My grandmother had died nine years earlier, the house had been sold and he had come to live with us way over in a different neighborhood. We knew Pop was old-fashioned and would want a wake, so we held one. But we never thought anybody would come. It had been years since he had lived in the old neighborhood. Besides, all his friends had died. Who would still remember him?

The evening of his wake was one we would never forget. People came and kept coming, and the family didn't know any of them. Over two hundred people came, of all races, religions and backgrounds. As we stood, stunned, in the receiving line, every person who shook our hands said the same thing: "I saw his name in the paper, and I just had to come and pay my respects."

All the people Pop had fed during those difficult war years had never forgotten. Twenty-five years later, they still remembered him. His gardens and generosity had changed their lives. Pop never saw the differences between people. For him, the food that comes from the earth belonged to everyone equally. On that night, I realized that the man who had wanted to be a farmer his whole life had finally fulfilled his dream.

Meredith Hodges

Just Keep Planting

The great French Marshal Lyautey once asked his gardener to plant a tree. The gardener objected that the tree was slow-growing and would not reach maturity for 100 years. The marshal replied, "In that case, there is no time to lose; plant it this afternoon!"

John F. Kennedy

Long before Paul Rokich was born, a copper smelter was built amid the lush trees and grasslands of northern Utah. The sulfur dioxide that poured out of the refinery turned the beautiful Oquirrh Mountains into a desolate wasteland.

One day when Paul was fourteen, he showed another boy around his birthplace. When the young visitor looked at this wasteland and saw that there was nothing living there—no animals, no trees, no grass, no bushes, no birds, just 14,000 acres of black and barren land that even smelled bad—well, this kid looked at Paul and said, "This place is crummy."

Paul knocked him down. He felt insulted. But he looked

around him and realized the boy was right. Paul made a decision: He vowed that someday he would bring life back to this land.

Years went by, but Paul didn't outgrow his dream. Now a young man doing construction work, he went to the smelter office. He asked the company bosses if they had any plans to bring the trees back.

"No," they said.

He asked if they would let him try to bring the trees back.

"No," they said again. They didn't want him on their land.

Paul realized he needed to be more knowledgeable before anyone would pay attention to his dream, so he went to college to study botany.

At the University of Utah, Paul met a professor who was an expert in the state's ecology. But the expert told Paul that the wasteland was beyond hope.

"Your goal is foolish," the professor and his colleagues said. Even if Paul planted trees, and even if they grew, the wind would only blow the seeds forty feet per year. That's all the dispersion he would get, the experts said, because there weren't any birds or squirrels to spread the seeds further. And the seeds from those trees would need another thirty years before they started producing seeds of their own. Therefore, it would take about twenty thousand years to revegetate that six-square-mile piece of earth.

"It would be a waste of your life to try to replant the Oquirrhs," Paul's teachers said. "It just can't be done."

So Paul tried to go on with his life. He got a job operating heavy equipment, got married and had some kids. But his dream would not die. He kept studying up on the subject, and he kept thinking about it. And then one night he stopped worrying about the so-called "unattainable" goal and began seizing the smaller opportunities right in front of him.

That night, under the cover of darkness, Paul sneaked out into the wasteland with a backpack full of seedlings and started planting. For seven hours he planted seedlings.

He did it again a week later.

And every week after that, he made his secret journey into the wasteland and planted trees and shrubs and grass.

Most of them died. But many survived and grew.

For fifteen years he did this. When a whole valley of his fir seedlings burned to the ground because of a careless sheepherder, Paul broke down and wept. Then he got up and kept planting.

Freezing winds and blistering heat, landslides and floods and fires destroyed his work time and time again. But he kept planting.

One night he found that a highway crew had clawed up tons of dirt for a road grade, and all the plants he had painstakingly planted in that area were gone.

But Paul just kept planting.

Week after week, year after year, he kept at it, against the opinion of the authorities, against the trespassing laws, against the devastation of road crews, against the wind and rain and heat . . . even against plain common sense. He just kept planting.

Slowly, very slowly, more and more plants took root and spread. Then gophers appeared. Then rabbits. Then porcupines. Nature was coming home to the Oquirrhs.

The administrators at the old copper smelter eventually took notice of Paul's work and gave him permission to keep replanting. Later, in the face of political pressure to clean up the environment, they actually hired Paul to do what he was already doing. They gave him machinery and crews, and his progress accelerated.

Today this former fourteen-thousand-acre wasteland is

filled with trees and grass and bushes, rich with elk and eagles. And Paul Rokich has received almost every environmental award Utah has.

He says, "I thought that if I got this started, when I was dead and gone people would come and see it. I never thought I'd live to see it myself!"

It took him until his hair turned white, but Paul managed to keep that impossible vow he made to himself as a child.

Paul Rokich planted a wasteland. And, one tree at a time, it grew.

Adam Khan

Food from the 'Hood

The purpose of agriculture is not the produc-tion of food, but the perfection of human beings.
Masanobu Fukuoka

I was in junior high school when the verdict came out: The four policemen filmed beating Rodney King were acquitted. South Central L.A. exploded in riots. I was out-raged at the looting and burning that took over our city. I thought, *Why burn your own neighborhood?*

At the age of fourteen, I had experienced some tumul-tuous times myself. My mother had always been in and out of jail. There were times I didn't know where my next meal would come from. But I had never been driven to the point of violence. The events of that spring made no sense to me.

The next fall I enrolled at Crenshaw High School, one of the most notoriously gang-ridden high schools in South Central L.A. One day, my biology teacher, Tammy Bird, asked a few students to meet her during lunch hour. She introduced us to Melinda McMullen, a business executive who was looking for a way to help rebuild our community. Together, they proposed that we turn the abandoned plot of land behind our classroom into an organic garden. With Ms. Bird offering extra credit and Melinda offering pizza, it was an offer too good to refuse.

For the next few weeks, about a dozen of us spent our time after school cutting down the weeds in the garden, most of them taller than we were. The ground was so hard and dry that we had to take an extra Saturday to prepare the soil. Then we planted herbs and vegetables. Before long, we were growing more than we could eat—so the idea of selling our bounty was a natural.

In September of 1993, we held our first official business meeting. We named ourselves "Food from the 'Hood" and decided to use our profits to fund college scholarships.

That April, we took our vegetables to Santa Monica's Farmer's Market, which is in a pretty ritzy part of Los Angeles. At first we felt out of place. People ignored us. I don't think that they knew what to make of a bunch of Latino and African-American teenagers at a vegetable stand touting "Food from the 'Hood." Finally, one of the guys bounced out of the booth and walked up to people saying, "Hi, I'm Ben Osborne from Crenshaw High. We've grown some organic veggies that are just too good to pass up!" People started buying our produce like crazy. For the rest of the school year, we had sell-out weekends.

But even with the success of our farmer's markets, we ended the school year with a profit of only $600 to put toward the scholarships. (Farming is so expensive!) It was clear we had to find an additional route to profits if we wanted to go to college. That's when we decided to go into the salad dressing business. After all, as my friend Karla Becerra said, "We grow ingredients for salads, so why not make what goes on top?"

Our next step was to develop a recipe. Our first priority: low sodium. High blood pressure is a serious issue among minorities in our community. Our second priority:

low fat. We wanted to make people healthy, as well as make money!

That December, we got a tremendous surprise. Rebuild L.A., a nonprofit organization formed out of the riots, gave us start-up funding of $50,000. Armed with our "seed" money, we found someone to manufacture our dressing and made our first large batch. We also used the money to buy office equipment and set up shop in a storage room near the garden. Also, we hired Aleyne Larner, one of our adult volunteers, to be the company's full-time advisor.

I'll never forget our first sales call. It was with the senior vice president of Vons, one of the largest grocery store chains in California. The room was full of men in suits and us—a group of kids from South Central! We told them about our product and how well it would sell, and they agreed to stock it! Other large grocery chains also decided to carry our dressing.

On April 29, 1994, on the second anniversary of the Los Angeles Uprising, we announced to the community that Food from the 'Hood's Straight Out of the Garden salad dressing was available in 2,000 supermarkets. No one had ever dreamed we could be so successful.

Soon after that, we heard that England's Prince Charles would be visiting Los Angeles. Carlos Lopez, our fourteen-year-old PR manager, wrote and invited him to visit us. We didn't know it at the time, but Prince Charles is a huge fan of organic gardening and has his own company that helps build economic empowerment in the inner cities of England. No one thought that he would come. But a few weeks later, we got a call from a representative of the British consulate saying, "The prince would be delighted."

Three weeks before the prince was due to arrive, our office was vandalized. All of our computer equipment, fax machines and telephones were stolen or destroyed. Some of us burst out crying. But Ben said, "Whatever doesn't kill us makes us stronger." We decided to come back stronger than ever. Many people from the community helped with repairs, and a few businesses donated money to replace the stolen equipment. Our school district even donated a telephone. We were back in business.

The day of the prince's visit finally came. I shook hands with the Prince of Wales! Karla, who used to be really shy, showed him around our garden. There were lots of reporters trying to crowd around, but Prince Charles waved them back and said, "I'm afraid you're trampling on their lettuce." He had lunch with us and ate an entire plate of salad with our salad dressing on it. Then he said, "Your garden is truly remarkable." After the prince's visit, the British consulate gave us a gift: a company delivery truck. We call it the Chuck Wagon.

Today, Food from the 'Hood is seven years old and the biggest success ever seen at Crenshaw High School. Our salad dressings—we now have three flavors—are sold in grocery and natural food stores in twenty-three states. To date, we've had more than seventy student-owners participate in Food from the 'Hood. Most have gone on to pursue higher education. This year, many of us are graduating from colleges all over the United States, including UC Berkeley, Stanford and San Diego State.

I feel like I owe a lot to that quarter-acre plot in back of my old classroom. We all do. The garden is where it all started. Ms. Bird always said one of the most important things about gardening is composting—how you can take leftovers and garbage and turn them into fertile soil for growing great things. Well, truer words were never spoken. I've never seen a bigger waste than the riots—and look what great things we grew out of that!

Jaynell Grayson

Angel of Mercy

Great opportunities to help others seldom come,
but small ones surround us every day.

Sally Koch

"Want a vegetable garden, but can't dig it yourself? Call and I will plant one for you. Free of charge," the card said. "I want to help."

Those were the words on the sign I tacked up on the church bulletin board. As I finished it, the secretary came over and said, "An angel of mercy, huh?" The way she said it, I wondered if she might be poking fun at me.

"I just want to help," I said.

A week later I had my first call. I parked in front of a dingy-white apartment building with numbered doors. Weeds sprouted all through the lawn. Mrs. Searing, a thin black woman with graying hair, answered my knock. She walked with me through the tall weeds, smiling and nodding. I suggested I put stakes in to mark a plot. She answered, "Let's go in, have some tea and think about it."

Inside a teakettle whistled, and cookies were heaped on plates.

"This is great," I said, jiggling the hot teacup on my knee. "There's room for as much garden as you could want. Getting water to it will be easy."

Mrs. Searing looked out the window. "My grandmother taught me about plants. When she was young she'd cut her hands picking cotton. Some herb she knew of grew in the rows. She chewed the leaves and rubbed them on her hands to heal them."

I set my cup down. "I could find out what herb it was. If you like, we could plant some in your garden."

Mrs. Searing sipped her steaming tea carefully. "I enjoyed gardening. I never got to it when my sons were growing up. I had seven sons. Only one's left now. He drives a taxi in Atlanta," she said.

We had a long talk about her life and about mine and what I wanted to do with myself. Finally it was time for me to go. There had been no progress toward a garden. I looked with regret at the unused tools in the back of my car. This had been a day wasted.

Mrs. Searing smiled and waved as I drove off. "Thank you for coming to see me!"

My next assignment was a couple of weeks later at a big green clapboard house. A cheery voice met me: "I'll be right out. Just let me get a sweater!" A small, heavyset woman bustled out the door. "There we are," she smiled, pushing her dentures in place with her tongue. "Call me Hazel. Come on, I'll show you my yard." She came down the steps sideways, holding onto the railing with both hands.

"I gardened quite a bit when my husband was alive. He built this trellis here for me, and this strawberry planter."

I made mental notes: Rebuild the porch steps. Reinforce the leaning trellis. Replant the barren strawberry planter.

Hazel was talking nonstop, cheerful and excited. She dug a half-dozen young shoots and pushed them into my hands, a gift for me to try in my garden. "These are some of my favorite bulbs," she said. I looked at the weed-choked sprouts. *Weed the bulbs,* I thought.

"I have my tools in the car. I'll start with weeding, if you want."

"Oh, honey, you have better things to do!" She laughed. "Come, have some lemonade. You like lemonade?"

A week later, I pulled into the driveway of my third assignment, full of resolution. This time I would carry my shovel as I walked in. As I lifted my trunk lid to reach for it, my smile faltered. Past the garden gate sat a round white table spread with glinting plates, a pitcher of something pink and a white frosted cake.

Coming through the creaky gate toward me, a woman in a navy flowered dress tucked a wisp of silver hair into place. She worked her hands together and smiled shyly: "So glad you could come!"

For two years, I went on gardening errands and my tools never left my car. In my work clothes, I visited, helping in the way help was most needed. I listened and ate cookies, crackers and cake. I drank lemonade, tea and soda pop. I left full of stories and advice, and often, with my hands full of gifts.

I was an angel of mercy. I let them do for me.

Erica Sanders

Calcutta Neighbors

Anything which grows is always more beautiful to look at than anything which is built.

Lin Yu Tang

Like so many gardens in the cities of India, ours was created by chance. It was a tiny scrap of unclaimed land, a town planner's nightmare. But under the heavy raindrops of the monsoon, the barren patch blossomed with a vivid carpet of rapidly growing flowers and weeds.

In time, the local authorities granted it official status, walling it and appointing a gardener. Within a few years, it became a local landmark, and everyone who lived nearby was proud of it. In crowded, industrial Calcutta, a garden was rare and precious.

It was a dainty little thing, about the size of ten saris stretched out to dry on a hot summer day; or, if you will, a badminton court. It had a low brick wall to keep the cows and goats away. There was a revolving blue gate to let the children and their nursemaids in, for amid the bougainvillea, jasmine and roses, there were a small slide and a swing.

The garden had been there for at least three generations. Even the old blind beggar, the oldest man in the
neighborhood, had played there as a child. And though
he could no longer see the swing or the slide, the jasmine
still smelled the same.

In an Indian city, each block holds its own religious fes-
tivals, cricket and football matches, clean-up drives and
cultural programs. Shekhar Roy was our block committee
secretary at the time of my story. Roybabu, as we called
him, was a friendly, outgoing retired professor. Gardening
was one of his hobbies. When our community gardener
passed away, the city refused to hire a replacement. Other
people in the neighborhood grumbled about bureaucrats
and budget cuts, but Roybabu volunteered to care for the
garden himself.

"After all," he said, "I have all the time in the world, and
I need something to keep me active." His enthusiasm
caught on; within days, all the retirees on the block
chipped in to help. Together, they pruned the bougainvillea. They planted new saplings. They watered the rosebushes and watched out for insects and litterbugs. They
included things like new hoes and spades, trowels and
fertilizer on their shopping lists; whatever each of them
could afford, and whenever they could afford it. And they
surprised themselves by doing more than they had ever
thought they could.

Then came the 1990s, and money was in the air. With
India's economy surging, people suddenly had more in
their pockets. Naturally, expectations went up, and with
them, the price of real estate.

One morning, a well-dressed gentleman appeared at
Roybabu's doorstep. He introduced himself as a developer and outlined his plan: He wanted to buy eight
houses in the block, including three that bordered the
garden. The owners and the city had agreed to allow him

to merge the plots, tear down the homes and build an apartment complex. His customers had already paid substantial advances. All that stood in his way was the garden. It would have to go.

It was hard news. Roybabu knew everyone who had sold off their homes; some were his friends. The next day, Roybabu visited them, one by one. Soon the truth came out: Not only had they received enormous offers and new homes in the proposed complex, but they had also been "advised" by the local political leadership to accept the developer's offer. Refusal, they were told, would only cause trouble.

It was evening when Roybabu walked home. He had spent all his life in this neighborhood, beside this garden. There, between the jasmine and the roses, he had found the strength to smile when he was blue, to bear up when he was weighed down.

The gate creaked slightly as it swung to let him in. He walked past the slide and the swing, past the roses and sat down on the grass. A gentle breeze blew the scent of jasmine through the air. The crickets had come out, their insistent calls resonating through the dusk. A tired smile floated on Roybabu's lips. He bowed his head and gave up his worries to the garden.

A week later, Roybabu called a meeting in the community hall. The entire neighborhood turned up. In quiet tones, he informed them of the city's decision to allow the old houses to be torn down and replaced with the apartment complex.

"As far as the garden goes," he continued, "the final decision has been left to us, the residents. It is our garden, and it cannot be destroyed without our permission. The thought of losing it breaks my heart, but the decision is not mine alone. It is for all of us."

Then the developer spoke. He showed drawings of the new buildings. He talked of how the complex would enhance the neighborhood, how many more people would be able to live there. "Times are changing. We should be flexible," he urged. "No one shall be inconvenienced by my project. Please say yes!"

The room was quiet for a few moments. Then a man stood up in the back.

"I know the times have changed, and we should accommodate the need for new housing," he said. "But I didn't know you wanted to take our garden, too. It belongs to everyone: us, our children and even their children. I think the garden should stay, unless you can assure us you'll build a new garden inside the complex, where we can all go whenever we like. I can't approve of this complex otherwise."

The developer shook his head firmly. "That's impossible! I've already booked a number of customers for this project. We can't just redesign everything now. And think of the extra cost! How can you say this?"

A woman stood up. "He can say that, Mister, because like the rest of us, he knows what we stand to lose if you have your way. Do you think that just because it's a small patch of land, it means nothing to us? We don't count our blessings in square feet. If you can't agree to his proposal, fine. You can kiss all your customers good-bye!"

Someone cheered. One by one, people rose to speak for the garden.

"I've spent all my life beside that garden, and now my grandchildren play there. It's part of our family."

"I got my first date with a flower I pinched from that garden forty-five years ago."

"No way, sir. You can build over the houses, but not over our garden."

"Roybabu, *amra apnar songey achhi*—we are with you!"

Roybabu couldn't believe his ears or his eyes. All his neighbors were on their feet. The developer shouted to be heard, but it was useless. Finally the man stood up, waved his hands in despair and walked out.

At that, the hall went quiet. Everybody stared at one another, astonished at what they had just done. Someone smiled, then laughed. Soon, everybody was crying or laughing, and hugging each other. It was one of the most touching moments of their lives.

Eight months later, the new apartment complex was complete. Its earth-colored tones blended perfectly with the other houses on the block. And it was built around our garden, allowing sunshine and visitors to enter freely.

Every morning, the retirees on the block come to work in the garden, drink tea and gossip. The children and their nursemaids come to play in the afternoons. In the evening, working people stroll in the quiet, green space. It is our garden, now more than ever.

Anirban Gupta

To Diana with Love, from Canada

The best method of overcoming obstacles is the team method.

Colin Powell

The death of Diana, Princess of Wales, left me in shock. I was watching TV when the announcement of her car crash was made. Completely stunned, almost numb, I followed the coverage throughout the week that led to her Saturday funeral.

That week was also one of nonstop work. I'm the executive director of the Composting Council of Canada—and it's a very busy job. We were facing a lot of deadlines at the time and our "to do" list seemed to get longer by the day.

At the same time, I was dealing with my own reaction, and that of everyone else, to the loss of Diana. Canada is still part of the British Commonwealth, and much of the country feels a deep kinship with Britain. The loss hit us very hard.

Here in Toronto, people began placing flowers, cards, candles and other remembrances in front of the Princess of Wales Theatre, a theater that, a few years before, had been named in Diana's honor.

Each time I passed the theater that week, I stopped and looked at all the notes and photos and flowers being left there. It had become somewhat of a shrine in her memory— a place for people to come and pay their respects.

I awoke early on Saturday to watch her funeral and the procession that followed on television. Once it was over, I caught myself thinking about how she had made a difference for so many and what an impact her death had on everyone. My mind then skipped to all the flowers placed at the Princess of Wales Theatre.

What was going to happen to them? Sure, the ones that were still fresh could be given away. But what about those that had been there for most of the week and had already begun to turn?

It suddenly hit me: We should get those flowers and have them composted! As part of my job, I spend a lot of time convincing people that organic materials such as fallen leaves, garden debris and food scraps should be composted and used to improve the quality of the soil, not thrown into the garbage.

Suddenly, composting those flowers became a way for me to do something that I believed in. And somehow, I sensed it could also become a fitting tribute to Diana. I had to find the owners of the theater—Ed and David Mirvish—and convince them to let the flowers be composted.

I called the theater, but all I could do was leave a message on the answering machine. I drove there, but the attendant could only suggest I leave my business card for the manager. The weekend passed, but no word came.

On Monday, buried in work, I asked my colleague Lyne to try phoning again. She came back with a partial answer: We would have to write a letter to Ed Mirvish, explaining what we wanted to do with the flowers. Apparently he had already received hundreds of suggestions.

I panicked. I had absolutely no time to write that letter. But if I didn't do it then and there, the chance would be lost forever.

First, though, I called the farm of one of the members of the council to ask if they would compost the flowers. They agreed but asked that we deliver the flowers ready for composting. That meant that we would have to remove plastic wrap and any other nonorganic materials.

Then I turned to the letter. I asked Mr. Mirvish to let us compost the flowers. I told him we would then use the compost to plant a tree in Diana's memory the following spring. That finished, I faxed it off and rushed back to work.

About an hour later, there was a shout in our office. Mr. Mirvish had faxed us back to say that our idea was wonderful. The flowers were ours for the taking. We were thrilled. But then we went back to work and forgot about it. We had so much to do.

At three o'clock that afternoon we got the call to come and pick up the flowers. For me, the world stopped with that phone call. I hadn't planned on getting the flowers that day. We barely had time to do what we were supposed to be doing.

So, like so many other times when my life had gotten rough, I phoned home. "Dad," I said, "we need help. We have the chance to compost all those flowers at the Princess of Wales Theatre, but we need to pick them up today. Can you please go rent a van for us?"

"How big a van?" he replied.

"Oh, I don't know. Just one of those cube-shaped vans. I'm sure it'll be big enough. We'll plan on going down there around six o'clock. We can park right outside the theater and get it done in no time."

Get it done in no time. What a small, naïve phrase for what lay ahead.

Just before 6:00, Dad picked up Lyne and me. "Let's take a few bags for the flowers," I said. "We should be finished by 7:30."

When we drove up to the curb by the theater, the three of us suddenly got quiet. Very quiet.

There they were. Diana's flowers. Hundreds and hundreds of bundles. They made a wall that must have stretched fifty feet long and two feet high. Never did I anticipate such a huge amount.

"Well, I guess we'd better get started," Dad said.

So we did. Almost every bundle was wrapped in plastic. We removed all of it by hand—without gloves. Given all the roses, gloves would have been nice. But I hadn't thought of that.

People passed us, headed out for the evening, and asked what we were doing. Some even stood and watched. As the time passed, our eagerness to explain ourselves waned. There was so much to do!

It was now past 8:00 P.M. and beginning to get dark. Despite nonstop work, we hadn't even made a dent in the wall of flowers.

I started to panic. We would never get this done! What had I got us into?

We needed help. I called a local radio station to ask for volunteers. They agreed to announce it on their 8:30 news.

That done, we went back to work. In a little while, a big car pulled up beside us. A tall man in a security uniform got out.

Oh great, I thought. *Somebody heard this on the radio and is coming down to check us out.* This was not going to be good. We had no permission papers. The theater was closed. I silently promised myself that I would never again do anything that I didn't have to do. *Oh, well, if he's going to kick us out, let him make the first move,* I thought.

The security guard walked up. "I heard about you on the radio," he said. I drew my breath.

"I just got off work. I'm here to help."

If I had known him better, I would have given him a big hug.

Then others started to show up. Dozens and dozens of people. They came from all over Toronto to help. Before long, the theater curb was crowded with willing volunteers.

By 11:00 P.M. we were finally done. Despite the late hour, no one seemed in a hurry to go home. Everyone needed to talk about Diana, to share their grief and shock. Many people were still talking outside the theater when Dad, Lyne and I finally said good-bye.

The next day, Dad and one of our staffers drove the flowers up to the farm that would do the composting. Then it was back to our work at the council. The compost wouldn't be ready until spring.

That April, as we prepared to plant our memorial tree, we began receiving requests from all over the country. Schoolchildren, mayors, leaders of other provinces—all over Canada people wanted to plant trees using the compost made from those flowers.

What had started out as personal gestures of respect for Diana at the time of her death became a wellspring of celebrations of her life and legacy. A chance for thousands of people to, symbolically, compost their grief and turn it into something good. That spring, more than 100 trees were planted in Canada in Diana's honor. And every one was graced with a bit of compost from the flowers that had been placed, in her memory, in front of the Princess of Wales Theatre in Toronto.

Susan Antler

The Loveliest of Gifts

I know what I have given you. I do not know what you have received.

Antonio Porchia

It was my first year of teaching. I was young, idealistic and certain that I could make my high schoolers appreciate the beauty of poetry. I started with A. E. Housman's "Loveliest of Trees" because it was short and about youth. Clearing my throat, I read aloud:

> *Loveliest of trees, the cherry now*
> *Is hung with bloom along the bough,*
> *And stands about the woodland ride*
> *Wearing white for Eastertide.*

My students listened and read along, but when I asked them what the first stanza was about, not a single one raised a hand. Maybe the second verse would make more sense to them. At least it had a mathematical problem:

> *Now, of my threescore years and ten,*
> *Twenty will not come again,*

And take from seventy springs a score,
It only leaves me fifty more.

Once again, no response. They didn't even realize that the poet was twenty years old and expected to live to be seventy. Once I put the numbers on the chalkboard, they understood the arithmetic, but they didn't grasp the passion in Housman's heart. They didn't sense his sadness that youth passes too quickly.

This poem was one of my favorites. I'd first grown to admire it when I was in college. I knew that, thanks to Housman, for the rest of my life I would look with new eyes at "things in bloom." I really wanted my students to appreciate it.

Still, the last stanza of the poem couldn't fail to move them, could it? I read:

And since to look at things in bloom
Fifty springs are little room,
About the woodlands I will go
To see the cherry hung with snow.

The students sat on their hands. I tried one last thing to get this message across.

"Put your papers down," I said. "Close your eyes." I walked over to the window and slowly, with as much emotion as I could muster, recited the poem from memory. But, afterward, I couldn't bear to ask my students again if they understood. I merely asked them to read the poem on their own and see if it didn't speak to them about life.

At the end of class, one student asked, "Miss Hoffman, do you have a cherry tree?"

"Why, no," I answered, surprised. "I live in an apartment."

After that day, I made a mental note not to teach "Loveliest of Trees" again. They were good kids, but sharing something I loved that much was too painful for me unless I knew they would understand and appreciate it.

That spring I got to share something else special with my students: the news that I was getting married over Easter break. We'd be going on a short honeymoon afterward, so they'd have a substitute teacher for two days.

The students pretended to be glad I wouldn't be in class, but I could tell they were happy for me. Still, they did seem to be getting a little restless: In the last days before spring break, I noticed a lot of whispering and note-passing. I was too happy to discipline them.

When I came back from the honeymoon, my students asked if they could take some class time to make a presentation "as a wedding present." I was in such good spirits, how could I say no? I sat at the back of the class, wondering what surprise was in store.

"Miss Hoffman, er, Mrs. Waterman," Andy said, "we know how much you like poetry. So we've memorized some poems for you today." Then one student after another came up to the front and recited short poems from Housman's *A Shropshire Lad*. Students who had rarely spoken up in class or who had done poorly on the poetry test—they all recited their poems easily.

I was speechless. How had they found the book, chosen the poems and learned them so well? I was so happy I wanted to cry.

But they weren't done yet. "Close your eyes, Mrs. Waterman," Andy said, repeating my instructions of so long ago. As I did, I heard some shuffling around. I thought I also heard the door open. Then another student said, "Let's begin" . . . and in unison they all recited "Loveliest of Trees." It was a beautiful moment.

When I opened my eyes, I saw all the students standing by the classroom door. And in front of them, in a container, was a large cherry tree. I could only imagine how much trouble it was for them to find that tree, buy it and get it to school. There was a note tied around a branch. It read, "We got the message. Thanks."

I planted that cherry tree right by the front drive of our new home. Every spring when it is covered with snowy blooms, it reminds me that young people often learn more than adults give them credit for. And, every spring, I vow never to underestimate my students again.

You see, I got the message, as well.

Pamela Waterman

The Kids on the Point

Joint undertakings stand a better chance when they benefit both sides.

Euripides

Shortly after Barbara Longworth moved into her little old house, she began to notice them—a boy and a girl, about ten.

Troublemakers, she thought, when she saw them tearing flowers off the stems in her neighbor's yard.

"Stop doing that!" she yelled at them, again and again.

But nothing changed.

One day, as they scattered torn petals amid the weed-choked grass, Barbara confronted the troublemakers.

"Do you know how long it takes a flower to grow?" she asked sternly. "Have you ever planted a garden?"

They didn't. They hadn't.

Barbara hesitated. She really didn't need this. But somehow, she heard herself asking the two if they'd like to help her plant a garden in her yard. And to her surprise, the troublemakers said yes.

It wasn't an easy time for Barbara. She was newly divorced, starting out in a new job. She had sunk every penny she had in the little house in the rundown Algiers Point section of New Orleans. She didn't have money for a garden; she hardly had money for herself. But something told her this was important.

So Barbara bought plants. She gave one to each of the troublemakers—Frank and Lisa. Now each had their very own plant to take care of. And every day, they came to water and weed and help in her garden. In *their* garden.

That was the beginning.

Barbara's neighborhood was like many others in New Orleans: full of character and charm, but threatened by crime and drugs, scarred by boarded-up buildings and abandoned cars. It was a neighborhood with lots of children, but little for them to do.

Frank and Lisa thrived on the attention Barbara gave them. They liked playing with her soft brown cat and her big black chicken.

As the two boasted of their garden, their friends wanted one, too. Soon, more children were banging on Barbara's door.

"Please, Miss Barbara," they'd say, "will you show us how to plant a garden, too?"

Soon she had irises and gardenias, periwinkle and Mexican heather, where she used to have nothing but weeds. Together, Barbara and the children unearthed a beautiful old brick sidewalk in Barbara's yard she didn't know was there.

When they ran out of room in the yard, the children decided to plant flowers down the street for Mr. Earl, an old man with cancer. They wanted him to have something to look at from his front porch. The gift was repaid with the old man's smile, and the children became his "adopted" grandchildren.

By the next spring, the group had grown to about twenty kids. They gave themselves a name: The Kids on the Point Society. They chose officers—The Rememberer (to remember what everyone was supposed to do) and The Eye (to make sure no one took their stuff).

The Kids on the Point had something to do now. They cleaned up their neighborhood; then they planted more flowers and moved around the corner onto Pelican Street, where they planted a vegetable garden—radishes and cherry tomatoes and cucumbers.

They weeded and watched. They hauled water all the way from Barbara's house. They shared their harvest of three cucumbers.

While they worked, they learned how long it takes a flower to grow. They saw tiny yellow blossoms become hard green balls, then sweet red tomatoes that exploded in their mouths when they bit into them.

It was frustrating for Barbara at times; all those kids, all that energy and no resources. But people in the neighborhood began to notice what was happening with The Kids on the Point. A bicyclist who saw them out weeding rode to the store and came back with a pile of gardening gloves. Another resident gave them eight new trowels. A landlord donated plants to go in front of his building, a neighbor brought lamb's ear from her garden and the man across the street gave them monkey grass.

Sometimes, when Barbara got home from work, she would find cuttings or fertilizer or a pack of seeds by her front door.

"This is not the kind of neighborhood where you expect to come home and find extra stuff on your porch," she would say to herself. Then she'd smile and gather up the gifts.

She noticed, too, that the children's attitude started to rub off on others. No one in the neighborhood threw trash around the little gardens and the areas the children had cleaned. Neighbors respected the gardens and enjoyed them together.

Finally, word made it to city hall, and the mayor of New Orleans gave The Kids on the Point a special proclamation in honor of their hard work. A newspaper writer who covered the story praised Barbara for giving the kids something to do, for finding an alternative to drugs and crime, for founding The Kids on the Point.

But Barbara doesn't think what she's doing is anything special. "It makes me feel good," she told the newspaper lady.

"People say, 'You do this for free?' I don't. I do it for me."

And for the troublemakers.

Sheila Stroup

A Healing Place

Although the world is full of suffering, it is full also of the overcoming of it.

Helen Keller

I came to the University of California at San Francisco to start the Mount Zion Breast Care Center. As physicians, we know we will touch our patients' lives. But we are also touched in surprising ways by the lives and stories of our patients.

Anne was one of my first patients. She was diagnosed with breast cancer in the winter of 1993. During a visit after her surgery, Anne was looking at a Monet poster on the wall of the exam room. "I wish the garden out there could look like that painting," she said.

"Really?" I asked. "How much do you wish that?"

And that was the beginning of the beginning. From this remarkable conversation, the Story Garden grew. At that point, the courtyard was largely concrete with trees and a few bushes along the edges. We secured a grant from the Creative Work Foundation and Anne organized a series of workshops. The first was a forum of inspiring work by other gardeners who had used their craft to enable people to develop a connection with the earth, and to use gardens and gardening as a source to reawaken the spirit of life.

I watched the garden grow. Gray concrete began to give way to color bobbing and swaying in the San Francisco fog. On Saturday afternoons, the garden was full of volunteers, planting seeds and blossoms they brought, while sharing stories in the sunshine. They came to grow a garden. They came to be together. As people worked in the garden, Anne collected and recorded their stories.

Sometimes she would spend hours in the infusion center, bringing people seeds to plant and talking to them about their stories. As they came for chemotherapy, they would watch the seeds turn to flowers, a metaphor for the life within them.

Once, an administrator concerned about the dirt being tracked into the infusion center told me that I had to "do something about Anne." We cleaned up the dirt, but everyone came to realize that Anne brought "health" of her own vintage that made everyone feel well.

Then Anne taught me another important lesson in healing. She told me that the voices of the patients were absent at the center. The walls were covered with pictures that celebrated technology and science, but few were about warmth and kindness. Patients, she told me, sometimes felt isolated and frightened in this place. I realized that, unintentionally, we had created a center that was more about medicine than healing—too much about science and not enough about people.

Anne had an idea, a way for people to share their stories, work in the garden and create tiles, art that could become the walls of the center. And the idea evolved.

The idea was to balance the constant change of the garden with the permanence of tiles—story tiles, where people etched their stories onto the walls and the fabric of the center. There were expressions of grief, faith, anger, love, philosophy; messages for loved ones and themselves. These stories expressed the range of emotion and humanity that is awakened in a time of crisis. Each was written beside an impression of a leaf or flower growing in the garden. The clay tablets were fired and glazed, then hung in the hallway around the garden, bringing the garden and its warmth and life inside.

I continue to learn. One of my patients told me she always spent an hour in the garden before she came up to see me. She watched the garden change. Some flowers faded, others were just beginning, soon to be brilliant. It inspired her to believe that her illness may have its season, too. To her, the garden was hope.

The voices of people touched by cancer are no longer absent in the center. The garden and the tiles represent the power of community, of people coming together to help one another.

The Story Garden is a place of refuge and beauty for staff, patients and families. For all of us who work at the cancer center, it serves as an ever-present reminder of why we come to work every day. It is our hope that the voices and stories of our patients, their friends and loved ones will be present in our center, that their humanity will be our humanity, and that as a community we can touch the lives of others. In any time of need, no one should be alone. These tiles are a reminder of the enduring strength, support and tenderness that we give to one another.

The inscription on Anne's tile reads:

> *This year in the garden I learned to live with my eyes on the sky, to love the peachy pinkness of the pansy, to lie belly down on the warm cement as the wind picks up and watch the golden coreopsis dance and bob like exploding fireworks. This year, I learned to live like a plant.*

Laura Esserman, M.D.

A Room Full of Roses

The love of our neighbor in all its fullness simply means being able to say to him, "What are you going through?"

Simone Weil

When Bonnie Bewley-Jaunbral went to work at the Anchorage Neighborhood Health Center, her little office wasn't much to look at. The small, windowless room was big enough for her mammography equipment, but not much more. The nonprofit clinic, which served a low-income neighborhood, didn't have the money for frills.

But as a mammogram technologist, Bonnie knew her clients needed a little pampering. Many of them were elderly. Many were Hispanic or Asian and didn't speak English well. And nearly all were nervous, bracing themselves for an uncomfortable exam or a frightening diagnosis in a strange, sterile environment.

I'm a woman, and I'd be nervous here, too, Bonnie thought to herself. *This is such a cold, stark room.* So since she was the only mammogram tech at the clinic, she decided to decorate her room *her* way.

She started by bringing in a little vanity table, just like the one she'd had as a girl. The frilled skirt and mirror added a homey touch to the room. After the mammograms were taken, clients were invited to use the powders, lotions, hair spray, deodorant and other niceties spread out on the table.

Bonnie made a point of wearing bright scrubs to work—pink, orange, yellow. She hung artwork in the plain little room, along with pictures of herself, her daughter, her dog and cat. She cracked jokes. She hung up cartoons and holiday decorations. She even brought in a heating pad to warm the cold metal plates of the mammography machine. Clients seemed to relax a little when they stepped into her cozy space.

And then Bonnie met Mike.

On their first date, the two went out for Sunday dinner. The next morning, a dozen roses arrived at the clinic for Bonnie.

She displayed them in her mammography room. Everyone in the clinic stopped in to sniff and admire.

"How beautiful! Who gave them to you? Don't they smell lovely?" her clients exclaimed.

That week, an elderly Hispanic woman came to Bonnie's examining room. She was obviously nervous, in awe of the massive mammography equipment and uncomfortable with the entire process. When the exam was over, Bonnie impulsively handed her one of Mike's roses.

Tears came to the woman's eyes. She beamed with happiness. And Bonnie suddenly realized she had another way to reach out to her clients, to say "I'm sorry" to uncomfortable and frightened women.

"Do you mind if I give away those roses?" she asked Mike.

"They're your roses," he said with a shrug. So for the rest of the week, Bonnie handed out the roses.

The following Monday, another dozen roses arrived. And the Monday after that. And the Monday after that.

From then on, whenever Bonnie had a client who was nervous or tense, one who didn't speak English or was having a difficult mammogram, or just seemed to be having a bad day, Bonnie tried to lift her spirits. She presented a rose, wrapped in a sheet of cleared X-ray film, sometimes with a ribbon or a sprig of baby's breath. Clients responded with tears, smiles and hugs of gratitude. Some of them had never been given flowers before.

At the end of the week, if there were roses left over, Bonnie dried them and hung them in bunches on the walls. Red roses, yellow roses, purple and orange and white and lavender—a rainbow of roses. The colors drenched the little mammogram room, and their scent perfumed that corner of the clinic.

Word spread. When the door was open, other patients and staff stuck their heads into Bonnie's room to admire the roses. The local newspaper and television station did stories. The florist who sold Mike his weekly roses agreed to give Bonnie free pink carnations for every mammography patient during October, Breast Cancer Detection Month.

It's been three years now. Three years with a fresh dozen roses arriving every Monday. Three years of women leaving the mammography room with a rose and a smile. Three years of a rainbow of roses filling the room, along with the vanity table and the pictures of Bonnie and her daughter and her dog and cat—oh, and pictures of Bonnie and Mike, too.

When her clients hear the story, they often say, "Marry that man!" But Bonnie just laughs. "I'm fifty-seven," she says. "We don't want to rush into anything. These days, we're just really enjoying being romantic."

Now and then, Bonnie gets a new client, one who walks in for the first time and is caught off guard by all the roses surrounding the mammogram machine. "What's all this?" they ask in astonishment.

"I have the best boyfriend in the world," Bonnie answers. "Come on in, and I'll tell you about him."

From the compliments piling up in the clinic's suggestion box, Bonnie's clients feel just as lucky. They think they have the best mammogram tech in the world.

Carol Sturgulewski

A Row for the Hungry

Never look down on anybody unless you are helping him up.

Reverend Jesse Jackson

It was a cold night in Washington, D.C., and I was heading back to the hotel when a man approached me. He asked if I would give him some money so he could get something to eat. I'd read the signs: "Don't give money to panhandlers." So I shook my head and kept walking.

I wasn't prepared for a reply, but with resignation, he said, "I really am homeless, and I really am hungry. You can come with me and watch me eat." But I kept on walking.

The incident bothered me for the rest of the week. I had money in my pocket, and it wouldn't have killed me to hand over a buck or two even if he had been lying. On a frigid, cold night, no less, I assumed the worst of a fellow human being.

Flying back to Anchorage, I couldn't help thinking of him. I tried to rationalize my failure to help by assuming government agencies, churches and charities were there to feed him. Besides, you're not supposed to give money to panhandlers.

Somewhere over Seattle, I started to write my weekly garden column for *The Anchorage Daily News*. Out of the blue, I came up with an idea. Bean's Cafe, the soup kitchen in Anchorage, feeds hundreds of hungry Alaskans every day. Why not try to get all my readers to plant one row in their gardens dedicated to Bean's? Dedicate a row and take it down to Bean's. Clean and simple.

We didn't keep records back then, but the idea began to take off. Folks would fax me or call when they took something in. Those who only grew flowers donated them. Food for the spirit. And salve for my conscience.

In 1995, the Garden Writers Association of America held its annual convention in Anchorage and after learning of Anchorage's program, Plant a Row for Bean's became Plant a Row for the Hungry. The original idea was to have every member of the Garden Writers Association of America write or talk about planting a row for the hungry sometime during the month of April.

As more and more people started working with the Plant a Row concept, new variations cropped up, if you will pardon the pun. Many companies gave free seed to customers and displayed the logo, which also appeared in national gardening publications.

Row markers with the Plant a Row logo were distributed to gardeners to set apart their "Row for the Hungry."

Garden editor Joan Jackson, backed by *The San Jose Mercury News* and California's nearly year-round growing season, raised more than 30,000 pounds of fruits and vegetables her first year, and showed GWAA how the program could really work. Texas fruit farms donated food to their local food bank after being inspired by Plant a Row. Today the program continues to thrive and grow.

I am stunned that millions of Americans are threatened by hunger. If every gardener in America—and we're seventy million strong—plants one row for the hungry, we can make quite a dent in the number of neighbors who don't have enough to eat. Maybe then I will stop feeling guilty about abandoning a hungry man I could have helped.

Jeff Lowenfels

[EDITORS' NOTE: *For more information regarding Plant a Row for the Hungry, contact: PAR Campaign, 10210 Leatherleaf Court, Manassas, VA 20111, phone/fax: 877-GWAA-PAR, E-mail:* par@gwaa.org, *Web site:* www.gwaa.org/par.]

The Timely Letter

Every act of kindness moves to a larger one till friendships bloom to show what little deeds have done.

June Masters Bacher

Years ago—okay, decades ago—I did my graduate thesis work on powdery mildew and muscadine grapes. And oddly enough, that led to one of the most remarkable experiences of my life.

Let me explain, starting with the thesis part. Powdery mildew is a serious disease problem in grapes. Muscadine grapes, a species that's native to the southeast United States, have great disease resistance. My idea was that if you could cross muscadines with commercial grapes, maybe you could come up with new varieties that wouldn't get powdery mildew.

I studied all the literature I could find on the subject. But, truthfully, I couldn't find much. Not many people had tried anything like this. You see, muscadines don't cross easily with other grapes—the offspring are almost always sterile. One of the few people who had had success was

Dr. Robert Dunstan. His name kept cropping up in my research. His papers were good reads, less formal than most scientific writing. I got a lot from them and ended up referring to them quite often in my thesis.

Eight years later, I joined NAFEX, the North American Fruit Explorers. NAFEX members are dedicated fruit fanciers. They do such things as hunt for "lost" varieties, breed new ones and try to grow fruits outside their normal range. The group had been started by a few avid fruit fanciers; one of them, I was pleased to discover, was Dr. Dunstan.

By the time I joined NAFEX, the group had over fifteen hundred members, but it still had an informal, friendly air about it. So when I saw Dr. Dunstan's name on the membership list, I took the liberty of writing him. He sent me a pleasant reply and explained that grape breeding was actually something he did as a hobby. He even let me know that he was the shortest of eleven children and used to consider himself "the runt pig of the litter."

Early in 1987, I learned that Dr. Dunstan was ill with cancer. The news saddened me. Over the next few months, I'd occasionally hear a little more news about his condition. He wasn't doing well. I started feeling that I should write him another, probably last, letter.

Finally, in early July, the urge to write became almost overpowering. It was so strong it amazed me. I didn't know where it came from. I wrote, thanking him for all his work, especially with grapes, and praising his accomplishments. I then put the letter in the mail as fast as I could get to the post office.

A few weeks later, I heard that Dr. Dunstan had passed away in July. I wondered: *Had he even gotten my letter before he died? Why had I felt such an overpowering urge to write, anyway?* The whole thing puzzled me.

A few months after that, I went to the NAFEX annual

meeting at Oregon State University. During a break between talks, I was approached by a very pleasant-looking young man. He introduced himself as Bob Wallace, actually Robert Dunstan Wallace, the grandson of Dr. Dunstan. What he told me next made my hair stand on end.

Apparently, during his final months, Dr. Dunstan had been very depressed. Not only was he sick, he was also feeling as though his life hadn't amounted to much. As the weeks went by, he became less and less responsive and alert. Then the time came when he was in and out of a coma and not expected to live much longer.

During one of these last days, Bob Wallace went to visit his grandfather and bring him my letter. Amazingly, he found Dr. Dunstan fully alert and lucid. Bob read him my letter, with its praises for his work. It broke the spell of his depression. He and Bob talked for several hours, much to the amazement of his family, discussing Dunstan's life and work. When they were done, Bob said, his grandfather finally seemed to be at peace, accepting that his life really had been worthwhile.

Dr. Dunstan slipped back into a coma soon after that. A day or so later, he was gone.

Bob's words affected me strongly, as little else in my life has. I felt like I had just finished running a marathon. I had a wonderfully light and happy feeling inside, as though I'd just felt something in the universe itself click into place.

And, you know, I think I had. We who grow plants like to think of ourselves as guiding and caring for their lives. But now it's obvious to me, more than it ever was before, that we ourselves are being guided and cared for, as well.

Lon J. Rombough

A Million Trees

He who plants a tree plants hope.

Lucy Larcom

Camp was great fun that summer of 1970. The roasting of marshmallows and the woodsy smell of the fire made fifteen-year-old Andy Lipkis fall in love with the great outdoors. But as he looked out over the forested mountains above the city of Los Angeles, his heart sank. He knew from his biology class that bark beetles were killing the pollution-weakened trees at a rapid rate.

Andy couldn't just stand by and watch them die. So he rallied his fellow campers in a tree-saving adventure. They started by planting smog-tolerant trees in an old parking lot at the camp. As they swung picks and sowed seedlings, they brought life back into that piece of earth. When camp was over, one fellow camper put his hand on Andy's shoulder and said, "Let's visit the trees when we're old." Andy smiled back, knowing they would someday.

For Andy, that summer inspired an idea. *We need to spread this work to more places and more people,* he thought. Then he suddenly felt afraid: not of failure, but of success.

He knew that if he got people to join him, he would be responsible for something very important. It might mean he would be planting trees for the rest of his life! But he decided to follow his heart, wherever it might lead.

A few years later, Andy heard that the California Department of Forestry was about to destroy 20,000 surplus seedlings. Andy asked if he could have them for another tree planting project. "That would be considered a 'gift of public funds,'" the department spokesman told him. "We're prohibited by law from giving them to you."

But Andy did not give up that easily. He called newspapers, senators and anyone else who could pull some strings. He told them what was about to happen and begged them to do something. His calls paid off. When the *Los Angeles Times* called the governor's office to confirm the story they were planning to run, the governor's office responded by ordering the bulldozers stopped—just as the seedlings were being plowed under.

Andy was allowed to adopt the remaining seedlings. Then he brought together kids and counselors from twenty summer camps for a major replanting project. Newspaper coverage led to more donations, more volunteers and a new law requiring the government to give surplus trees to nonprofit groups who wanted them. People from all backgrounds joined Andy and his growing pack of citizen foresters. The group's nickname, "TreePeople," took root.

In 1980, Los Angeles Mayor Tom Bradley heard about TreePeople's success. He'd read that massive tree-planting could reduce pollution and wondered if planting a million trees in Los Angeles could breathe life back into his city. The mayor was told that it would take twenty years and $200 million to accomplish such a project. But the city couldn't wait twenty years; it had to start now. So Mayor Bradley asked TreePeople to take up the challenge. Los

Angeles had just been selected as host of the 1984 Olympics. Andy saw this as a perfect opportunity to show the world the power of people working together. He told the mayor he was sure the people of Los Angeles could do it, at virtually no cost to the government.

Response to the Million Tree Campaign was enthusiastic from the beginning. One nursery offered to donate 100,000 surplus trees if TreePeople could find a way to transport them. The U.S. Air Force came through. Early one morning in November 1981, eight massive trucks arrived in a convoy that stretched a quarter-mile on the freeway to move the seedlings across the L.A. Basin. The Million Tree Campaign was underway. Three hundred volunteers and airmen worked side by side all day long to move the seedlings.

As the Air Force crew prepared to leave at day's end, they were stopped by a beautiful sight. Standing before them, a group of volunteers holding hands had formed a circle, the sunset's glow bathing them in a warm light. The airmen were so moved that they stopped and joined the circle, making it twice as big. Hand in hand, they celebrated not just the day, but their power to contribute to life.

With this auspicious beginning, TreePeople inspired hundreds of volunteers with an ambitious goal: They would plant the millionth tree by the 1984 Summer Olympics. For the next three years, this goal united people from all over Los Angeles to work together to create an urban forest. Billboards proclaimed, "Turn Over a New Leaf, Los Angeles." Bumper stickers read, "Rooting for the Future." People were connected by the hope that the trees they had planted could help heal their home and the planet, too.

Four days before the Olympic flame was lit, the millionth tree was finally planted. The people of Los Angeles were amazed that they could do something so profound with their own hands. To celebrate, volunteers gathered in the mountains overlooking the city. Old and young, men and women, leaders from corporations, gangs and government agencies shared smiles and even danced on the mountain together.

Since the Million Tree Campaign, TreePeople has been training young people to become "managers of the environment." They teach kids that the city is a living ecosystem that can be healed and nurtured only by the informed actions of caring citizens. They deliver fruit trees to low-income families across the city so they can grow their own fresh fruit. On Martin Luther King, Jr. Day, they got thousands of Angelenos to plant the largest living memorial to Dr. King ever created. Five hundred trees now line the entire seven miles of King Boulevard. TreePeople's citizen foresters are now organizing neighborhoods to plant and care for trees throughout Los Angeles.

Andy's summer camp dream has become the gift of a lifetime. Andy now tells city kids across the country, "Believe in your dreams. That's what made mine grow."

Skye Trimble

PEANUTS *reprinted by permission of United Feature Syndicate, Inc.*

An Angel in Shirtsleeves

It's easy to make a buck. It's a lot tougher to make a difference.

Tom Brokaw

Mickey Weiss was technically retired from the family produce business. Even so, he still enjoyed dropping in now and then to check up on things. Early one morning in 1987, he headed over to pay a visit.

On the way, Mickey couldn't help slowing the car as he passed a small encampment of homeless people. They were just beginning to stir in the cool Los Angeles dawn. He sighed with helplessness at the sight of such poverty.

Minutes later, he pulled up at the family's vegetable company, one of many located at the Los Angeles Wholesale Produce Market. And there, waiting for the garbage truck, were two hundred pallets of slightly dam-aged strawberries.

Mickey exploded. "Why are we throwing away berries when eight blocks away, people are frying stale bread over open fires for their first meal of the day?" he demanded.

That was the beginning of a crusade. In the years that

followed, Mickey Weiss helped feed hundreds of thousands of hungry people in California by salvaging edible food destined for Dumpsters. He once calculated that in just two years, he gave away more than eight million dollars' worth of food.

Every morning in Los Angeles, big semitrailers deliver produce to the wholesalers' market. And every morning, food is deemed unfit to sell. Maybe a few tomatoes in a crate are molding, although the rest are fine. Maybe the peaches are blemished, though still sweet and firm. Maybe cartons are improperly labeled, or paperwork is incomplete. Until Mickey came along, nearly all that was thrown away.

Mickey was in his early seventies, but he knew the produce industry inside out. He'd dropped out of college to help his father with a struggling produce business, after his brother-in-law gambled away the profits. Together, father and son built up the one-truck business until they served the city's finest restaurants. Then came World War II. The man who knew his fruits and vegetables spent the war in Palm Springs, working in the officer's mess and scouring the L.A. produce markets for the bananas the troops loved.

After the war, Mickey went back to the family produce business and was soon known as "the mushroom king." After more than forty years, he handed over the business to his son. Then, Mickey was supposed to retire.

Until he saw those strawberries.

Mickey started working the phones. Using his contacts in the industry, he got other wholesalers to donate space at the produce market. He rounded up high school students to call Los Angeles charities to see who could use produce to feed the poor. He worked with the county agriculture department and other government agencies to cut through red tape that had kept unsaleable food from being given away.

Today, the center is the collection point each weekday morning for unsold fruit and vegetables from market merchants. Then, the donated produce is picked up by charities for distribution to soup kitchens, shelters and agencies that help the needy. Everything from apples to zucchini—along with more exotic fare such as fresh ginger, tomatillos and eggplant—goes into soup pots and salad bowls for homeless people, poor children, shelter residents and many more.

"Thank God, thank Mickey," they say.

So much for retirement. Until his death in 1996, Mickey was on the job at the distribution center three or four days a week. He was capturing donations of more than a million pounds of produce a month, and passing them directly to charities.

His work didn't go unnoticed. In 1989, President George Bush gave Mickey an End Hunger Award. Mickey's dream was to see similar food centers operating in every large produce terminal in America. "I'll be glad to go and help them," he said—and he did. Los Angeles was first; Houston followed; other cities fell in line. In 1991, Peter Clarke and Susan Evans were so inspired by Mickey's work that they established From the Wholesaler to the Hungry, a program to teach other cities to set up produce distribution programs. There are now more than seventy-five such operations around the United States.

Mickey once told an interviewer that the greatest lesson he learned from his charity was that "people give to people, not causes." She, in turn, described him as a silver-haired angel in shirtsleeves.

Mickey Weiss's cause lives on after his death. And to the people who benefit from his legacy of giving, he is now—and always has been—a real angel.

Carol Sturgulewski

5

LITTLE SPROUTS

Gardening has a magical quality when you are a child.

Barbara Damrosch

"A word with the manager . . ."

Iva Mae's Birthday

One of the luckiest things that can happen to you in life is, I think, to have a happy childhood.
Agatha Christie

Iva Mae Maples was the poorest girl in our first-grade class, and the thing she looked forward to above all else was her birthday. In 1936, her birthday fell on the third Friday of September, and she had invited us to her birthday party. In all her young life, she'd never had a birthday party before. "Not once!" she said.

Deep into the Great Depression, none of our families had much money. Our panties and dresses were sewn from the cloth of printed muslin flour sacks. Yet all of us, except Iva Mae, were fortunate enough to have sturdy shoes and socks and warm coats, though many were hand-me-downs or bought secondhand.

She wore shoes with holes in them, no socks, and she used one of her mother's cardigan sweaters as a coat. The sleeves were much too long. Even scrunched up as far as they would go, they still covered her hands. Which was just as well, since she didn't have any mittens either.

We all adored Iva Mae. She wore zinnias tucked into her pigtails. She was funny and adventurous and did outrageous things like bringing a squirrel to school and sneaking it into the teacher's desk drawer. Or belching loudly and then looking with total disgust at the unfortunate classmate seated next to her, saying, "Well! I sure hope y'all feel better now."

Another thing about Iva Mae: She brought wonderful lunches to school. Her mother raised all sorts of fruits and vegetables in their backyard. They would probably have starved otherwise.

What they didn't eat fresh from the garden, Mrs. Maples canned in quart jars. One of the best lunches Iva Mae brought to school was a thermos of homemade vegetable soup and a piece of buttered cornbread. The soup smelled so good we could hardly stand it. Occasionally she would give one of us a taste. It was glorious!

Finally, *the* Friday arrived. We were almost as excited as Iva Mae. Birthday day! Party day! Ice cream and cake day!

Since we were to walk directly over to Iva Mae's house after school, we arrived that morning carrying our wrapped presents. Our teacher placed them on a shelf in the cloakroom. All day we noticed Iva Mae glancing at the gifts every few minutes, eyes shining in anticipation.

When school let out at three, we gathered our gifts and trooped over to Iva Mae's. There were about twelve of us, laughing and chattering all the way. All except Iva Mae, that is. She seemed strangely quiet, and the closer we came to her house, the quieter she became.

We soon found out why. When twelve noisy little girls spilled through the door into Mrs. Maples' tiny two-room house, giggling and bearing gifts, the poor woman went into shock. Bewildered, she looked at Iva Mae as if to say, "What is going on here, young lady?"

We'd never known Iva Mae to be meek or shy, but now she squirmed uncomfortably and in a hushed little voice said, "I just decided to have me a birthday party, and I didn't think you'd mind. I plumb forgot to tell you and . . ."

We all fell silent. *Mrs. Maples didn't know about the party!*

Would she yell? Would she scream? Would she throw us all out and then give Iva Mae a spanking? Did this mean there would be no ice cream and cake? And wasn't it just like Iva Mae to pull a stunt like this?

"Oh," Mrs. Maples said, clutching her throat. "Oh. Oh my! Oh my, my, my!"

We watched as she struggled with her thoughts and feelings. What would she do next? She looked into the pleading eyes of her daughter. She gave a deep sigh. She rolled her eyes. She shook her head. Then she began to laugh and gave Iva Mae a big hug. "You're right," she finally said. "It's party time!"

We looked around. Their sparsely furnished home left plenty of wall space for shelves, which Mrs. Maples had built of old scrap lumber and bricks. And every shelf was laden with home-canned produce from her garden.

It was a beautiful sight of plenty. Clear glass jars brimming with jewel-toned fruits and vegetables, including dozens of jars of her famous vegetable soup.

She knew we expected refreshments, so she made do with what she had. She took four quarts of soup from the shelf to warm up.

"Now, girls," she said, "please go out to the garden and pick fourteen pears and a big bunch of zinnias to decorate the table."

We dashed out to the garden. Once outside, I said, "Gee, Iva Mae, how come your mother wasted garden space on something you can't eat?" I pointed to the zinnias that grew along the entire length of the garden. They were all different colors, bright and pastel. Big flowers, too; some ruffled and some plain. I had never seen so much beauty in one spot. And even though it was late September, they still looked beautiful.

"Oh, those," Iva Mae said. "Mother says those are food for our souls."

Back inside, we snacked on soup and crackers and soon forgot about ice cream and cake. Mrs. Maples arranged the pears on a round platter, and wedged a big candle in the center of the plate. Then she lit the candle and we all sang "Happy Birthday."

We ate the pears while Iva Mae opened her gifts. There were paper doll books, a coloring book, some bath salts, hair ribbons, a bottle of hand lotion, two pairs of socks, a handmade head scarf, some Old Maid cards, a puzzle, a yo-yo and a kaleidoscope. She glowed with joy to have so many new things.

Mrs. Maples glowed, too. Her little girl was happy!

And because she overheard us admiring her zinnias, she gave us each a handful of freshly gathered seed before we left. "Plant these next spring," she said, "and remember me when you see them bloom."

How could I *not* remember? Even now, sixty-five years later, I still think of her every time I see zinnias blooming in my garden.

I remember her good humor, her sweetness, her creativity, her courage in "making do" during a hard period in their lives. I remember her showing me that you don't need ice cream and cake to have a great party, and that no gardener is ever too poor to have something to share with others.

Perhaps, most of all, I remember how I no longer felt that Iva Mae was the poorest girl in our first-grade class.

Nita Waxelman

The Plum Pretty Sister

There is a garden in every childhood, an enchanted place where colors are brighter, the air softer, and the morning more fragrant than ever again.

Elizabeth Lawrence

Justin was a climber. By one and a half, he had discovered the purple plum tree in the backyard, and its friendly branches became his favorite hangout.

At first he would climb just a few feet and make himself comfortable in the curve where the trunk met the branches. Soon he was building himself a small fort and dragging his toy tractors and trucks up to their new garage.

One day when he was two, Justin was playing in the tree as usual. I turned my back to prune the rosebush, and he disappeared.

"Justin, where are you?" I hollered.

His tiny voice called back, "Up here, Mommy, picking all the plums for you!"

I looked up in horror and disbelief. There was Justin on the roof of the house, filling his plastic bucket with the ripe juicy plums from his favorite tree.

When Justin was three, I became pregnant. My husband and I explained to him that we were going to have another baby as a playmate for him.

He was very excited, kissed my tummy and said, "Hello, baby, I'm your big brother, Justin."

From the beginning he was sure he was going to have a little sister, and every day he'd beg to know if she was ready to play yet. When I explained that the baby wasn't arriving until the end of June, he seemed confused.

One day he asked, "When is June, Mommy?"

I realized I needed a better explanation; how could a three-year-old know what "June" meant? Just then, as Justin climbed into the low branches of the plum tree, he gave me the answer I was looking for . . . his special tree.

"Justin, the baby is going to be born when the plums are ripe. You can keep me posted when that will be, okay?" I wasn't completely sure if I was on target, but the gardener in me was confident I'd be close enough.

Oh, he was excited! Now Justin had a way to know when his new baby sister would come to play. From that moment on, he checked the old plum tree several times a day and reported his findings to me. Of course, he was quite concerned in November when all the leaves fell off the tree. By January, with the cold and the rains, he was truly worried whether his baby would be cold and wet like his tree. He whispered to my tummy that the tree was strong and that she (the baby) had to be strong too, and make it through the winter.

By February a few purple leaves began to shoot forth, and his excitement couldn't be contained.

"My tree is growing, Mommy! Pretty soon she'll have baby plums, and then I'll have my baby sister."

March brought the plum's beautiful tiny white flowers, and Justin was overjoyed.

"She's b'ooming, Mommy!" he chattered, struggling with the word "blooming." He rushed to kiss my tummy and got kicked in the mouth.

"The baby's moving, Mommy, she's b'ooming, too. I think she wants to come out and see the flowers."

So it went for the next couple of months, as Justin checked every detail of his precious plum tree and reported to me about the flowers turning to tiny beads that would become plums.

The rebirth of his tree gave me ample opportunity to explain the development of the fetus that was growing inside me. Sometimes I think he believed I had actually planted a "baby seed" inside my tummy, because when I drank water he'd say things like, "You're watering our little flower, Mommy!" I'd laugh and once again explain in simple terms the story of the birds and the bees, the plants and the trees.

June finally arrived, and so did the purple plums. At first they were fairly small, but Justin climbed his tree anyway to pick some plums off the branches where the sun shone warmest. He brought them to me to let me know the baby wasn't ripe yet.

I felt ripe! I was ready to pop! When were the plums going to start falling from that darn tree?

Justin would rub my tummy and talk to his baby sister, telling her she had to wait a little longer because the fruit was not ready to be picked yet. His forays into the plum tree lasted longer each day, as if he was coaxing the tree to ripen quickly. He talked to the tree and thanked it for letting him know about this important event in his life. Then one day, it happened. Justin came running into the house, his eyes as big as saucers, with a plastic bucket full to the brim of juicy purple plums.

"Hurry, Mommy, hurry!" he shouted. "She's coming, she's coming! The plums are ripe, the plums are ripe!"

I laughed uncontrollably as Justin stared at my stomach, as if he expected to see his baby sister erupt any moment. That morning I did feel a bit queasy, and it wasn't because I had a dental appointment.

Before we left the house, Justin went out to hug his plum tree and whisper that today was the day his "plum pretty sister" would arrive. He was certain.

As I sat in the dental chair, the labor pains began, just as Justin had predicted. Our "plum" baby was coming! I called my parents, and my husband rushed me to the hospital. At 6:03 P.M. on June 22, the day that will forever live in family fame as "Plum Pretty Sister Day," our daughter was born. We didn't name her Purple Plum as Justin suggested, but chose another favorite flower, Heather.

At Heather's homecoming, Justin kissed his new playmate and presented her with his plastic bucket, full to the brim with sweet, ripe, purple plums.

"These are for you," he said proudly.

Justin and Heather are now teenagers, and the plum tree has become our bonding symbol. Although we moved from the home that housed Justin's favorite plum tree, the first tree to be planted in our new yard was a purple plum, so that Justin and Heather could know when to expect her special day. Throughout their growing-up years, the children spent countless hours nestled in the branches, counting down the days through the birth of leaves, flowers, buds and fruit. Our birthday parties are always festooned with plum branches and baskets brimming with freshly picked purple plums. Because as Mother Nature—and Justin—would have it, for the last fifteen years, the purple plum has ripened exactly on June 22.

Cynthia Brian

Luther Burbank and the Disappearing Raspberries

Appearances often are deceiving.

Aesop

Our childhood home in Santa Rosa, California, was stuffed with plants and animals. If it grew, my folks grew it. Or, if we didn't grow it, we traded for it. If all else failed, Dad worked for it. Sometimes he worked for Luther Burbank, the world-famous horticulturalist known as "The Plant Wizard."

When I was a kid, I didn't know about Luther Burbank, or that Dad worked for him. There was something else I didn't know, either: why we didn't grow raspberries. That seemed odd just because two ten-foot rows of post and wires, definitely set up for raspberries, stood right beside our garden. But those wires were bare.

After I grew up, I became very close to my sister, Edith, who was ten years older than I. One Sunday afternoon when I was visiting, she leaned over and said, "Stu, I'll tell you something no one on this earth knows. This has to be our secret, though. You promise you won't tell anyone, at least as long as I'm still alive?" She looked at me most seriously.

"Yes," I said, intensely interested.

"You remember Dad's garden? How hard he worked?"

"Sure."

Edith leaned close and almost whispered, "Do you remember the raspberry patch? Just beyond the apple trees? The poles and wires were there for raspberries, but Dad stopped growing them."

"*Stopped* growing them?" I asked.

Edith rushed right ahead. "Oh, he grew them all right. Mr. Burbank gave Dad some to try. Through the years, Mr. Burbank gave Dad lots of plants to raise."

"Luther Burbank gave Dad plants?" I said.

"Yes. The Shasta daisies along Grandma's front fence were from him. That Indian peach tree by Grandma's back fence. And that awful big cactus by the chicken yard. I suppose there were other things I don't remember."

My sister paused, looked around, then said, "And the raspberries were from him. I remember Dad saying that Mr. Burbank wanted some planted in different soil than he had and that he'd want to keep track of how they did. So Dad brought them back and planted them right then and there. He wanted to do everything just the way Mr. Burbank would.

"I was just a kid, so I didn't give the berries another thought—until the day a year or two later when Dad brought in the first bowl of berries. I fell in love with them. They were just so good! When nobody was looking, I ate them all. I got heck from Mom for not saving some for others. This I could understand. However, we'd often been told we could help ourselves to any fruits or vegetables growing outside. So I started eating them right off the vine! I loved those berries. Every chance I got, I gobbled them up."

Edith told me our brother and sister liked them, too.

She laughed, "I soon learned that in order to have all the berries, I'd have to get up early. So, when I first heard Dad in the kitchen, I'd sneak out the front door, run around to the back, and eat all the ripe berries. When there weren't any ripe ones left, I'd eat the almost-ripe ones. Sometimes I even got a bit of a stomachache!"

As I laughed in amazement, Edith continued. "This went on for several seasons. I had the time of my life. Then one day I saw Daddy digging up the raspberries, throwing the dug-up plants into his old wheelbarrow, then hauling them off to the burning heap. I said, 'Dad, what are you doing? All your good raspberries!'"

"He answered, 'They just don't give berries, Edith. Lots of bloom, lots of green berries. But for some reason they don't hang on. Something in the soil, I guess. I had to tell Mr. Burbank. He said he'd ride his bike out one day and look at the soil. Maybe it's the apple tree or the leach line. In the meantime, I just won't plant anything here.' And, as you know, he never did."

My sister's next words came almost in a whisper: *"I never told him."*

I sat there playing back in my mind what I had just learned. It's not every day you learn your big sister's deepest, darkest secret.

Then a question came to me. "What did Mr. Burbank say?"

"Mr. Burbank was the Plant Wizard and all, but for once even he was stumped. He just said he didn't know what had happened, either."

Well, I thought, *that's not surprising. He'd have to have been a People Wizard, too, to have figured this one out!*

Stuart C. Vincent

Brian

Brian is seven. He's a dreamer and drives his teacher crazy. She's stiff as taffy in December.

One day Brian got to school an hour late. His teacher stormed from the classroom, down to the office, and called Brian's mother. "Brian was an hour late today," his teacher said. "I've just about had it!"

Brian's mother worried all day. Finally, Brian got home.

"Brian, what happened at school?"

"I was late. My teacher got mad."

"I know, Brian. She called me. What happened?"

"Well," Brian started, "it must have rained. There were worms all over the sidewalk." He paused a while and went on. "I knew the kids would step on them, so I tried to put them back in the holes."

He looked up at his mother. "It took a long time because they didn't want to go."

His mother hugged him. "I love you, Brian," she said.

Jay O'Callahan

Gone Fishin'

Roses are red,
Violets are blue;
But they don't get around
Like the dandelions do.

Slim Acres

It was my third year of trying to create the perfect lawn.

I was doing quite well this summer. I'd reseeded the bare spots from winter's ravages. I'd found just the right grass seed for our soil conditions. I'd created a sprinkler system that worked well for both the lawn and for entertaining my four children.

All was going well, until one day I noticed several sprouting dandelions. *No problem,* I thought. I hurried to the store and bought an herbicide. I figured that by the next weekend, I'd have those yellow devils whipped.

But when I got home, I took a closer look at the instructions. Reading the cautionary statements made me shudder; we live in a rural area with a nearby pond and have cats and dogs and children. I didn't want to inflict toxic chemicals on any of them. So I made the mixture weaker than the directions called for. Weak and ineffective: By the next weekend, those tough little dandelions didn't have so much as a withered leaf.

I had promised my four-year-old daughter Kayla we'd go fishing on Saturday. Kayla loves to fish and is very good at it. But when Saturday arrived, I found the little yellow splotches in my lawn had multiplied.

I'll have to deal with the dandelions before we go fishing, I told myself. *The lawn is less than half an acre; how long can it take?*

With screwdriver and garbage sack in hand, I attacked the pesky weeds.

"Pickin' flowers, Daddy?" Kayla asked.

"Yes, dear," I said, digging furiously at a tough root.

"I'll help," she offered. "I'll give some to Mommy."

"Go ahead, sweetie," I answered. "There's plenty."

An hour passed, and yellow splotches still remained.

"You said we's going fishin' today," Kayla complained.

"Yes, I know, dear," I said. "Just a little more flower picking, okay?"

"I'll get the fish poles," Kayla announced.

I labored on, prying up one stubborn root after another.

"I found some worms under a rock, Daddy," Kayla piped up. "I put them in a cup. Are you ready?"

"Almost, honey."

More minutes dragged by.

"You picked 'nough flowers, Daddy," Kayla insisted impatiently.

"Okay, honey, just a few more," I promised. But I couldn't stop. The compulsion to finish the job was overwhelming.

A few minutes later, a tap came on my shoulder.

"Make a wish, Daddy!" Kayla chirped.

As I turned, Kayla took a big breath, puffed, and sent a thousand baby dandelion seeds into the air.

I picked her up and kissed her, and we headed for the fish pond.

David Clinton Matz

A Garden So Rich

Life affords no greater responsibility, no greater privilege, than the raising of the next generation.

C. Everett Koop, M.D.

I watched out the window as they started turning over the soil. Of course, my husband did most of the work, while our five-year-old son spent most of his energy fingering through the dirt looking for worms. Still, the sight of the two of them "working" side by side, preparing the ground for a spring garden, brought a smile to my face.

For just a moment, I considered joining them. Then I remembered the excitement I'd heard in my son's voice when he announced that Saturday morning, "Me and Daddy are going to plant a garden!"

I sipped my coffee wondering if joining in on the fun would be interfering in a male-bonding project. Right then I heard my son call out, "Hey, Dad, bet you can't find a worm this fine."

"Oh, yeah? Look at this one," my husband countered.

I could see the two squirming creatures that dangled from their fingers in some sort of "fine" worm contest. For a second, I wondered how one went about qualifying a fine worm. Cringing, I made up my mind. This was definitely their project. I'd leave it to them. Besides, it might be more fun to stand back and simply see what grows out of this garden.

I watched as they poked the seeds into the black top-soil. They planted tomatoes, squash and green beans. I watched as they carefully transplanted the tomato plants into the ground. I listened to the spurts of laughter, the dialogue that passed back and forth.

"When will they grow, Daddy?"

"Soon," my husband replied.

"Tonight?"

"Not that soon."

"Tomorrow?" my son asked.

"In a few days. The seeds have to sprout, then grow."

"Then we'll have vegetables?"

"No, it takes a while."

"One day?" my son questioned.

"Longer," my husband replied.

"Two days?" his anxious young voice queried.

I saw the smile touch my husband's expression, and at that moment I knew I was already seeing the first of many fruits the garden would bring. My son would learn that some things in life aren't instant. My husband would learn how to better deal with a five-year-old's expectations and endless questions. Patience . . . what a wonderful fruit to grow.

In the evenings that followed, they knelt to the ground and looked for signs of new life. The sight of them, so close and with common goals, warmed my heart and made me happy I'd decided to watch from afar.

More days passed, and each afternoon I watched the

two of them water their garden. My son always managed to get as wet as the garden, and, more times than not, even my husband came in drenched. The laughter that followed them in made the muddy tracks and extra laundry tolerable. Well, almost tolerable.

Finally, the plants appeared. From the distance I enjoyed my son's look of glee, as well as the look of wonder on my husband's face as he, too, watched our son. And like the tiny plants breaking through the earth, I saw fruit number two appear. Pride . . . what a wonderful fruit to grow.

The weeks passed; the garden grew. At the first fruit-bearing blossoms, I watched the two men in my life study and examine each plant. My son would ask questions and my husband did his best to explain.

"Why do they call squash, squash?" the smallest and dirtiest gardener questioned.

"I don't know," came my husband's answer.

"I wonder how many worms live in this garden?" my son asked.

"I don't know," my husband replied.

"A million?"

"Probably," my husband said.

"Can we catch them?" Excitement radiated from his voice.

"I don't think so," my husband answered with a chuckle. "But look at this blossom."

"Will it really become a tomato?" came yet another question.

"It will." My husband smiled.

I smiled, too. For just as plants grow, I knew I was watching a relationship take root—watching cherished moments being framed for future memories.

They continued to water, to weed and to care for their small garden. And after all the work and effort they proudly produced ten tomatoes, several medium-size squash and three pots of beans.

One afternoon, as he placed a few dusty tomatoes on the kitchen table, my husband shook his head ruefully and said, "We probably spent ten hours out there for each of these tomatoes. Was it worth it?"

Our smiles met at the same time. There was no need to answer. Relationships, memories, patience and pride. Who knew a garden could bear so much?

Christie Craig

The Sock Garden

If you can give your son or daughter only one gift, let it be enthusiasm.

Bruce Barton

Some people grow corn. Some people grow roses. But who ever heard of growing socks?

I guess you have to be a special kind of gardener—and a special kind of dad!

One day last fall, Dad said, "Go get your oldest, rattiest wool socks!"

My sister, my brother and I thought this sounded weird. But it was better than sitting around until Mom got back from the store.

When we all met outside with our socks, I asked, "What are we doing?"

"We're making a sock garden, of course!" Dad said with a smile.

We carried our socks and hiked down the road. I wondered where we were going. But then we stopped at an old field. Dad looked out at the dead, gray weeds. "Remember how this field was full of flowers this summer?" asked Dad. We all nodded. "Good," he said. "Pull your socks over your shoes and follow me."

So we did, feeling silly.

Dad walked. We walked.

Then my sister Sara hopped. Dad hopped, too.

I liked that. So I stomped. We all stomped and giggled.

Dad pulled a seed pod off a plant. It snapped just like a bean. He touched a pod of another. It exploded with a noise—tsssk!—and flung out seeds. Soon we were all touching the popping plants.

We found a plant with tiny cups. We tilted them sideways and out poured seeds. They fell with a hiss, like cereal pouring from a box.

Then we got really wild. Dad taught us a kooky dance: the Woodchuck Waddle. He said his aunt had taught it to him as a kid.

I made up another: the Squirrel Skip. Sara invented the Deer Dance. David twirled around until he was so dizzy, he fell over. We danced and laughed some more.

By this time, we were sagging in our socks. Then, "All done," said Dad.

"All done?" I wondered out loud. Dancing is never all done. Then I realized Dad was looking at our socks, but I was still clueless.

On the way out of the field, we played follow-the-leader. I was in charge. I pulled the white fluff from some milkweed pods.

"Whoosh!" I yelled as I let it go free. We watched the seeds, on downy parachutes, float and fly away in the wind.

Then we took off our socks and carried them all the way home. Back at the house, Dad plopped down on the ground in the backyard. He held up his socks for us to see. They were covered with dirt and plant bits. But there was more . . . there were prickly seeds: little ones and big ones in all kinds of shapes.

Finally, I understood. While we'd been playing with seeds, our socks had been collecting them. Dad told us that animals caught seeds in their fur just like we caught them in our socks. When the seeds fall off the fur, they grow in a new place. And that's what our seeds would do, too.

That afternoon, we buried our seedy socks in the yard. "Let's make it a secret!" said Sara. We didn't say a word to Mom.

But when the next summer came, we had flowers growing in funny, sock-shaped clumps. The flowers were pretty. Mom brought in jars full of them, and even put some in her hair.

"Where did they come from?" she asked Dad.

We all stayed quiet. "The rain or wind must have brought them," said Dad, trying not to grin.

David and Sara hid their faces behind pillows. But I couldn't keep quiet. I giggled. Soon we were all laughing . . . and our sock garden secret was out for good!

Some people grow corn. Some people grow roses. But my dad grows socks—and a whole lot of fun!

April Pulley Sayre

My Mother's Cure

*Gardening requires lots of water—most of it in
the form of perspiration.*

Lou Erickson

To break the spell of a long, cold Minnesota winter, my
mother and I pored over seed catalogs making plans for a
garden. "Maybe we should plant tomatoes," my mother
suggested. "Grandma had good luck with tomatoes. Wish
I could remember what she said about growing tomatoes.
Hmm. Maybe it will come to me."

"I hope we have better luck with tomatoes than we did
last year with flowers," I grumbled. Ever since I had
turned fifteen in the fall, I seemed to grumble about
everything.

"Oh, come on, Jeanie. Cheer up. We'll have lots of fun in
our tomato garden. It'll be a real mother-daughter project.
Two by two, we'll see them through, from seeds to soup,"
my mother said, adding a little soft-shoe step to her
words.

When the precious seeds came to our house, my
mother sowed them in what she called a "baby" flat.

When they grew too big for that flat, she transplanted them into bigger flats. "Sixty plants!" she exclaimed. "Why, we've got our work cut out for us this summer, that's for sure."

"How many tomatoes do you think we'll get from each plant?" I asked, looking dubiously at the spindly little things.

"Well, if we had a bigger plot, we'd have hundreds. But the yard is too small for that. We'll have to stake them. That way, we'll decrease the number of tomatoes per plant. It will mean we'll have to trim some 'kiddos' from each mother plant."

"Oh, Mom!" I wailed. "That sounds horrible!"

"Oh, don't be silly, Jeanie," Mom said, with a touch of impatience. "Honestly, you teenagers are all alike. The merest little thing and you go into hysterics. A summer of good, hard work will be the cure for what ails you. As soon as there's no longer any danger of frost, we'll get these plants outside."

It was barely daylight one Saturday morning when my mother yanked me out of bed. As she tossed me a pair of overalls and a trowel, she said, "We haven't a minute to lose. Weatherman says we are in for rain by mid-morning. Let's get those plants in so they can soak up that nice spring rain."

I kept up a constant stream of complaints as I worked along with my mother. She brushed them all aside with a song she said Grandma always sang as they gardened together. "Just wish I could remember what she said, though, about growing tomatoes. Might still come to me as we go along here, two by two, from seeds to soup."

My mother was relentless in her "cure" for whatever it was that ailed me that summer. I had barely recovered from my planting experience when she informed me that it was time to hoe and weed our garden plot. If we weren't hoeing and weeding, we were warding off cutworms by wrapping the bases of the plants with paper. The more I griped about all the hard work, the louder my mother sang about the joys of working together.

As the summer slipped away, out came the canning equipment. We spent a long, boring weekend boiling and rinsing each item with great care.

"We'll have to labor away on Labor Day," Mom said. "I wouldn't want to waste even one tomato. We'll have tomato juice, some we'll can whole and some we'll boil down for soup. And I have the recipe for Grandma's chili. I sure wish I could remember what it was she said about growing tomatoes. Still hasn't come to me. Oh, say, Jeanie, run down the street, will you, and get Mrs. Nelson's Mason jars? She has a sack set aside for me."

I barely recognized the boy who opened the Nelsons' backdoor. Could that really be Eddie, the Nelsons' grandson? Where was the gangly, awkward Eddie of last summer? I was so stunned by his movie-star good looks I felt a peppy tune building up inside me. When I stumbled down the steps, Eddie offered to carry the sack of jars and walk me home. When my mother saw him, she was as surprised as I had been. She stammered out something about fixing iced tea.

"Are you here for the Labor Day weekend?" she asked, when I was unable to break the silence.

"Uh—well, no. I mean, yes," Eddie blushed. "I'm going to the academy this year, and I'm here early for football practice. I'll be living with my grandparents while I go to school."

"Isn't that wonderful!" my mother glowed.

"Yeah, it's great," Eddie said. "We're having a team picnic on Labor Day. Uh—hmm—uh, say, Jean, maybe you'd like to come with me—I mean, if you're free Labor Day," Eddie concluded, looking directly at me.

I looked around at the kitchen counters heaped high with tomatoes and canning equipment, gazed with great pain at the sack of Mason jars, and dared not meet my mother's eye. I had been by her side all summer. She had met my gripes and sass with as much love and care as she had lavished on her tomatoes. She had wanted us to be a mother-daughter team, seeing this project through from seeds to soup. But I hoped she would realize how much I wanted to go to that picnic. At the same time, I hated to think of her working alone in our kitchen, humming and singing her little tunes to herself.

My mother took off her glasses and wiped them slowly on a corner of her apron. Surveying the kitchen counters, she seemed to be looking far beyond the tomatoes and canning equipment. Perhaps that is why she said softly, "I remember now what Grandma said about growing tomatoes. She said, 'Children and tomatoes grow much too quickly. But at least you can preserve tomatoes when they blossom.'" In a stronger voice, my mother added, "Of course, Jean may go to the picnic. I'm sure you two will have a wonderful time."

I was so happy I couldn't speak a word, so I couldn't thank my mother until after Eddie left. I was smiling—beaming—for the first time in months. I kissed my mother, and I kissed every tomato within reach. Then I thanked my lucky stars I had a mother who knew how to raise tomatoes—and a daughter.

Jean Jeffrey Gietzen

6

THE SEASONS OF LIFE

From the earth we were formed,
  To the earth we return.
  And in between, we garden.

Nelson Eddy

Mike and the Grass

The love we give away is the only love we keep.

Elbert Hubbard

When Mike was three, he wanted a sandbox, and his father said, "There goes the yard. We'll have kids over here day and night, and they'll throw sand into the flower beds, and cats will make a mess in it, and it'll kill the grass for sure."

And Mike's mother said, "It'll come back."

When Mike was five, he wanted a jungle-gym set with swings that would take his breath away and bars to take him to the summit, and his father said, "Good grief, I've seen those things in backyards, and do you know what they look like? Mud holes in a pasture. Kids digging their gym shoes in the ground. It'll kill the grass."

And Mike's mother said, "It'll come back."

Between breaths when Daddy was blowing up the plastic swimming pool, he warned, "You know what they're going to do to this place? They're going to condemn it and use it for a missile site. I hope you know what you're doing. They'll track water everywhere and have a million water fights, and you won't be able to take out the garbage without stepping in mud up to your neck. When we take this down, we'll have the only brown lawn on the block."

"It'll come back," Mike's mother said.

When Mike was twelve, he volunteered his yard for a camp-out. As they hoisted the tents and drove in the spikes, his father stood at the window and observed: "Why don't I just put the grass seed out in cereal bowls for the birds and save myself the trouble of spreading it around? You know for a fact that those tents and all those big feet are going to trample down every single blade of grass, don't you? Don't bother to answer. I know what you're going to say: 'It'll come back.'"

The basketball hoop on the side of the garage attracted more crowds than the Olympics. And a small patch of lawn that started out with a barren spot the size of a garbage can lid soon grew to encompass the entire side yard.

Just when it looked as if the new seed might take root, the winter came and the sled runners beat it into ridges. Mike's father shook his head and said, "I never asked for much in this life—only a patch of grass."

And his wife smiled and said, "It'll come back."

The lawn this fall was beautiful. It was green and alive and rolled out like a sponge carpet along the drive where gym shoes had trod . . . along the garage where bicycles used to fall . . . and around the flower beds where little boys used to dig with iced-tea spoons.

But Mike's father never saw it. He anxiously looked beyond the yard and asked with a catch in his voice, "He will come back, won't he?"

Erma Bombeck

God's Mountain Garden

Keep a green tree in your heart and perhaps the singing bird will come.

Chinese Proverb

I grew up on a farm in the mountains of northwest Arkansas. As children, my brother and I roamed every inch of the little mountain facing my parents' house. We knew where every giant boulder and animal burrow was on that little piece of mountain bordering my dad's farm.

One day, my grandpa came to visit from his home several miles away. We sat on the front porch swing looking at the mountain, and he began to tell me a story. It was a delightful tale about him and me living in a little cabin on the mountain.

"Can you see it?" he asked. "It's right there by that big acorn tree. See it?"

Of course I saw it. What eight-year-old child wouldn't see what her imagination wanted her to see?

"We're gonna live in that cabin. We'll catch a wild cow for our milk and pick wild strawberries for our supper," Grandpa continued. "I bet the squirrels will bring us nuts to eat. We'll search the bushes for wild chickens and turkeys. The chickens will give us eggs, and we'll cook us a turkey over the big ol' fireplace. Yep, we'll do that some day."

From that day on, every time I saw my grandpa, I asked when we would go to live in that little log cabin on the mountain. Then he'd once more spin the story of how the two of us would live in the cabin with the wildflowers and wild animals around us.

Time raced on; I grew into my teens and gradually forgot Grandpa's story. After graduating high school, I still saw Grandpa and loved him dearly, but not like that little girl did. I grew out of the fantasy of the log cabin and wild cows.

Before long, I married and set up my own house. One day, the phone rang. When I heard my daddy's sorrowful voice, I knew my grandpa had left us. He had been in his garden behind his house and died there, his heart forever stopped.

I grieved alongside my mother for my dear grandpa, remembering his promises of the cabin in the woods with all its animals and flowers. It seemed I could once again hear his voice telling me the fantasy we shared. I felt my childhood memories being buried with him.

Less than a year later, I went to visit my parents' farm. Mama and I sat on the front porch admiring the green foliage of the mountain. It had been ten months since Grandpa had passed away, but the longing to hear his voice one more time was still fresh in my soul.

I told Mama about the story Grandpa had always told me, of the cabin in the woods, the wild cow, the chickens and turkey. "Mama," I said after I had finished my story, "would you mind if I went for a walk by myself?"

"Of course not," was her reply.

I changed into old jeans and put on my walking shoes. Mama cautioned me to be careful and went on with her chores.

The walk was invigorating. Spring had come to the country, and everything was getting green. Little Johnny-jump-ups were springing up all over the pastures. New calves were following their mamas begging for milk. At the foot of the mountain, I stopped. Where did Grandpa say that acorn tree was?

"Straight up from the house," I thought I heard him say.

I began my journey up the little mountain. It was steeper than I remembered, and I was out of shape. I trudged on, determined to find that tree.

Suddenly the ground leveled out. I was amazed to see what was before me. Soft green moss covered a small, flat clearing. Dogwood trees, smothered in pastel blooms, surrounded it. Off to the side stood a tall oak tree—Grandpa's acorn tree! Scattered among the tufts of moss were vibrant colors of wild wood violets. Green rock ferns and pearly snowdrops were scattered about as well. I could hardly catch my breath.

I don't know how long I stood there—several minutes, I suppose. Finally I came to my senses and sat down on the moss. In all my childhood wanderings on the mountain, I had never seen this magically beautiful place. Was this what Grandpa meant when he pointed out our special spot on the mountainside all those years ago? Did he know this was here?

A squirrel darted in front of me. He had a nut in his mouth. I watched as he scampered up the oak tree. No, I didn't see a wild cow or chickens. But in my heart, I knew they were there somewhere.

I decided to go tell Mama what I had found. She would want to see it, too. Before I left I took one more look. It was the most beautiful place I could have ever imagined.

It didn't take me as long to get back to the house. I burst into the kitchen babbling about the clearing on the side of the mountain. Mama calmed me down enough so she could understand what I was talking about. Daddy heard the conversation and tried to convince me there was no such place up there. He knew the mountain and had never seen anything like that.

On my insistence, he and Mama decided to go see the amazing place I was raving about. Once again I climbed the mountain straight up from the house. Before I knew it, we were at the top.

"We must have missed it," I told my dad.

He just nodded and we retraced our steps. We searched for over an hour for that little place on the mountain. We never found it. I was devastated.

On the way back home, Mama put her arms around my shoulders.

"Sissy," she said, "you know what you saw, don't you?"

"Yeah, I know what I saw, and I know it's there somewhere. We just missed it."

"No, sweetie, it's not there anymore. You saw God's garden. Only special people can see that. Your grandpa loved you so much, and he knew you were grieving inside. Hold that memory in your heart."

I'm fifty-two years old now. Every time I go back to Mama's house and sit on the porch, I remember the secret garden Grandpa told me about. But I no longer go out and look for it. No, I know just where it is.

Bertha M. Sutliff

Rusty Nails

*Beyond talent lie all the usual words: discipline,
love, luck—but, most of all, endurance.*

James Baldwin

*James A. Michener was one of America's finest and most pro-
lific writers. He was eighty-five when he wrote his autobiography,*
The World Is My Home. *Of it, he wrote:*

I have been impelled to attempt this project because of
an experience that occurred eighty years ago when I was
a country lad of five. The incident was of such powerful
import that the memory of it has never left me.

The farmer living at the end of our lane had an aging
apple tree that had once been abundantly productive but
had now lost its energy and ability to bear any fruit at all.
The farmer, on an early spring day I still remember, hammered eight nails, long and rusty, into the trunk of the
tree. Four were knocked in close to the ground on four
different sides of the trunk, four higher up and well
spaced about the circumference.

That autumn a miracle happened. The tired old tree,

having been goaded back to life, produced a bumper crop of juicy red apples, bigger and better than we had seen before. When I asked how this had happened, the farmer explained: "Hammerin' in the rusty nails gave it a shock to remind it that its job is to produce apples."

"Was it important that the nails were rusty?"

"Maybe it made the minerals in the nails easier to digest."

"Was eight important?"

"If you're goin' to send a message, be sure it's heard."

"Could you do the same next year?"

"A substantial jolt lasts about ten years."

"Will you knock more nails in then?"

"By that time we both may be finished," he said, but I was unable to verify this prediction, for by that time our family had moved away from the lane.

In the 1980s, when I was nearly eighty years old, I had some fairly large rusty nails hammered into my trunk—a quintuple bypass heart surgery, a new left hip, a dental rebuilding, an attack of permanent vertigo—and, like a sensible apple tree, I resolved to resume bearing fruit.

James A. Michener
Submitted by Marci E. Brown

CLOSE TO HOME

JOHN McPHERSON

"I see you had a little problem with the Weed Eater."

Flowers for a Newborn Child

Flowers are words which even a babe may understand.

Bishop Arthur Cleveland

It was a cold, drizzly day. Mist nudged up against the windows and doors of the house. I was adding more wood to the fire when I heard a knock at the front door.

Judy was standing on the doorstep, wearing her usual faded green sweatpants, a hand-knitted sweater—and a silver tiara. She only wore her tiara on special occasions. She held a large, crumpled plastic bag in her arms. We smiled warmly at each other.

"Flowers for the newborn child," she declared, holding out the bag. I welcomed my friend and accepted the package. There was no sign of any flowers, but I said "thank you" anyway.

Judy has always been full of surprises. If she said she brought flowers, then sooner or later, flowers would appear. I have never known anyone even vaguely like her. She has always approached things differently, danced to her own tune. At seventy-six, she still considered such practical things as umbrellas or raincoats unnecessary on rainy days. She would simply stride out into any weather, defying rain or snow. "I've yet to hear of a person dissolving because of a little extra moisture in the air," she'd say.

That particular morning, there were tiny jewels of rain nestled in the weave of her sweater, a cascade of droplets adding sparkle to her wiry gray hair, rain still clinging to the tip of her nose. She shook her head vigorously back and forth, like a dog after a swim, then matter-of-factly straightened her tiara.

"Where is the little darling?" she asked. "I'm dying to meet her, dear."

I led the way to the sky-blue door at the end of the narrow hall. We both looked in, barely breathing.

The curtains in the little room were open. Low square windows framed a dripping wisteria vine in full flower. My daughter lay fast asleep in her grandfather's wicker baby basket. She was loosely swaddled in a cotton blanket. From the walls around her, pale pink and blue sheep grazed peacefully in her newborn baby landscape.

I looked at Judy. She was gazing intently at my child.

At first, she said nothing. Then she whispered, "Alisaundre. Alisaundre." She leaned over the wicker basket, ran her knotted brown hand lightly across Alisaundre's pale, sleeping cheek. Judy's bright eyes shone at the sight of a smudge of black hair splayed out on the white sheet like a charcoal drawing.

"I've brought flowers for you, Alisaundre," Judy said. She glanced briefly in my direction before she continued. "Your mother has them, dear, in that plastic bag she's holding. But these flowers are the kind that will last forever."

I opened the bag and peered into it. I looked up, confused. Judy straightened herself and began to explain.

"I've made her a blanket, dear. I used the wool from my sheep. I searched until I found a variety of plants and organic materials to create the brightest pigment dyes. Then I matched the first letters of the natural colors with the letters in Alisaundre's name."

She took the bag from me, unfolded the blanket, and scattered a summer garden into the room. I caught my breath. Alisaundre stirred in her sleep.

I stood entranced as I listened to Judy name the colors she had knitted into this exuberant striped blanket, a work of art that both described and spelled my first child's name:

"Aloe, Lichen, Iris, Sage, Alum, Ultramarine, Nasturtium, Dandelion, Red iron oxide and English marigold. Alisaundre."

Judy spread her worn hand over the rainbow. Wool the color of softest sand separated each of the colored rows. "I dyed the wool in my tin tub, then spun it into skeins," she went on. "I used my longest, thickest needles to knit the colors. With time, the weave will stretch and the blanket will grow, just as Alisaundre will."

I didn't know what to say, or how to say it. The blanket was more than beautiful, more than profound, more than fantastic. I gathered it in my arms and burrowed my face into it. It smelled of distant fields and lazy sheep, summer flowers and the rich earth's perfume. I draped it lightly over my daughter as she slept. Judy bent down to kiss her gently on the forehead, and together we tiptoed out of the room.

That was fourteen years ago. The same small blanket that fit the wicker basket grew with the baby to fit the crib, comforted my toddler in her day bed, and followed my girl to her full-size bed. Every night, Judy's flowers snuggle close to the lovely long-limbed young woman who is my daughter, Alisaundre.

Claire Beynon

The Day the Lilies Bloomed

Heaven is under our feet as well as over our heads.

Henry David Thoreau

A statue of a young fighter pilot stands in front of the old capitol building in Phoenix, Arizona. His name was Frank Luke, Jr., and his tour of duty in World War I was brief but spectacular. Downing eighteen enemy aircraft in less than a month, he became one of only four fighter pilots awarded the Congressional Medal of Honor in that war.

But there's more to the Frank Luke story than brave deeds in the skies above France. A most unusual event is recorded in the family Bible. It took place six thousand miles from the war, back home at Frank's parents' house in Phoenix, Arizona.

In September 1917, at age twenty, Frank was a handsome, happy-go-lucky lad. Fascinated by the new flying machines as a teenager, he joined the army and was accepted into flight training. At the end of his training, he was commissioned as a second lieutenant and given a fourteen-day leave. He went to Phoenix to be with his family one last time before going off to war.

One day during the leave, Frank was heading off to pal around with some old classmates. On his way out the door, his mother, Tillie, stopped him. She laid a hand on his arm and said, "Frank, dear, I've been meaning to ask you to plant some lily bulbs for me. The weather's so perfect for it today. Would you mind terribly?"

Tillie was known for her sweet and amiable nature, and Frank was happy to oblige her. He took the bag of bulbs and spent some time alone in the front yard before leaving to find his friends. Just a few days later, he shipped out to join the war in France.

Frank's tour of duty was uneventful until September 1918. During that month he came to specialize in the destruction of German observation balloons, as well as other enemy aircraft. In a seventeen-day period, Frank broke every record for downing enemy aircraft. Dubbed the "Balloon Buster," he destroyed one after another, sometimes with his partner and sometimes on his own. On one astounding mission, he shot down three planes and two balloons in just ten minutes. All together, in those few days Frank accounted for fourteen balloons and four German planes. He was christened the American "Ace of Aces" of his day.

Back in Phoenix, the family read about Frank's brave exploits in the newspapers. Then, on September 29, his mother stepped into the front yard to find an amazing sight. The lilies that Frank had planted on leave had suddenly burst into bloom—strangely out of season in September. But that wasn't all. Once blooming, it was clear that they formed the cross-like shape of a World War I airplane! Frank was crazy about airplanes and also a devout Catholic, so his intention could have been either.

The family members gathered and exclaimed at the sight, saying those lilies should have bloomed in June, not September! And, how like Frank it was to have planted them in some special way. Word of the marvel spread. A newspaper photographer came to the house and that week the Sunday paper ran a photo of Tillie standing beside the cross of lilies.

But, from the first moment she saw them, Tillie's response to the flowers was one of sorrow. She brushed away tears, certain that something must be wrong with Frank.

On November 25, two weeks after the Armistice ended World War I, Tillie's fears were realized. The family received notification from the Red Cross that Frank was missing in action. They would learn much later that Frank had single-handedly shot down three German observation balloons on his last mission. He was wounded in flight and managed to land without crashing in Murvaux. But his wounds were severe, and he died later that day.

Frank Luke Jr., had made his final heroic flight on September 29—the day the lilies bloomed.

Jane Eppinga

The Bubbup Bush

What one loves in childhood stays in the heart forever.

Mary Jo Putney

We stood hand in hand at the edge of the garden. The summer sunshine was warm and comforting on our backs as we gazed out upon the neat, loamy rows of carrots, beans, lettuce and squash. I was three, nearly four then, and my father, strong and impossibly tall, was the gentle, fairy-tale giant who completely owned my heart.

"Mama tells me you don't want to give up the bubbup," he said. His deep voice was solemn as he bent his head to catch the worried look in my eyes.

I gave the pacifier, my beloved bubbup, a few good tugs with my lips and tongue, my cheeks hollowing with the effort. I could sense Mama watching us from the kitchen window, but I didn't dare look back.

"You're almost four years old now, honey. No longer a baby. Only babies suck on bubbups all the time."

I looked away. Looked toward a noisy bumblebee sipping nectar from the face of a marigold flower. I loved my bubbup. Loved the giggly sound of the name I'd given it. Loved the comfort it gave me as I drew on its slippery, rubbery tip. I didn't want them to take it away.

My father gave my small hand a gentle squeeze, then tugged the pacifier out of my mouth. It made a hollow sound, like a cork popping from a bottle. He crouched down in front of me, low enough to bring us to eye level. Then he squeezed my hand again and made me look at him.

"Did you hear what I said?" he asked gently.

I nodded. I wanted to cry. My bubbup dangled from Papa's long fingers, just out of reach.

"Do you remember a few weeks ago," Papa said, his eyes briefly wandering toward the garden, then back to mine, "when your mother and I brought you out here to help plant all these vegetables?"

"I remember," I said, giving a sniff.

"Do you remember how we planted seeds from packets with pictures of all the different kinds of vegetables on the fronts?"

Again I nodded, remembering the tender pleasantness of that day.

"And then we watered them and watched very carefully every day until we saw the tiny plants beginning to grow?"

"Mmm-hmm."

"Well, I bet if we plant your bubbup just like we did those seeds, in a few days, maybe even tomorrow, we can come back to find a bubbup bush growing right where we planted it."

I stared at him. Big-eyed, I said, "Really?"

"Really. But, of course, it would mean your giving it up so that we could plant it," he said. "Do you think you could do that?"

"Would it have bubbups on it?"

"No, Paula. But it would have something else very special."

"What?"

"Well, with a bubbup bush, you have to grow it to find out."

He kept fingering the bubbup, and I kept looking at it, trying to decide. *It would be fun to grow a bubbup bush*, I thought.

But . . .

"We could dig a big hole in a very special place that you alone get to choose. We'll cover it up with some soft soil, just like a blanket. Then we'll sprinkle it with water from the watering can. You know how you love to sprinkle," he said, the corners of his mouth tipping upward in one of his special daddy smiles.

I kept eyeing the bubbup. Eyeing the long fingers grasping the pink ring on the end of it. "How—how long would it take to grow?"

"That depends. If I remember correctly, I think bubbups don't take very long to grow at all. If we plant it right now, go away, then come back tomorrow morning, I bet we'll find a bubbup bush growing."

I looked the garden over, searching for a special spot.

"There," I said, pointing with my tiny finger toward the huge, yellow, nodding blossoms standing like merry-maids-all-in-a-row near the fence. "Next to the sunshine flowers."

"Excellent choice," Papa said. "Just where I would have picked." He smoothed my hair from my cheek. "Let's go get the shovel."

I followed him to the shed, tightening my lips and tongue as if to suck on the bubbup that wasn't ever going to be there anymore.

I didn't sleep very well that night, dreaming about the bubbup. Missing it terribly, but also wondering dreamily what a real, live, bubbup bush would look like. Would it truly be there in the morning when Mama, Papa and I went out to look for it?

"Is it there?" I cried, first thing the next morning. Still in my jammies, I raced out of the house and across the lawn toward the garden to see.

"I think so," Mama said, her voice full of laughter as she followed close behind.

"I think I see it," Papa said. He took Mama's hand, keeping in step. And then I saw it, too. A plump, silvery-green bush nestled between two sunshine flowers, right where we'd planted the bubbup. As I drew closer, my bare feet barely skimming the warm earth between the rows, I could see that the bush was abloom with dozens of purple spear-like fronds. *Fairy wands,* I thought.

I knelt in the dirt and touched a fragrant spear, bending my nose toward its familiar fragrance. "Mama!" I squealed, breathing deep. "It smells like Mama!"

I looked over my shoulder. They were standing at the edge of the garden and Papa was kissing Mama's cheek. I watched him take a deep breath, too, and then he nuzzled her neck.

"Yes, it does," he said, grinning. "Would you like to cut a stem? You could wear it in your hair."

"Oh, yes! Then I'd smell like Mama, too!" I looked at Mama. "Can I?"

"Why, of course, dear," Mama said. "Here, let me help."

She laughed and gave Papa a big hug. Then she came over and helped me twine one of the fragrant purple stems into my hair. I was grinning from ear to ear, the proudest three-year-old in the world.

I'm sure I must have missed my bubbup for some time, but all I remember is the happiness. To this day, the scent of lavender reminds me of my mother. And of my gentle father in all his wisdom, and that summer day so long ago we planted a little girl's babyhood and grew something magical in its place. A bubbup bush—and a garden of memories.

Paula L. Silici

Reprinted by permission of Kathy Shaskan.

A Hug from Heaven

Gardens are our link with the divine.

William Howard Adams

It was an autumn morning in 1971, shortly after our family moved into our first house. The children were upstairs unpacking boxes, and I was looking out the window at my father. He was moving around mysteriously on the front lawn. My parents lived nearby, and Dad had visited us several times already.

"What are you doing out there?" I called to him.

He looked up, smiling. "I'm making you a surprise."

What kind of a surprise? I wondered. Knowing my father, an engaging and imaginative man, it could be just about anything. But Dad would say no more, and caught up in the busyness of our new life, I eventually forgot about it.

Until one raw day in late March when, again, I glanced out the window. Dismal. Overcast. Little piles of dirty snow still stubbornly littering the lawn, as boots and wet mittens cluttered our closets. I had always hated winter—would it *ever* end?

And yet . . . was it a mirage? I strained to see what I

thought was something pink peeking out of a drift. And was that a dot of blue across the yard, a small note of optimism in this gloomy scene? I grabbed my coat and headed outside for a closer look.

They were crocuses, not neatly marching along the house's foundation in typical garden fashion (where I never could have seen them from the window), but scattered whimsically about the front lawn. Lavender, blue, yellow and my favorite pink—little faces bobbing in the bitter wind, they offered the hope I'd almost lost. "See?" they seemed to say. "You've survived the long dark winter. And if you hang on a little longer, life will be beautiful again."

Dad. I smiled, realizing he must have secretly planted these last fall. What could have been more perfectly timed, more tuned to my needs? How blessed I was, not only for the flowers, but for him.

My father's crocuses bloomed each spring for the next four or five seasons, bringing that same encouragement every time they arrived. *Hard times almost over, light coming, hold on, hold on . . .*

Then, apparently, the bulbs could produce no more. A spring came with only half the usual blooms. The next spring, about 1979, there were none. And none the years after that. I missed the crocuses, but my life was busier than ever, and I had never been much of a gardener. *I should ask Dad to come over and plant new bulbs*, I thought. But I never did.

My father died suddenly, on a beautiful day in October 1985. We grieved deeply, but cleanly, because there was no unfinished business. We had no regrets or lingering guilt. Our family had always had a strong faith, and we leaned on it now. Of course, Dad was in heaven. Where else would such a beloved person go? He was still a part of us; in fact, he could probably do even more for his family now that he was closer to God.

And if I wondered sometimes, just a little, about where and how Dad was, no one else ever knew. We suffered. We handled our pain. We laughed and cried together. Life went on.

Four years passed, and on a dismal day in spring 1989, I found myself running errands and feeling depressed. *Winter blahs,* I told myself. *You get them every year. It's chemistry.*

Perhaps.

But it was something else, too. Once again I found myself thinking about my father. This was not unusual— we often talked about him, reminiscing and enjoying our memories. But now, in the car, my old concern surfaced. How was he? *I know that I know that I know,* I told God in the familiar shorthand I often use. *But do You think You could send a sign, just something little, that Dad is home safe with You?*

As I turned in to our driveway, I suddenly slowed, stopped and stared at the lawn. Small gray mounds of melting snow. Muddy grass. And there, bravely waving in the wind, one pink crocus.

Hold on, keep going, light is coming soon. . . . There was no way, I knew, that a flower could bloom from a bulb more than eighteen years old, one that had not blossomed in over a decade. But there the crocus was, like a hug from heaven, and tears filled my eyes as I realized its significance. God had heard. And He loved me, so much that He had sent the reassurance I needed in a tenderly personal way, so there would be no doubt.

The pink crocus bloomed for only one day, April 4.

My father's birthday.

Joan Wester Anderson

Robbie's Mission

I dream of giving birth to a child who will ask,
"Mother, what was war?"

Eve Merriam

Every April, my school's eighth-grade class travels to Washington, D.C., for their class trip. It's a long ride from New Jersey, but it's always exciting to get to visit places so important in our history. One year back in the mid-eighties, history really came alive for my students. That was the year Robbie Brown was on a mission.

One by one, in the early morning darkness, my eighth-graders and I boarded the bus. When Robbie Brown got on, he was holding a four-inch pot with a white hyacinth. The delicate flowers were in full bloom. There was a small American flag stuck in the soil. Everyone asked Robbie what the flower was for. All he'd say was that he was on a mission.

Robbie became the talk of the bus. What mission was he on? Some of the girls in the back of the bus started spreading rumors. The hyacinth was really a present for Nancy Reagan, with whom Robbie was secretly in love.

He'd give it to her when we toured the White House. Or maybe it was a present for our tour guide, the pretty young woman in the front seat.

After a long ride, our bus finally arrived in Washington. We stopped at the White House, got off the bus and went on the tour. The girls watched Robbie closely. But when we got back on the bus, Robbie was still carrying the flower.

We drove down Pennsylvania Avenue to the Capitol. Robbie carried the hyacinth with him on the Capitol tour. No one let Robbie get out of sight. What was his mission?

Around noon, we went to lunch. Robbie put the hyacinth down—just long enough to eat a burger and fries.

Next, we drove past the Washington Monument and around the Tidal Basin, where the famous cherry trees were in bloom. Everyone watched Robbie like a hawk at Arlington National Cemetery. He walked past JFK's grave, then down the stairs to Bobby Kennedy's grave. At the pool there, he put the plant down, cupped his hands, and scooped some water into the pot. Robbie left Arlington just the way he had entered it—plant in hand.

Finally, the bus drove back to Washington and let everyone off at the Lincoln Memorial. A sense of urgency filled Robbie's steps. Everyone followed as he headed down to the wall of the Vietnam War Memorial. He scanned the many names, then put the hyacinth down under one particular name.

Robbie turned to find his classmates watching with fascination. "So, what's the story?" one finally asked.

"My mother's sister is named Katie," Robbie began slowly. "She fell in love with Chip. Chip would always send Katie white hyacinths for Easter. He'd get the bulbs from Holland and grow them himself in his garden. When they bloomed, he'd dig them up, put them in a pot, and give them to her.

"In 1965, Chip was drafted," Robbie went on. "The next year, he went to Vietnam. He never came back. Twenty years later, Aunt Katie still talks about Chip. This flower is from her to him. She asked me to leave it here."

We all walked back and boarded the bus. Nobody kidded Robbie about the flowers anymore. For a long time, even the girls in the back were strangely silent.

Many years have passed since then, and all those eighth-graders are now adults. They've probably all forgotten that the Washington Monument is 555 feet tall and that Abraham Lincoln was assassinated at Ford's Theater. But I'm sure they all remember a soldier named Chip, a white hyacinth and Robbie's mission.

George M. Flynn

A Garden for Four

Love has nothing to do with what you are expecting to get—only with what you are expecting to give—which is everything.

Katharine Hepburn

In San Francisco, where the houses rub shoulders and squat only steps from the street, we don't have gardens. We have backyards. And if you find a place to live with a backyard that has not been cemented over or gone to the dogs, you consider yourself lucky, indeed.

Four years ago, I found a new apartment. It had a backyard with a small concrete center patio, as so many of them do. A leaning fence corralled three sides of the yard. Between the patio and the fence, deep beds held a mishmash of bottlebrush and pine. The trees stood in weed patches and everything was tangled in climbing clematis that was busy strangling sweet-smelling jasmine.

This apartment happened to sit less than a block from my parents' big, but yardless, condo. They had just retired and were busy with bridge tournaments, guitar lessons and international travel. Dad was still a Hercules of a man, silly, creative and kind. Mom was The Planner. When they enthusiastically offered their gardening services, I was thrilled. I had no idea what would happen next.

It started innocently enough. For Christmas, they gave me one of those plastic green scooter seats—"to save your back," Mom said. For my birthday in February, Dad and my brother spent two entire weekends removing the top three inches of "bad dirt" and replacing it with Dad's "good dirt," a secret concoction of who-knows-what mixed with beer dregs. Mom and Dad got a set of keys to my place, "just in case" they felt like puttering in the garden while I was at work.

As spring warmed to summer, I began to feel as if leprechauns had moved in; each evening, I'd come home from work to find all sorts of garden mischief. A fragrant, fifty-pound bag of chicken manure materialized in the work shed. His and her watering cans stood at either side of the yard, to save steps and arguments about who last left what can where. And our gardening tool collection grew so fast that I suspected the shovels had married and started a family of little spades, hoes and picks.

Had I slept through moonlight work sessions? Window boxes changed their dresses nearly as often as I did. And each time the fog rolled in, rows of bumblebee wind whirligigs clattered in beds of purple petunias and pink impatiens.

I would wake up early on Sunday mornings, pull back the drapes and spit coffee at the sight of my parents' dungareed fannies pointing skyward, beginning another full day of planting and pulling. Mom developed a mania for combinations of orange and purple. She planted salvia, marigolds, poppies, golden aster and lavender. The jolts of color blanketing the yard made my eyes hurt. I took to reading my paper wearing sunglasses.

Dad, meanwhile, proclaimed himself paramedic to all sick and injured plantings—mainly because he stepped on them himself in his size-thirteen workboots. His gardening prescription? "Give it another week."

But my parents' gardening mania was shortlived. Less than a year later, and just six weeks before I was to be married, Dad was in a hospice, dying of brain cancer. A ferocious biological weed had sent its tendrils deep into his memory, robbing him of speech and sight. Yet he insisted that whatever happened to him, we mustn't postpone the wedding. I promised him solemnly that we would honor his wish, and we did.

I had learned a lot watching my parents enjoy themselves, shaping that city garden in their precious last summer. Working, planning, bickering, experimenting and learning side by side, they built memories for all of us. I realized how much Mom treasured those months when she gave my husband and me a splendid patio set with a gigantic umbrella. "So you can enjoy your garden like your dad and I did," she said with a smile.

Recently, my husband—out of the blue—decided to plant a gigantic candy-colored bougainvillea. Nurserymen and neighbors galore warned him that bougainvillea roots are extremely sensitive and that they often get shocky, keeling over dead the minute they are put in the ground. Sure enough, two weekends later, it looked like a tumbleweed, no more than a collection of brittle twigs.

"Should we rip it out?" he asked me.

I remembered Dad's favorite gardening cure.

"Give it another week," I said.

Dad and I were right. I think that cheerful bougainvillea will be cresting our fence by this summer.

Rayne Wolfe

Roses for Rose

The sweetest flower that blows, I give you as we part.
For you it is a rose, for me it is my heart.

Frederick Peterson

Red roses were her favorites—her name was also Rose—
And every year her husband sent them, tied with pretty
    bows.
The year he died the roses were delivered to her door.
The card said, "Be my Valentine," like all the years
    before.

Each year he sent her roses, and the note would always
    say,
"I love you even more this year than last year on this day.
My love for you will always grow with every passing
    year."
She knew this was the last time that the roses would
    appear.

She thought, "He ordered roses in advance before this
    day."

Her loving husband did not know that he would pass
    away.
He always liked to do things early, way before the time.
Then, if he got too busy, everything would work out fine.

She trimmed the stems and placed them in a very
    special vase,
Then sat the vase beside the portrait of his smiling face.
She would sit for hours, in her husband's favorite chair,
While staring at his picture and the roses sitting there.

A year went by and it was hard to live without her mate,
With loneliness and solitude that had become her fate.
Then, the very hour, as on Valentines before,
The doorbell rang, and there were roses sitting by her
    door.

She brought the roses in, and then just looked at them
    in shock,
Then went to get the telephone, to call the florist shop.
The owner answered and she asked him if he would
    explain,
Why would someone do this to her, causing her such pain?

"I know your husband passed away more than a year ago,"
The owner said. "I knew you'd call, and you would want
    to know,
The flowers you received today were paid for in
    advance.
Your husband always planned ahead, he left nothing to
    chance.

"There is a standing order that I have on file down here,
And he has paid well in advance; you'll get them every
    year.

There also is another thing that I think you should
    know:
He wrote a special little card . . . he did this years ago.

"Then, should ever I find out that he's no longer here,
That's the card that should be sent to you the following
    year."
She thanked him and hung up the phone, her tears now
    flowing hard,
Her fingers shaking, as she slowly reached to get the card.

Inside the card she saw that he had written her a note.
Then, as she stared in total silence, this is what he
    wrote. . . .
"Hello, my love, I know it's been a year since I've been
    gone,
I hope it hasn't been too hard for you to overcome.

"I know it must be lonely, and the pain is very real,
For if it were the other way, I know how I would feel.
The love we shared made everything so beautiful in life.
I loved you more than words can say. You were the
    perfect wife.

"You were my friend and lover, you fulfilled my every
    need.
I know it's only been a year, but please try not to grieve.
I want you to be happy, even when you shed your tears.
That is why the roses will be sent to you for years.

"When you get these roses, think of all the happiness
That we had together, and how both of us were blessed.
I have always loved you, and I know I always will.
But, my love, you must go on, you have some living still.

"Please try to find happiness, while living out your days.
I know it is not easy, but I hope you find some ways.
The roses will come every year, and they will only stop
When your door's not answered when the florist stops
    to knock.

"He will come five times that day, in case you have gone
    out.
But after his last visit, he will know without a doubt
To take the roses to the place where I've instructed him,
And place the roses where we are, together once again."

James A. Kisner
Submitted by Bonny Eiffert

Buddies

It's a happy talent to know how to play.

Ralph Waldo Emerson

Grandfathers and three-year-old boys are natural buddies. On this particular day in May, the grandfather was pleased to have the company of his best little pal when planting the vegetable garden. For a while, the boy seemed to like it, too. His small fingers were just the right size to pick up tiny seeds and drop them into Granddad-made holes. They were a great team.

But before long, the boy became restless and directed his irritation at the seeds themselves.

"What's this one, Granddad?"

"Beets."

"Ugh, I hate beets."

"Well, then, let's do the zucchini instead."

"Yuck. I *really* hate zucchini."

"Okay, buddy. What would you like to plant?"

"How about . . . doughnuts?"

Just in time, the grandfather stopped himself from saying there was no such thing as a doughnut seed. Looking at the unhappy little face, he suddenly got an inspiration.

"Wait a sec. I have to go inside and get the right seeds."

Granddad returned with a handful of Cheerios. He and the small boy solemnly planted them in a special corner of the vegetable garden.

Weeks later, when the real seeds began to break through the soil, the boy became entranced with the tiny seedlings. He spent many afternoons helping Granddad water and hoe and watch them grow. And when the first baby vegetables were harvested, he liked them after all.

For weeks, he forgot all about the doughnuts. But then one day at lunch, he said, "Granddad, what happened to our doughnuts? How come they didn't grow?"

Granddad paused a moment. "Well, you know, dough-nuts are tricky. Some years when you plant them, you get lots of doughnuts." He sighed. "But other years, all that comes up are the holes."

Maggie Stuckey

A Lesson in Love

The best things in life aren't things.

Art Buchwald

Many years ago, I lived in a small cottage on Southern California's coast. I was lonely. My husband, a physician, was hardly ever home. We had no children. The high brick walls that surrounded our tiny yard left little room for me to fulfill my longing for a garden of my own.

I had one prime gardening spot: Centered on our small, perfectly manicured front lawn was a stone planter just large enough for five tea rosebushes. These I had lovingly chosen, nurtured and coaxed into perfection. Every leaf was manicured, every thorn symmetrical. The plants were fertilized with rich, homemade compost full of earth-worms. The lush blooms, which in the Laguna climate lasted all year, were spectacular both in number and their velvet beauty.

This miniature garden was my escape, my refuge, my chapel. But after a time, I began to notice that every Sunday morning when I came out the door to fetch the weekend paper, there was a small, gaping hole in my flowers. A beautiful bud that had been full of promise would be gone, with only a severed branch to mark its passing.

I was outraged at this offense. How could someone cut buds off my roses over and over, without asking permission? My anger grew until, pushed to my limit, one Saturday evening I crouched behind the stone wall near the rose planter.

Just after sunset, old Mr. and Mrs. Palmer, the reclusive couple who owned perhaps the most desirable property in the entire bay, came doddering down the sidewalk and stopped in front of my roses. Slowly, painfully, they bent over the blooms, inhaling as deeply as their frail lungs would allow, their eyes closed, lost in some distant memory.

As I watched, Mr. Palmer took out an ancient penknife and carefully cut a single bud from the bush. With a creaking bow, he presented it to his plump and bent little wife.

Something about their gaze left me embarrassed, almost ashamed. I suddenly felt I could never understand, let alone ever find, such depth of feeling for another soul. Humbled, I could only watch from my hiding place as they slowly shuffled down the sidewalk to the sea.

Time passed. I had a baby, one I'd yearned to have for years. Old Mr. Palmer died, but Mrs. Palmer stayed on. Every Saturday evening, Mrs. Palmer, now alone, made her tortuous way down the sidewalk to my rose planter. And every Sunday morning I would find one of my plants partially but carefully denuded.

Despite the touching interlude I had seen between my elderly neighbors, I still resented this thievery. Finally I had enough. One evening I decided to intercept Mrs. Palmer. I was going to confront her about respecting other people's property. As she made her way toward me, I stepped outside and sat down on the stone planter in front of my house, my new baby on my lap.

Mrs. Palmer came up to me. "How lovely your roses are this evening," she said in her thick, Germanic accent. "And the little one, such a blessing!" My infant son flashed her a grin. I said nothing.

She knew that I knew.

"Others?" she asked, indicating my child with a bristled eyebrow. The question pierced me like an arrow. My ten-year-old stepson, a brilliant but disturbed boy, had just lost his mother to a tragic accident. Now this shattered child was coming to live with us. From all our past encounters, I felt that any interaction between us was doomed to failure. Worse, I was sure that my new baby's needs would be overshadowed by the demands of this unwanted addition to our household.

Tears stung my eyelids. The essential unfairness of life overwhelmed me. "My stepson is coming to live with us next week," I sniffed as Mrs. Palmer nodded sympathetically. "His mother just died. I've just had this baby, my only child, and now. . . ."

"Honey," she said, seizing my wrist in her arthritic grasp. "You never know where love is going to come from."

Looking down at my wrist, I saw her wizened arm, and its faint blue tattooed numbers. She kissed my baby on the top of his head and reached over to the roses. With an ancient penknife, she cut a perfect blossom, handing it to me with a little bow. Then she waddled off down the sidewalk and out of sight.

Her actions stunned me like the sun breaking through a wintery sky. I had vowed to show her anger, but this elderly widow, who must have known such hardships, had shown me love. If she could do that for me, a complete stranger, surely I could do the same for both my baby and my stepson. I, too, could stand ready to welcome love in, to watch it unfold like a rose.

ahansen

Garden Crime

Now that we've retired and live in the country, I have finally started gardening, as I've wanted to all my life. I love it, and I'm learning a lot. My husband likes to help out. He often comes home with plants he's found along the side of the road.

Two years ago he came home with a plant about fifteen inches tall. He told me he had found a whole field of them. As always, I faithfully planted it in front of our house in a nice, sunny spot. It grew quickly, and I had a lot of admirers—people even took pictures. But I was disappointed because it produced no flowers. That was unfortunate. I wanted a flowering bush in that spot.

As I was digging it up to transplant it, a very nice police officer stopped and asked me where I had found that plant.

"You can have it if you want it," I told him. "It doesn't produce any flowers and I have no use for it. My husband says there's an entire field of them, so if you want more, he can tell you where to find them."

"Thank you, ma'am," he replied. "I think I would like to talk with your husband." He waited in his car in front of our house while I kept puttering in the garden, feeling rather strange.

Finally, my husband arrived home. When asked by the police officer where more of these "beautiful" plants could be found, my husband said, "I don't remember!"

Well, you can imagine my horror when the policeman informed us we were growing marijuana, which of course is against the law. But, since we are in our seventies, to my relief, he believed my husband's loss of memory and we weren't arrested! And, to my delight, the police officer dug up the plant himself and took it away, saving me the work!

The next time my husband goes on plant foraging expeditions, I'm sending along a plant identification book. Who knows what he could bring home?

Ursel Rabeneck

Yellow Irises

When I stand before God at the end of my life, I would hope that I would not have a single bit of talent left, and could say, "I used everything you gave me."

Erma Bombeck

As a mother of five, Mom had little time during the day to be out in the garden with her beloved rhododendrons or planting bulbs. But a loyal gardener always finds a way. As soon as we were tucked away in bed, she'd grab her garden tools and car keys and go outside into the night. Starting up the car, Mom shined the headlights onto a section of the garden. In peace and quiet at last, she'd settle into a gentle rhythm of weeding—a rhythm she hoped would soothe her nerves after another busy day.

With five kids comes a lot of energy, and my parents found relief in Washington State's trail system. Packing the car with lunches and a mess of kids, off we went to the mountains. The moment the car stopped at the trailhead, the doors flew open and we bounded up the path with my parents following in the rear.

Along the trail, I looked for unusual plants, ones I didn't think Mom would recognize. Whenever I came across an oddball, I would proudly present her with a sample. Thus challenged, she'd open her wild plants guide and together we'd flip through the chapters, looking for a match. Years later, I came across the battered book and discovered dried wafers of leaves and flowers still pressed between the pages.

On days the weather kept us indoors, sometimes we would flip through fine art catalogs or visit museums and art galleries. One day, a beautiful museum catalog arrived in the mail. Mom and I leafed through it, marking pages of our favorite flower paintings.

"Look!" I gasped, pointing to a Japanese print. Mom had seen it, too. It was a beautiful landscape. Tall green grass seemed to ripple in the breeze and clouds dotted the blue sky. A small hut, perhaps the family home, sat near a well-tended flower garden.

"We'll get that one," she smiled. And we filled out the order form.

During my senior year in high school, I took a forestry course. The end of the semester loomed, but thanks to Mom, I didn't have to take the final exam. The student who brought in and correctly identified the greatest number of native plants was exempt from the Big Test. The night before class, Mom and I toured the yard collecting samples and packed them in a cardboard box. The next day, I (we) won hands down.

Mom's creativity and love for children was reflected in everything she did, from setting the dining-room table with craft projects as an alternative to TV, to making houses out of grass and cattail reeds.

Life was not all fun and games, though. Sometimes, things weren't quite right with Mom. Sometimes she did things we didn't understand. She tired easily. She missed appointments and went on strange eating binges.

One night, my sister and I heard a commotion from outside our bedroom. We opened the door just enough to see two men wearing white coats carrying our mother away on a stretcher. As soon as they disappeared, we ran to find Dad.

"What's wrong with Mommy?" we cried.

"She's not feeling well," Dad said, his voice trembling. "Mommy's going to a special hospital for a couple of months."

From that point on, the family had to deal with the fact of Mom's mental illness. It was often hard for us to understand; doctors back then were still struggling with how to treat manic depression and schizophrenia.

The years went by, and we kids grew up and moved away. My parents divorced. Mom struggled with alcoholism, severe depression and loneliness. Unable to hold down a job, she ended up in low-income housing in downtown Seattle. Undaunted by living in the middle of the city, Mom was determined to be near flowers and green things, so each spring and summer she rode the city bus to and from her community garden plot.

Eventually I moved to Alaska, but Mom and I stayed in close touch, our letters and phone conversations laced with "garden speak."

"Someone's stealing my tomatoes," Mom once lamented. "What should I do?"

"Plant more!" I said, laughing. "You'll really make them happy!"

Then one autumn, Mom was diagnosed with pancreatic cancer. The doctors gave her a few months to live. Mom suffered immeasurable physical pain, but for reasons unknown to her doctors, she was suddenly free of the mental illness that had plagued her most of her adult life. It was as if all of the darkness just lifted and was gone. For the first time in many years, Mom was "there" more than she'd ever been, allowing us to share whole conversations, walks and meals together. I made several visits from my home in Alaska.

On a midsummer morning, I was out in my garden when my sister and older brother called to say that Mom was refusing any sort of care, food or water. She was fading fast. They promised to stay in close touch from her hospital room.

I wanted to be alone, so I returned to the garden. After a few hours, I picked a large bouquet of yellow irises and carried them into the house. The phone was ringing. It was my sister. Mom was slipping in and out of consciousness and hadn't responded in several hours.

My sister held the phone up to Mom's ear so I could talk to her. The yellow irises beside me misted into a golden haze as I held back tears.

Speaking slowly and deliberately, I told her that every time I'm in the garden I think of her. I told her I was grateful for all she had taught me.

"I will always love you, Mom."

She was so weak, she could only whisper.

"Thanks, honey." Those were her last words. Mom died that evening.

The next morning, I was going through a box of family papers and photographs, searching for memories of Mom. As I gently pulled back a handful of faded newspaper clippings, my heart stopped. There was the Japanese print Mom and I had picked from the catalog over thirty years before. The sunlit garden scene was as lovely and tranquil as ever. And in the foreground was a large clump of yellow irises.

Marion Owen

7

OVERCOMING OBSTACLES

The day the Lord created hope was probably the same day he created spring.

Bern Williams

Black Tulips

It is only with the heart that one can see rightly;
what is essential is invisible to the eye.

Antoine de Saint-Exupéry

When I was a child growing up in The Netherlands, I often begged my mother to tell me this story about an experience her family had at the end of World War II.

During the terrible last winter of the German occupation, the *hongerwinter,* food was very scarce in The Netherlands. People were so desperately hungry they began to eat small animals and many things not normally considered edible, including tulip bulbs. People discovered the bulbs could be cooked like potatoes or turnips, or even eaten raw.

For centuries, my mother's family, the Van der Veldes, had owned a highly successful tulip business, which provided jobs for many in our village of Ridderkerk. Their bulbs were popular throughout Europe and abroad, and the family name was known far and wide. But the war shut their business down, and during the winter of hunger, my grandfather, Arnoldus, donated all his tulip bulbs to feed the hungriest villagers.

All, that is, except for a few irreplaceable bulbs. For years, Arnoldus had been trying to cultivate a black tulip, something no gardener had ever been able to do. He was now very close. By careful selection, he had created a dark-purple tulip. These few bulbs he guarded vigorously to prevent people from stealing them for food. He did not even give them to his family to eat, because they would make just one meager meal, and eating them would destroy his chance of restarting his business and restoring his village after the war.

One day, underground Radio Orange announced that the war was over. There was great rejoicing, but more hardships were still to come. The German forces that had occupied and terrorized our country for five long years started to withdraw, battalion by battalion. But as they pulled back, some soldiers deserted and fled toward Germany, sacking and looting as they went. There was much destruction, and the Dutch people still faced grave dangers.

My grandfather, Arnoldus, looked at his pale, thin children and realized that the hunger could continue for a long time as the war left poverty in its wake. He wondered if it might be time to feed his precious bulbs to his children. Certainly it would be better than losing the bulbs to the marauding bands of fleeing German soldiers. After hours of agonizing, he made his decision. He seized a shovel and went into the garden. There he found my mother, Albertha, then just seven, looking flushed and agitated.

"Papa! Papa! I must tell you something," Albertha said. Over her shoulder, Arnoldus saw a band of drunken, looting soldiers coming toward them down the street. He whispered to Albertha to run inside the house and frantically began digging for his bulbs. Over and over his shovel came up empty. He was too late. Someone had already stolen them.

Crazed with grief and rage, he ran toward the street screaming, "They have stolen my tulip bulbs!" Albertha, watching from the doorway, cried out and ran to stop him. Before she could reach Arnoldus, a German soldier raised his pistol and shot him. Although the German surrender had been signed, a curfew was still technically in effect, and my grandfather had violated it.

Arnoldus survived his wounds and mended slowly. When he could finally leave his bed, he sat by the window staring out into the garden. He so regretted that he hadn't given the bulbs to his family sooner. The war was over and spring was coming, but life remained very hard. Many houses had been bombed. There was little food and few jobs.

Finally the weather warmed, and Arnoldus was able to sit outside. Albertha stayed close to him, attending to his every need, rarely leaving him even to play with her friends. She had become quiet and reserved, although she had been a happy, bubbly child before the war. Sometimes she would try to cheer her father by pointing to the pile of rubble next door, all that was left of their neighbors' bombed house. She reminded her father that at least their family still had each other and a roof above their heads. Arnoldus realized the truth in her words and often glanced over at the ruins to remind himself of how lucky they had been.

One day, he noticed something sprouting among the broken bricks and concrete. He pointed out the green leaves to Albertha. Suddenly, all her reserve left her. She began to cry hysterically. Between convulsive sobs, she told him that these were his black tulip bulbs. He held her close and listened with amazement as she told her story.

Just before her father was shot, Albertha had been in the garden when a friendly German soldier had approached

her. Carl Meier was stationed in the family's neighborhood during the Occupation. He had Van der Velde
bulbs in his own garden back home in Germany, and
appreciated their value. Carl had watched as Arnoldus
gave away the precious bulbs to feed his neighbors, and
he suspected that there were more hidden away. The
soldier warned Albertha that a band of German looters
was on its way down the street. He urged her to hide the
remaining bulbs away from the yard, which would
surely be searched. And he begged her not to mention
his name to anyone, as he could be court-martialed for
his warning.

Just then, the laughing and shouting of drunken soldiers
could be heard coming down the road. Carl Meier fled.
With no time to summon her father, Albertha scrabbled in
the dirt with her bare hands, scooped up the bulbs from
their hiding place, and reburied them in the rubble next
door.

As she clambered back over the fence into her own garden, she found her father digging with a shovel. She tried
to tell him what she had done, but he was so intent on his
work that he ignored her.

For some time, it was uncertain whether Arnoldus
would survive his gunshot wound. When he began to
recover, Albertha went to retrieve the bulbs, knowing
that seeing them would raise his spirits. She climbed over
the fence and gasped with horror. An unstable wall had
collapsed on the spot, covering the bulbs. It seemed
impossible to the little girl that anyone could ever move
the heavy slab. Overwhelmed with sorrow, Albertha
decided not to tell anyone what she had done.

However, during the last cruel days of winter, ice must
have formed in the cracks of the wall, gently forcing them
apart. With the warmth of spring, the ice had melted, and
the tender shoots had made their way up toward the sun.

Arnoldus had survived, and so had his bulbs. Now father and daughter stood looking at the young green leaves.

It took some time, but my grandfather rebuilt his business, starting with those few bulbs. The rare dark-purple tulips eventually became an enormous source of income for the people in Ridderkerk and provided many much-needed jobs. The recovery of Ridderkerk persuaded its people that there could again be happiness after so much misery, and new life after so much death. As the tulips rose from the ruins and came to bloom again, so did The Netherlands.

Although the Van der Veldes tried to locate Carl Meier, he was never found. But the family did find a way to honor his courage and kindness. When my mother's little brother was born the following year, the grateful family named him Karel, the Dutch version of "Carl."

Carin Klabbers-Ouwens
Translated by Philip Klabbers

Downwind from Flowers

We pardon as long as we love.

La Rochefoucauld

Several years ago in Seattle, Washington, there lived a fifty-two-year-old Tibetan refugee. "Tenzin," as I will call him, was diagnosed with one of the more curable forms of lymphoma. He was admitted to the hospital and received his first dose of chemotherapy.

But during the treatment, this usually gentle man became extremely angry and upset. He pulled the IV out of his arm and refused to cooperate. He shouted at the nurses and became argumentative with everyone who came near him. The doctors and nurses were baffled.

Then Tenzin's wife spoke to the hospital staff. She told them Tenzin had been held as a political prisoner by the Chinese for seventeen years. They killed his first wife and repeatedly tortured and brutalized him throughout his imprisonment. She told them that the hospital rules and regulations, coupled with the chemotherapy treatments, gave Tenzin horrible flashbacks of what he had suffered at the hands of the Chinese.

"I know you mean to help him," she said, "but he feels tortured by your treatments. They are causing him to feel hatred inside—just like he felt toward the Chinese. He would rather die than have to live with the hatred he is now feeling. And, according to our belief, it is very bad to have hatred in your heart at the time of death. He needs to be able to pray and cleanse his heart."

So the doctors discharged Tenzin and asked the hospice team to visit him in his home. I was the hospice nurse assigned to his care. I called a local representative from Amnesty International for advice. He told me that the only way to heal the damage from torture is to "talk it through."

"This person has lost his trust in humanity and feels hope is impossible," the man said. "If you are to help him, you must find a way to give him hope."

But when I encouraged Tenzin to talk about his experiences, he held up his hand and stopped me. He said, "I must learn to love again if I am to heal my soul. Your job is not to ask me questions. Your job is to teach me to love again."

I took a deep breath. I asked him, "So, how can I help you love again?"

Tenzin immediately replied, "Sit down, drink my tea and eat my cookies."

Tibetan tea is strong black tea laced with yak butter and salt. It isn't easy to drink! But that is what I did.

For several weeks, Tenzin, his wife and I sat together, drinking tea. We also worked with his doctors to find ways to treat his physical pain. But it was his spiritual pain that seemed to be lessening. Each time I arrived, Tenzin was sitting cross-legged on his bed, reciting prayers from his books. As time went on, he and his wife hung more and more colorful *thankas*, Tibetan Buddhist banners, on the walls. The room was fast becoming a beautiful religious shrine.

As winter began to fade, I asked Tenzin what Tibetans do when they are ill in the spring. He smiled brightly and said, "We sit downwind from flowers."

I thought he must be speaking poetically, but Tenzin's words were quite literal. He told me Tibetans sit downwind so they can be dusted with the new blossoms' pollen that floats on the spring breeze. They feel this new pollen is strong medicine.

At first, finding enough blossoms seemed a bit daunting. Then, one of my friends suggested that Tenzin visit some of the local flower nurseries. I called the manager of one of the nurseries. His initial response was: "You want to do what?" But when I explained the request, the manager agreed.

So, the next weekend, I picked up Tenzin and his wife with their provisions for the afternoon: black tea, butter, salt, cups, cookies, prayer beads and prayer books. I dropped them off at the nursery and assured them I would return at 5:00.

The following weekend, Tenzin and his wife visited another nursery.

The third weekend, they went to yet another nursery.

The fourth week, I began to get calls from the nurseries inviting Tenzin and his wife to come again. One of the managers said, "We've got a new shipment of nicotiana coming in and some wonderful fuchsias and, oh, yes! Some great daphne. I know they would love the scent of that daphne! And I almost forgot! We have some new lawn furniture that Tenzin and his wife might enjoy."

Later that day, I got a call from the second nursery saying that they had colorful wind socks that would help Tenzin predict where the wind was blowing. Pretty soon, the nurseries were competing for Tenzin's visits.

People began to know and care about the Tibetan couple. The nursery employees started setting out the lawn furniture in the direction of the wind. Others would bring out fresh hot water for their tea. Some of the regular customers would leave their wagons of flowers near the two of them. It seemed that a community was growing around Tenzin and his wife.

At the end of the summer, Tenzin returned to his doctor for another CT scan to determine the extent of the spread of the cancer. But the doctor could find no evidence of cancer at all. He was dumbfounded. He told Tenzin that he just couldn't explain it.

Tenzin lifted his finger and said, "I know why the cancer has gone away. It could no longer live in a body that is filled with love. When I began to feel all the compassion from the hospice people, from the nursery employees and all those people who wanted to know about me, I started to change inside. Now, I feel fortunate to have had the opportunity to heal in this way. Doctor, please don't think that your medicine is the only cure. Sometimes compassion can cure cancer, as well."

Lee Paton
Submitted by Linda Ross Swanson

Of War and Roses

The pursuit of science should constantly be betrayed by the love of beauty, and accuracy of knowledge by tenderness of emotion.

John Ruskin

He strode the length of the nursery walkway, inhaling the heady scent. To an untrained eye, the rows of methodically labeled roses might look identical. But Monsieur Francis Meilland knew better. As a rose breeder, he had dedicated his life to these plants. He knew each one intimately.

Pausing, he reached out to rub a particularly glossy leaf, its finely serrated edge curling slightly over his finger. Ah, this one . . . *this one* . . . Monsieur Meilland sighed.

A masterpiece! Unlike anything he had ever grown before. Of all his treasures, this plant produced the most heartbreakingly beautiful blooms.

Monsieur Meilland was anxious to experiment, to develop the rose further and to give it an appropriate name. But he was out of time. The year was 1939, and the threat of war hovered over Western Europe. He could only hope to preserve the rose from the terrible dangers on the horizon.

By June the following year, the German Army had occupied northern France. Now the Nazis cut across to the coast, then turned and moved toward Paris, never striking twice in the same place. Waging *blitzkrieg*, or lightning war, they had attacked first one town, then another, spreading defeat and disaster everywhere.

Pressed for time, Monsieur Meilland took cuttings from his beloved plant, still untested and still unnamed. Methodically, he packaged and shipped them to rose aficionados throughout the world. Would they get out of France? Would they arrive at their destinations? More importantly, would they survive? He could only hope. And pray.

One last plane left France just before the Nazis gained control of the airport. On board were the final rose cuttings, cushioned in a diplomatic pouch, destined for the United States.

Four long years passed. Throughout Europe, shelling resounded like a giant bell solemnly tolling the dead. And then it arrived: a letter from a rose grower in Pennsylvania praising the beauty of Meilland's discovery. It was ruffled. Delicate. The petals were of cameo ivory and palest cream, tipped with a tinge of pink.

His rose had survived.

But, for Monsieur Meilland, the crowning glory came later. On the very day that Berlin fell and bells of freedom rang across Europe, rose growers gathered far away, in sunny California, at a ceremony to christen his splendid blossom. To honor the occasion, white doves were set free to wing their way across a sapphire sky.

And, after so many years, the fragile rose that had survived a war finally received its name.

'Peace.'

Carol McAdoo Rehme

The Next Best Thing

Life is a great big canvas; throw all the paint on it you can.

Danny Kaye

When my parents reached their seventies and were having difficulty doing the things they had previously done with ease, a quote by test pilot Chuck Yeager became their favorite motto: "Do what you can for as long as you can and when you can't, do the next best thing."

My father in particular was challenged by a weakened muscular system that would cause his legs to sometimes give way without warning. Ever diligent that he might fall, my mother would periodically check to make sure he was still standing as he ambled around outside doing yard work.

One morning, Mom spied him lying flat on his stomach under an apple tree. Alarmed, she scurried out to help. Only when she got closer did she see that he had a trowel in hand and was weeding. Exasperated, she asked, "What are you doing?"

My father replied, "The next best thing."

Ann Pehl Thomson

Tough Love

Nothing can bring you peace but yourself.

Ralph Waldo Emerson

Growing up wasn't easy for my oldest daughter. Michelle was different, somehow. Despite her cherub's beauty and gentle soul, she stood apart from her peers, and they felt the difference.

Her high school years came and went without much mention of friends except for her small "group." Michelle stayed within their protective shell until they all gradually moved on or moved away, off to start their own lives. Only Michelle was left behind. I watched, trying to help yet not interfere, as she struggled to find new friends.

In her desperation to belong at any cost, Michelle found "friends" who were not friends at all. It was then that she tried drugs for the first time. The drugs made Michelle feel different, powerful. Then, they took her.

I lost my daughter that first year. It was as if she became possessed and lost her soul. Inside, she did not exist. Over the next year, Michelle stormed in and out of our lives. She was gone for days at a time. I later learned she lived, by choice, in her car with Jim, a go-nowhere drug addict. He hit her and pushed her and burned her with cigarettes. Yet she stayed with him, with the night life, with the drugs. When she was gone, I ached to see her, but I dreaded the times she did come home. Then, our house rang with shouts and tears, pleading and accusation. And after a few days, Michelle would be gone again.

That New Year's Eve, I sat alone on my sofa, wondering what the new year would bring. Thinking of the disaster that engulfed our dear daughter, I felt as if I were dying. I knew I had to make some changes.

Searching for hope, I cast back in my mind, seeking other times and other events that had brought me happiness. *What were the happiest times in my life?* I asked myself. *What past loveliness could help carry me through the ugliness of today?*

Memories rose to the surface, images of myself as a little girl in springtime. I recalled moments with warm mud between my toes, afternoons lying in the high grass, the smells of spring that gave my soul a joy I hadn't felt since my youth.

How could I relive those moments? Perhaps, I thought, the answer was right in my backyard. If my soul felt like dying, perhaps I needed to make something else grow.

At first, I thought I'd taken on too much; our dark, barren yard had little to offer in the way of inspiration. But then I recalled a saying: "Yard by yard, it's too hard; inch by inch, it's a cinch." I promised myself to go inch by inch in creating some beauty in our family's broken world.

We cut down trees and brush. I shoveled topsoil and pulled weeds and planted bulbs. As I worked in my new garden, I tried to focus on light and hope. I became quiet and at peace with God, my garden and myself. The healing began; the garden became my sanctuary from the sorrow and pain in my home.

I watched that first spring come. I'd pluck snails in my nightgown at 6:00 A.M. after a sleepless night spent praying that Michelle was safe and warm somewhere—though I knew she wasn't. Michelle roamed alone. But I survived, one day at a time. I learned to garden and I learned to pray.

The calm and clarity I found in the garden gave me the strength to finally take a stand against Michelle. For a year, we had always been there for her, waiting to welcome her back, providing money and a home, only to have her leave again, refueled for another round of drugs and abuse. "Inch by inch" wasn't enough now. I had to do something bigger. I told my daughter not to come home anymore.

"I have a key to the house. I'll come back whenever I want," Michelle retorted angrily.

I reached deep inside for the strength to reply.

"I'll change the locks," I said in a trembling voice. "I can't watch while you kill yourself."

The "tough love" broke through. Truly alone, Michelle suddenly started crying like a lost child.

"All I want is to be happy," she sobbed.

In my garden, I had prayed many times for Michelle's sobriety. In that moment, with the faith I had found in my garden, I caught a glimpse of her soul struggling back to us.

Soon after, Michelle was accepted into a women's recovery home. I went to my sanctuary and got down on my knees. I thanked God for the hope of answered prayers.

Later that week, I found a bare-root rosebush at a nursery. Its name was 'Betty Boop,' Michelle's pet name. I went to visit Michelle in the recovery house and told her about "her" rosebush.

"When you come home from the recovery house, the rosebush will be blooming," I said. "It's like you: simply beautiful."

Michelle's recovery was not easy, but she made it. She, too, learned to put her faith in the old saying, "Yard by yard, it's too hard; inch by inch, it's a cinch." Today, Michelle has hope for a future. She has met a wonderful young man, and they are engaged to be married. They are so in love, and Michelle is blooming at last, just like the 'Betty Boop' in my garden. That garden truly saved us both, for it gave me the strength to stand up to my daughter and give her what she really needed: not just love, but tough love.

Mary Harrison Hart

"I feel a lot better now.
Thanks for being such a great listener."

A Tree House for Everyone

Dreams are extremely important. You can't do it unless you imagine it.

George Lucas

I often say I have the best job on earth. But the truth is, for a passionate gardener, working at the Cleveland Botanical Garden isn't really a job at all! And when we decided to build a half-acre garden for children, well, it got even more interesting.

We thought it was important to involve children in the design process. That way we could learn what children themselves wanted to see and do in a garden. So we invited the public to come help us design the garden. On February 4, 1996, more than one hundred parents, grandparents and children showed up.

We rolled out big sections of white butcher paper on the floor and passed out lots of crayons. Then I asked the children to draw their fantasy garden. I also told them to place themselves somewhere in the picture.

Soon, close to seventy-five children were down on the floor, drawing intently. A dazzling, colorful mural began to emerge, filled with apple trees, streams, grape arbors, huge pumpkin patches, boulders, scarecrows, corn and a crazy quilt of flowers. They drew black bears, deer, raccoons, rabbits, watermelons, rainbows, ponds, forts, sunflowers, acorns, frogs, tomatoes and more.

An eight-year-old boy named Alan came late to the workshop. He had cerebral palsy and was strapped into a wheelchair. "Alan saw the special invitation asking children to the workshop," his mother said. "He insisted on coming." She wheeled him over to a table, and we gave him some paper and crayons. He went right to work—he knew exactly what he wanted to draw.

When all the children were done, I asked them to show everyone their drawings and describe them. When it was Alan's turn, his mother helped him hold up his drawing and point to it. He had drawn a very tall tree with a tree house teetering right at the top. Sitting in this high tree house was a boy in a wheelchair.

My heart went to my throat. It was both heartbreaking and inspiring to see how much a wheelchair-bound boy wanted to feel what it would be like to be way up in a treetop, looking down just like the other boys and girls. I turned to Deborah Hershey Guren, one of the Botanical Garden's biggest supporters. She looked as moved as I was. "A tree house for everyone. Wouldn't that be wonderful?" she murmured.

"Yes, but I don't know how you'd ever get a wheelchair up there," I replied.

Deborah said nothing, but kept her eyes on Alan and his drawing.

More than three-and-a-half years later, after many long hours of planning, building and planting, we were ready to host the grand opening of the new Hershey Children's Garden. With several hundred people there and all the opening festivities going on, no one noticed a young boy in a wheelchair waiting patiently for the garden to open. As soon as the invited dignitaries cut the ribbon, dozens of children ran inside. Most of them headed straight toward a large water fountain that had been designed especially for kids to play in and get wet.

Meanwhile, Alan directed his motorized chair right up the long ramp that led into the new tree house. As he rolled higher and higher, his smile kept growing brighter.

It just so happened that Deborah had headed over to the tree house, as well. She was looking down on all the children enjoying the garden below, when up rolled Alan, beaming with excitement and pride. He looked out over the tree house railing and said loudly to everyone in earshot, "This was my idea!"

When Deborah recognized Alan as the same young boy who had touched everyone so deeply with his desire three years earlier, she had to wipe away tears of joy. Her gift had made one child's dream come true. Alan had ached for something most of us take for granted. And she had helped to make it happen. Didn't it sound so simple, yet so profound?

A tree house for everyone.

Maureen Heffernan

Mandela's Garden

Watching something grow is good for morale.
It helps you believe in life.

Myron S. Kaufman

Nelson Mandela, leader of the African National Congress that helped end apartheid in South Africa, winner of the 1990 Nobel Peace Prize, and president of South Africa, was also, for twenty-seven years, a political prisoner. There, although separated from the outside world and his loved ones, he never lost his dedication to his cause. Mandela worked in mines, studied, and organized his fellow prisoners.

He also gardened. These are his words:

To survive in prison, one must develop ways to take satisfaction in one's daily life. One can feel fulfilled by washing one's clothes so that they are particularly clean, by sweeping a hallway so that it is empty of dust, by organizing one's cell to conserve as much space as possible. The same pride one takes in more consequential tasks outside of prison one can find doing small things inside of prison.

Almost from the beginning of my sentence on Robben Island, I asked the authorities for permission to start a garden in the courtyard. For years, they refused without offering a reason. But eventually they relented, and we were able to cut out a small garden on a narrow patch of earth against the far wall.

The soil in the courtyard was dry and rocky. The courtyard had been constructed over a landfill, and in order to start my garden, I had to excavate a great many rocks to allow the plants room to grow. At the time, some of my comrades jested that I was a miner at heart, for I spent my days at the quarry and my free time digging in the courtyard.

The authorities supplied me with seeds. I initially planted tomatoes, chilies and onions—hardy plants that did not require rich earth or constant care. The early harvests were poor, but they soon improved. The authorities did not regret giving permission, for once the garden began to flourish, I often provided the warders with some of my best tomatoes and onions.

While I have always enjoyed gardening, it was not until I was behind bars that I was able to tend my own garden. My first experience in the garden was at Fort Hare where, as part of the university's manual labor requirement, I worked in one of my professor's gardens and enjoyed the contact with the soil as an antidote to my intellectual labors. Once I was in Johannesburg studying and then working, I had neither the time nor the space to cultivate a garden.

I began to order books on gardening and horticulture. I studied different gardening techniques and types of fertilizer. I did not have many of the materials that the books discussed, but I learned through trial and error. For a time, I attempted to grow peanuts, and used different soils and fertilizers, but finally I gave up. It was one of my only failures.

A garden was one of the few things in prison that one could control. To plant a seed, watch it grow, to tend it and then harvest it, offered a simple but enduring satisfaction. The sense of being the custodian of this small patch of earth offered a small taste of freedom.

In some ways, I saw the garden as a metaphor for certain aspects of my life. A leader must also tend his garden; he, too, plants seeds, and then watches, cultivates and harvests the result. Like the gardener, a leader must take responsibility for what he cultivates; he must mind his work, try to repel enemies, preserve what can be preserved and eliminate what cannot succeed.

Nelson Mandela

You Forgot Something

A strong positive mental attitude will create more miracles than any wonder drug.

Patricia Neal

A monk was working in his garden when his students came up to him and asked, "What would you do if you had fifteen minutes to live?" He responded, "Continue to do what I am doing."

That did not impress me. So I asked one of our sons what he would do. "I'd buy a quart of chocolate ice cream and eat it." That revealed enlightenment to me until someone came up and said, "Perhaps you're being too harsh with the monk. What if his chocolate ice cream is his garden?" Ah, then I remembered.

Spring was in the air. However, this was the year John Florio planned to retire. So this spring he would not be doing any commercial landscaping as he had for his entire life. John had planted thousands of bulbs, plants and trees over the years and had created a beautiful world for all to enjoy. He was known best for surrounding office buildings with flowers so everyone's workday was made a little easier by the beauty he created.

When John developed a burning sensation in his stomach he took some antacids. When the distress continued he saw his physician, who ordered a GI series. His physician suspected an ulcer caused by John's depression and the stress related to his retirement, which the X ray confirmed. Stronger medication did nothing to relieve John's symptoms. Further X rays and tests revealed an enlarging ulcer, and a biopsy was obtained which diagnosed a carcinoma of the stomach.

It was at this point that John appeared in my office. "John, I have a week's vacation coming up in March and I don't want to delay your operation, so let's get you right into the hospital."

"You forgot something."

"What did I forget?"

"It's springtime. I'm going to go home and make the world beautiful, and when I'm done I'll return for the operation."

I returned from my vacation. Many weeks went by. One day John appeared in the office.

"I'm ready for the operation now."

John was admitted to the hospital and at the time of surgery I found a large malignant tumor which could not be completely removed. I sat down at his bedside the next morning.

"John, I couldn't remove all the cancer. You need more treatment, possibly chemotherapy and radiation."

"You forgot something."

"What did I forget?"

"It's still springtime. I don't have time for your treatment. I'm going home to make a beautiful world, and if I die I'll leave a beautiful world."

I didn't argue with him; nor did his family. He was discharged home and did not return to the office as scheduled.

A year later I came into the office and noticed his chart in one of the examining-room racks. I turned to my nurse. "You have the wrong chart. He is dead. We must have two patients by that name. Get me the correct chart."

"Why don't you open the door?"

I opened the door to the examining room and there sat John.

"Hi, Doc. I have a hernia from lifting boulders in my landscape business."

We fixed his hernia as an outpatient because John wanted no part of hospitals. There was no sign of cancer anywhere.

A few months later John was back in the office. I was told by the office staff he was having problems with his diet. This time I was sure it must be his cancer recurring and obstructing his stomach.

"Doc, I know you took out half my stomach, but I'm hungry and I need to talk to you about my diet." Needless to say, John had no problem eating whatever he desired. From then on the only calls I had from John were for treatment of various aches and pains related to his work.

I began to spend time with him outside the office. He became my teacher, showing me how beautiful the world was when seen through his eyes. I began to see tiny flowers and colors everywhere that I had never noticed before. I felt like an extraterrestrial landing on this planet, seeing it for the first time. I still collect flowers as I jog or bike that I bring home to plant in our yard while thinking of John and how he taught me to see beauty everywhere.

My wife and I were invited to the Florios' seventieth wedding anniversary, and it was a thrill to see all the lives he had touched and helped to make beautiful. When John's wife became ill they moved into a nursing home where he still kept making the world beautiful. John lived to be ninety-four with never any sign of cancer. He outlived his wife and wrote an autobiography before he died. In it he said, "I always hope I'll die working in my garden."

He did, because the world was his garden. Someday I hope the world will be filled with John Florios who make it their garden. What you consider your garden is up to you. Just don't forget springtime is a state of mind, and spend your lifetime working to create a beautiful world. When you do, you will be planting the seed of life within every cell in your body. So grow, bloom and blossom, and use the difficulties of life to fertilize your growth.

Bernie Siegel, M.D.

Lean Times

My mother is a woman who speaks with her life as much as with her tongue.

Kessaya E. Noda

Life in central California's San Joaquin Valley was hard in the 1950s. Jobs were scarce. Dad took whatever seasonal work he could find, and Mom worked two jobs.

Nearly everything we ate came from the garden. We didn't grow potatoes or yellow onions or the delectable asparagus we loved so well, because there just wasn't room for them. But it didn't matter; the public was invited to take what was left after the harvest on the large corporate farms. Gunnysacks in hand, we'd spend hours searching for large, dirt-encrusted potatoes, or strong-smelling onions.

In my childish innocence, it never occurred to me that we did this because we were poor. I thought that those of us gathering the leftovers were happy to be digging in the soil and finding treasure—treasure we could eat. After all, we never went hungry—until one autumn when my aunt and uncle and two cousins came to visit.

We had harvested our garden, and all the food that could be canned was tucked neatly in the pantry. There was just enough to see us through the winter months. Dad wasn't working, but Mom made most of our clothes, and her paying jobs took care of other staples like milk, cheese, pinto beans—and shoes.

Then Uncle Wes's family came and stayed. And stayed. They had come to California hoping to find work, but they weren't having any luck. Mom and Dad were generous. They never dreamed of suggesting that the long visit was a bit of a hardship.

"Man doesn't make the garden; the garden makes the man," Mom said. "Every gardener shares with others, because the earth gives to us, and we should give in return." So she kept sharing and patiently waited for the extra mouths to move on.

Finally, their departure day arrived. In her usual generous manner, Mom invited Uncle Wes and his family to help themselves to some of the home-canned jars of food when they left. She said her good-byes and then left for work as the visitors finished their packing. We kids were in school, and Dad was out doing some odd jobs.

When Mom arrived home that night, she went to the pantry to select the main course for dinner. She stepped inside and let out a loud gasp. Every last jar of her home-canning was gone—the entire winter's supply. She looked behind the jellies, around the bags of flour and still, not one jar was to be found. We all knew what had happened, but no one uttered a word.

Tears filled Mom's eyes, but she never said a mean word. "Let's have breakfast for dinner, okay everyone?" she asked and began to stir up a batch of pancakes. But there were many more nights to eat before our garden would grow again. Even I knew this was serious.

I don't know how, but some way or other, word spread

through our church and the neighborhood. A few days later, we started finding grocery bags filled with mostly home-grown food sitting on our back porch in the mornings. No one knew where they came from. We did notice that different bags would appear, so more than one person was helping to keep us fed. Times were lean for everyone. But people—some who, I suspect, didn't even know us—were sharing from their own meager pantries.

We had some hungry times that winter, but we made it. And I learned that Mom was right about gardens making the man. I've never yet met a gardener who wasn't kind enough to share.

Dyann Andersen

Hummingbirds in Hell's Kitchen

Every man's neighbor is his looking glass.

English Proverb

I used to live in Hell's Kitchen in New York City, and that's where I learned how to garden. We lived on the third floor of a crumbling brownstone—the kind of place where the landlord has no phone number, just a post-office box for the rent.

One day, a salesman sent me a flyer for mail-order roses. I looked out my window at the empty, forlorn lot below me and then sat down and ordered three rose-bushes. They came about a week later, three eighteen-inch thorny sticks in a plastic bag filled with soggy newspaper.

"What are you going to do with them?" my husband wanted to know.

"Well," I answered, "we need to build a window box, and then we'll hang it up outside the window and plant them."

"What 'we'?" he asked, and started off for the lumber-yard over on Tenth Avenue.

Filled with potting soil and roses, the window box weighed about three hundred pounds. I was terrified that the people who lived downstairs might come out into their yard just in time to get flattened as the box pulled free of the deteriorating brick wall. But it hung there, and in June, pink buds began to swell.

One Sunday, as we sat reading the newspaper, I suddenly smelled them—at least ten blossoms had burst open in the hot morning sun. They sat blushing and nodding as a city breeze wafted their perfume, along with the sound of the M-11 bus, into our apartment.

Soon, wonderful things started happening. People would stop me on the street.

"I know you!" they'd exclaim. "You're the one with the flowers. Very nice!"

People would call up from Forty-eighth Street, "What are they?"

"Roses!" we'd shout back.

"*Que bonita!*" they'd yell.

"*Gracias!*" we'd yell back.

Eventually, my first-floor neighbors moved out. We grabbed their apartment sight unseen because those roses had made us so land-hungry. In the tiny courtyard, I planted nicotiana and foxgloves, columbine and ferns, hellebores and viburnum, all of which could thrive in the dim light at the foot of the tenement. Woodpeckers visited, and hummingbirds the size of bumblebees. At night, bats swooped by, devouring mosquitoes and moths.

One morning, I found a local hooker-junkie asleep under the gardenia on a sheet she had swiped from my clothesline. She was very thin and her pale face was covered with welts. I suspected she had AIDS.

"You got a very nice yard," she remarked. "It don't smell like the city." As I led her out through the dingy hallway, she turned and said, "From here you'd never know somethin' so nice was back there." She walked away swinging her skinny arms and singing cheerily.

About a year ago, we moved to New Hampshire, to a house built by the Shakers. From my kitchen, I can see a lilac bush planted 150 years ago. With all the windows shut against the cold spring night, its scent still fills the house.

I designed an elaborate garden made of boxed beds in geometric shapes, divided by gravel paths and with a tree at its center—a potager, it's called. It's based on the medieval gardens grown behind monastery walls. It's a little paradise—my Garden of Eden—and I love it.

But I learned my most important gardening lesson back in the big city. I don't ever forget that there are hummingbirds in Hell's Kitchen, that roses grow on tenement balconies and that a garden prompted a prostitute to sing. It's our nature to find beauty, even in the most unexpected places. Without it, humankind would have died out long ago from sheer misery.

And that is why I give thanks for gardens.

Hillary Nelson
Submitted by Connie Goldman
Excerpted from Goldman's book,
Tending the Earth, Mending the Spirit

Sunflowers in Beijing

Where flowers bloom, so does hope.

Lady Bird Johnson

I grew up in Beijing, China, during the turbulent years of the Chinese Cultural Revolution. My parents, both medical doctors, belonged to the group of intellectuals the revolution intended to "purge" and "educate." In 1966, when I was twelve years old, the revolution was at its height.

Each day when I came home from school, I saw my parents' mood grow more somber. Some of their friends had already been imprisoned, while others were dragged into the streets, beaten and humiliated. Our house seemed shrouded in an eerie silence and sadness. I feared the worst for my parents.

I tried to focus on happier times. Two years earlier, my father had turned the tiny patch of dirt in front of our house into a garden. Each spring Father and I dug into the dry soil, fertilized it with chicken manure and planted sunflower seeds. The sunflowers grew tall and their faces turned to the sun, as if smiling.

Father loved to sit in the sun, watching the garden until his smile matched that of the sunflowers. In the fall, after we harvested the seeds, we roasted them with a sprinkle of salt and snacked on them through the long winter.

Would my father want to plant the garden this spring? Would he and my mother even be at home to harvest in the fall?

One spring afternoon, my father came home from the weekly political meeting, looking sadder than usual. When I greeted him at the door, he led me to the tiny shed where he kept his gardening tools. Without a word, he walked over to the garden and started tilling the soil. I followed him with relief. I was sure the gesture meant that everything would be all right.

Three days later, the soldiers came for him.

He was taken to the labor camp, in the poorest section of the province. The charge against him was straightforward—he was labeled a counterrevolutionary because of his profession and his family background. His father had been a landowner before the Communists took over China in 1949. Anyone who owned land, had factories or money or property before 1949—or had relatives who did— was considered an enemy of the poor. For that reason alone, one could be persecuted.

My mother's punishment was not as severe. Although she was a doctor, her parents were far from wealthy, so her family background was not considered as vile as that of my father's. She was no longer allowed to practice medicine, but at least she was not sent to a labor camp. She cleaned rooms in our local hospital, read Chairman Mao's books and heard lectures on her husband's misdeeds.

When the sunflowers were ready for harvest, I collected them alone and cried the whole time. I vowed not to eat a single seed until my mother and I visited my father during the Chinese New Year. When we arrived at the labor camp, the first thing I did was set a bag of roasted seeds into Father's hand. His pale, bony face broke into a sad smile. I hoped the seeds would nourish him, body and spirit, and help keep him alive.

When the next spring came, I planted the garden alone, and I did not cry this time. It was as if the warm, familiar earth filled me with renewed hope for Father's return. I took special care of the garden. Watching the sunflowers grow was my only link to my father.

The New Year arrived, but I was ill. Mother had to go alone to visit the labor camp. I gave her a big bag of sunflower seeds to take.

When she returned home, she was in tears. Through muffled sobs, she said, "Your father's suffered so. He's so thin, so sickly. He didn't smile once in the two hours I was there. Not even when I gave him the seeds."

I couldn't believe it. I wouldn't believe that Father might lose hope. The next spring, Mother told me not to bother with the garden. "It won't make any difference to your father," she said sadly. I was so angry at her lack of faith that I refused to speak to her until I finished planting the garden.

In July 1968 my father was released from the labor camp. When I went with my mother to bring him home, he did not smile; he looked numb, frozen. He barely spoke. But when he saw our garden, the sunflowers standing tall in the warm summer afternoon, a smile quivered on his lips.

My mother sighed with relief. I cried.

Ten years later, the Cultural Revolution was over. Both my parents had been restored to their posts as doctors. When their hospital built new housing for the medical staff, Mother and Father were assigned a large, sunny apartment. They were eager to leave the small, dark house, but Father would not leave the garden.

After much pleading and begging by my parents, the housing administrator agreed to let Father have a small patch of land in a community garden. Only then would he move.

I have left China, but my parents and I write often. Mother says Father still grows his sunflowers and still sits in the sun watching them smile. An ocean away, so do I.

Linda Jin Zou

8

THE FAMILY TREE

*The most important work you and I will
ever do will be within the walls of our
own homes.*

Harold B. Lee

The Burning of the Leaves

Nothing in this world is really precious until we know that it will soon be gone.

Donald Culross Peattie

Papa, my grandfather, loved the fall. Every year, at the end of October, he would gather all the yard's leaves in neat piles along the curb and begin burning them.

All along the avenue, as far as one could see, leaves would be burning. I used to wonder if it were pre-arranged, this ritual of disposal. Yet I never heard Papa phone anyone and say, "Well, today is the day. I'll see you at the curb." No, it just sort of happened. The fires would start in the late afternoon, when the winds were low, and continue into the early hours of dusk, the dying embers barely discernible by the time we children had to go in.

Leaf-burning was a family affair, a part of autumn I looked forward to every year. Adults raked all day, trying to keep the laughing children from running and jumping into the leaves before they got to the curb. At an early age, I delighted in the crackling sounds the flames made, and learned respect for fire, as well.

Neighbors talked and caught up with the latest goings-on. The men said things like, "Seems like there are twice as many as last year." Nana baked pies and invited folks in for food and company. The visitors lingered long after the embers were cold, and spoke of the coming winter. Papa, though, stayed outside, standing guard lest some stubborn leaf try to reignite and escape.

As a child, I never asked Papa why he seemed to love the burning of the leaves. I just assumed that everyone burned leaves in October and he was just doing what was expected of him. As I grew into adolescence, I found myself sitting at the curb, talking into the evening with him. And I became aware that it was more than a yearly chore for him. He once shared with me the times his dad had burned leaves on their small plot in the Pennsylvania hills. My great-grandfather was a coal miner and had little time to relax with his family. Papa and his ten brothers and sisters all looked forward to spending precious time with their dad during the burning of the leaves.

Papa was a quiet man, not given to a lot of talk. After years of working in open steel pits, he was still in great shape, but he moved slowly and always with a purpose. He and Nana were the anchors in my formative years, always there: same house, same comfortable routines. My parents and I lived a migratory army life. My grandparents rarely traveled. They were a constant I held even more dear as I grew into adulthood.

Then, early one summer, Nana died. That fall, Papa moved in with my parents. With his flowers, his hobbies and his family, he seemed content. But then one weekend when I was home from college, I noticed that Papa was raking the leaves out to the curb. Mom hadn't told him. I realized that I was going to have to be the one to break the news. I went out and explained that here, in this new town, there was an ordinance against burning leaves. All that smoke wasn't considered environmentally sound, and the authorities were worried about spreading fires.

Papa never said a word. He walked away, shoulders as low as they had been at Nana's funeral. He put the rake against the house and went inside. The leaves remained at the curb until late fall winds scattered them back into the yard. A feeling of sadness stirred within me that autumn; I, too, had lost something that could not be replaced. For many autumns after that, Papa pruned, repotted and did other garden chores, but he never again raked leaves.

The year I got pregnant with my second son was also the year we learned Papa had cancer. The doctors didn't think he would make it to Thanksgiving. Papa was thinner and moved slower than ever, but we all lied to him and to ourselves, saying how good he looked and making plans for joyful, not empty, holidays.

In the middle of October, I took Papa out to the farm my husband and I had just bought. The air was crisp, and Indian summer was at its peak. Papa walked the few acres with Adam, his great-grandson, as if he were patrolling an estate, with a measured step and head held high. I watched from the yard as he delighted in my four-year-old's exuberance.

When they returned, I told Papa that out here in the country, we wouldn't get fined for burning leaves. Could he please give me a hand with the task? He smiled widely for the first time in a long time, hugged me and said, "Thank you, I'd be glad to help." Tears began to fill my eyes, and the closeness between us was cemented for all time to come.

I raked, Adam ran through the leaves and Papa supervised the careful placement of the leaves along the gravel drive. He instructed Adam on the hazards of fire. The lesson was like a favorite bedtime story heard and loved so many times before.

Then Papa lit the match and the first pile began to burn. The colors moved quickly together, swirling around. Leaves tried to escape, only to be brought back in by Papa's deft control of the iron rake. The pile burned into the early hours of the evening.

The pie and coffee Papa had that night before retiring were, he said, the perfect end to one of the best days he had had in a long time.

He died one week later in his sleep.

A few days afterward, I received a letter from the Department of Sanitation. It had a warning and a copy of the local ordinance against leaf burning. But I hadn't really lied to Papa; there was no fine.

I shall miss my grandfather always . . . and the burning of the leaves.

Edie Cuttler

The Perfect Garden

*E*ach flower is a soul opening out to nature.

Gerald de Nerval

It was over dinner, thirty years ago, that Dad first told me I had a younger sister. I was twelve. I thought he was joking, until I looked across the table at Mother. Her face was rigid, her gray eyes unfocused, and I could sense the magnitude of what she was holding back.

Stunned, I nodded silently while Dad told me about Annie. He kept his voice calm, as if to reassure me that my world was still intact. He said that she lived in a good hospital with other mentally handicapped children, but I imagined her tucked away in a shoebox in some dark corner of a closet. I thought our parents had filed her away in their minds and expected me to do the same. "That's how it's done," they seemed to say.

Though I never saw my sister while I was growing up, I sometimes wondered about her. *Was she as thin as I? Did she braid her hair, too?* I remembered Mother had said something about water on the brain. Years later, Dad told me that the doctors believed Annie would die shortly after birth. He and Mother debated whether to bring her home. Finally, they decided she'd be better off living "with her own kind."

Perhaps they were right. Ours was a polished world, rooted in self-restraint. Our house felt like a museum. The furniture was dark with age and laden with family history. Flower arrangements came from the florist, and a stiffness in the air discouraged easy conversation. Outside, the elegant garden was immaculate. Tidy clusters of iris stood in a sea of yellow daylilies. Peony blossoms were held aloft on stakes, and vines of flowering clematis clung neatly to a pair of arched trellises. Unblemished by weeds or fallen leaves, it was a model garden.

There was no niche for Annie at home. She'd have stood out like a weed in a proper English garden.

In 1993, I finally went to meet her. I was thirty-nine. She was thirty-six. I went knowing little about her likes and dislikes, except for tidbits I had gleaned over the phone from a social worker: her favorite color, red; her dress size, ten.

I found her home in a line of brick rowhouses not far from where I'd grown up. The curtains in the windows were closed. The tiny porch was shedding its paint; the child-size garden bed out front was a barren patch of soil.

I sat in the car for a moment, feeling uncertain. Then I started across the road carrying a shopping bag full of presents. Earrings, chocolates, a red pocketbook, sweat pants, red tennis shoes. My heels tapped along the pavement, then up the three front steps to her house. Lanky men smoking cigarettes on a porch next door followed my movements with dull eyes.

The social worker ushered me into a dimly lit room. A TV blared from the corner. Several young women approached me at the same time. There were four of them. They peered up at me, jostling each other for a better view. I scanned each face, confused. "Annie?" I said to them all.

The women became silent. Then one of them grabbed my hand, and there she was, looking as startled as I felt. There was something familiar about her face. We had the same brown hair and green eyes, though her complexion was pasty and she was shorter than I. I handed her the bag of presents.

Annie looked right into my eyes. "I've missed you," she said loudly, her voice husky as a schoolboy's.

"Annie, open your presents," the social worker said. "See what your sister has brought you."

Annie tore the wrapping paper off each present eagerly. She hugged the pocketbook to her chest. She asked me to put the earrings on her and then admired herself in a mirror. She pulled the sweatpants on under her skirt and danced around the room. When we went upstairs to her room, she chattered to me as if she'd stored up words for years. She gave me a pad of paper and asked me over and over to write down my name, the date and the exact time I would call her the following week.

Five years have passed. Seeing her often, I've become used to Annie. I've learned to hear her say "I've missed you" without cringing at the emotion in her voice. I've been delighted when she announces, "I'll see you next month, don't you worry." And when she leans over and sniffs me, announcing loudly, "You smell good today," I no longer stiffen with embarrassment.

Today, as I drove her to my house, I said we'd plant some flowers. She said, "I'll watch you." But when we arrived, she said, "Okay, buddy, I'll help you out. Yes, I will." She'd already spotted the marigolds waiting beside my bedraggled garden. When she shoved the little plants into the holes I had dug, I flinched. She gripped the stems with her fist and ground the roots into the dirt until I put my hand over hers. She relaxed her fist, looked straight into my face and said, "Am I doing good?"

"You're doing great!" I said quickly, patting dirt around the flower. My words sounded shrill to me. I was afraid I'd offended her. But she had already grabbed another plant.

She cupped the flower in her hands and thrust her nose into the tiny polished petals and wisps of green. She breathed them in as if she were breathing in the fragrance of the world. "This flower smells good," she said, her face lit with pleasure. Then, stepping closer and holding the plant out like a gift, she pressed it against my nose and lips. I sniffed at the flower in her hands. Breathing in the marigold scent, I could almost taste its briny bitterness sliding down my throat. But the delight Annie took in presenting it to me was disarming. Something seemed to lift from the air between us, softening the barriers raised by years of separation. For a moment, the flower resting in the cup of her hands was all that mattered to us.

Now, after taking Annie home, I pause to admire our marigolds. Only a few of the tufted yellow heads hang from their stems. I hardly notice that some of the tiny blossoms are crushed. Most of the flowers will surely survive. For there is a whiff of Annie's presence all around, a vitality and a bittersweet bite to the air. No doubt our parents would think this bed of marigolds an eyesore. But to me, it's perfect.

Molly Bruce Jacobs

A Bedside Story

Good cheer is the best physician.

Pindar

My dad was a doctor, the old-style family physician. His patients loved him. Each Christmas he'd get so many presents—homemade fruitcakes, pipes with $100 bills stuffed in them, baskets with forty-eight different-colored pairs of socks—that he'd still be opening them that night.

As a child, while I knew his patients loved him, I didn't really know why. I figured part of it was his dedication: From 6:00 A.M. hospital rounds to 9:00 P.M. phone calls, he was there when they needed him. Part of it was probably his southern storyteller's charm—he could spin yarns with the best of them (a trait I, of course, did not inherit).

But I never realized what most of his appeal was until one summer evening. I happened to be playing behind the honeysuckle vines when Dad came down to his vegetable garden. He didn't know I was around. Even so, he sure didn't act like he was alone. Instead, he knelt down at the edge of his garden and started talking.

"Good evening, Miz Lettuce. You're looking mighty pretty tonight, young lady. What's that? Wilted? No, you don't look a day over thirty. In fact, I was hoping you might drop by for supper tonight."

He pulled a few leaves and set them in a peck basket, then moved over to a different section of the garden and started straightening up some fallen vines.

"Hey there, old bean, old rascal! Been chasing after the marigolds again, I see. You're going to have to start staying where you belong—you're all the flowers talk about anymore, you know. Now sit up straight and let me check you over. Hmmm, leaves normal. Flowers, um-humm. Pods, look good. You're the picture of health, Chief. We just need to fix a few weeds around your roots."

After a couple of minutes of quiet weeding, he got up and started checking some vines tied to thin, green stakes.

"Now, don't worry, Miz Tomato, I wouldn't ignore you. After all, you know you're one of the gals on my short list. Yes, Ma'am, you bet—right there at the top."

The corn plants were next on his rounds. He stopped at one, pulled out his small pocketknife—Dad always carried a pocketknife—and picked away at something.

"Calm down, Corn, old pal, you gotta expect a few ear problems now and then as you grow up. This'll be over in a jiffy. There now, let me give you a good, long drink; it'll give you a sense of well-being."

Whistling—Dad was a great whistler—he went off to get the hose. I tiptoed out of my hiding place.

What made my father such a great doctor? Well, sir, by now you know the answer as well as I.

It was his bedside manner.

Pat Stone

off the mark   by Mark Parisi

Reprinted by permission of Mark Parisi.

Lilacs for Mother's Day

The true measure of an individual is how he treats a person who can do him absolutely no good.

Ann Landers

The family had just moved to Rhode Island, and the young woman was feeling homesick that Sunday. It was Mother's Day—and her own mother was 800 miles away in Ohio.

She had called home that morning to say "Happy Mother's Day." Her mother had mentioned how cheery and colorful the yard was now that spring had arrived. And as they talked, the young woman could almost smell the tantalizing aroma of the purple flowers hanging on the big lilac bush just outside her mother's door.

Later, when she told her husband how she missed those lilacs, he popped right up from his chair. "Let's go get some. I know where we can find all you want. Get the kids and c'mon."

So off they went, driving into the sparkling May countryside, up past the small villages and new housing developments, past the abandoned apple orchards, back to where trees and brush have devoured old homesteads.

Where they stopped, dense thickets of cedars and junipers crowded the roadway on both sides. There wasn't a lilac bush in sight.

"Come with me," said the man. "Right over that hill is an old cellar hole, from somebody's farm of years ago, and there are lilacs all around it. I know the man who owns this land, and he said I could poke around here anytime. I'm sure he won't mind if we pick a few lilacs."

Before they got halfway up the hill, the fragrance of the lilacs drifted down to them, and the kids started running. Soon, the mother was so excited she, too, began running. When she reached the top, she stopped in amazement.

There, far from view of passing motorists, were towering lilac bushes, so laden with the huge, cone-shaped flower clusters they almost bent double. Smiling with delight, the woman ran to the nearest bush and buried her face in the flowers, drinking in the fragrance and the memories it recalled.

While the man examined the cellar hole and tried to explain to the children what the house must have looked like, and where the fields were, the woman slowly drifted among the lilacs. Carefully, she chose a branch here, another one there, and clipped them with her husband's pocketknife. She was in no hurry, relishing each blossom as if it were a rare and delicate treasure.

Finally, though, they climbed back over the hill and returned to their car for the drive home. For miles, while the kids chattered and the man drove, the woman sat in silence, surrounded by her flowers. Her smile was now one of contentment, and in her eyes was a faraway look.

When they were within three miles of home, she suddenly shouted to her husband, "Stop the car! Stop right here!"

The man slammed on the brakes. Before he could ask

why she wanted to stop, the woman was out of the car and hurrying up a grassy slope with the boughs of lilacs.

At the top of the hill was a nursing home. Because it was such a beautiful spring day, many patients were outdoors, strolling with relatives or sitting on the porch.

The young woman went straight to the end of the porch, where an elderly lady was sitting in her wheelchair, alone, head bowed. Across the railing went the flowers, into the lap of the old woman. She lifted her head and smiled. For a few moments, the two women chatted, both aglow with happiness, and then the young woman turned and ran back to her family.

As the car pulled away, the woman in the wheelchair waved and clutched the lilacs to her bosom.

Inside the car, the kids asked, "Mom, who was that? Why did you give her our flowers? Is she somebody's mother?"

The mother said no, she didn't know the old woman; she had never seen her before. But it was Mother's Day, and she seemed so alone, and who wouldn't be cheered by flowers?

"And besides," she added, "I have all of you, and I still have my mother, even if she is far away. That woman needed those flowers more than I did."

That satisfied the kids, but not the husband. The next day he purchased half a dozen young lilac bushes and planted them around their yard. And several times since then he has added some more.

I know. I was that man. The young mother was, and is, my wife.

Now, every May, our own yard is fragrant with lilacs. And every Mother's Day, our kids gather purple bouquets for their mother, just as she gathered them that first year.

And every year I remember that smile on a lonely old woman's face, and the kindness that put it there.

Ken Weber

Nona's Garden

There's nothing like a good family when you're really up a tree.

Carolyn Hax

When my grandparents emigrated from Italy to this country, they joined the rest of their clan who'd already settled in the small town of Oelwein, Iowa. Here the men had found jobs working for the railroad. Because most of Oelwein's population was of German descent, the newcomers had a hard time fitting in. So, to give them a sense of community and belonging until they "learned the ropes," the heads of each family pooled their money and bought a square city block of homes.

In Italy, my people had loved their gardens. So when they settled into their new homes, the backyard fences came down and all that open space became flower and vegetable gardens. Cobbled pathways connected each house, while grape arbors provided shade, fruit and wine.

"What's wrong?" Nona, my grandmother, asked me one day when she caught me sulking in my room.

"Nothing," I said, not wanting to tell. The truth was too painful. I was tired of being the brunt of jokes at the playground. Tired of being the "different" girl everybody picked on because of my dark coloring and simple, handmade clothes.

"You got nothing to do?" she said. "Then you come with me. Maybe you learn something today."

There was no saying "no" to Nona. I knew she knew what was wrong, and it was lesson time. I set my stubborn jaw and followed her downstairs where she snatched up her basket and garden shears. "You come," she said again.

We headed toward the herb garden first, a sunny spot that butted up against *Zia* Amalia's zucchini patch.

"See here?" Nona said, pointing to a thick bush, its rangy stems lifted toward the sun. "This is oregano."

Snip went the shears, and a handful of stems and leaves went into the basket. "Look," she said. "See the leaves? Small. Hardly anything to them."

She waited for me to nod in agreement.

"Smell." She rubbed a few teardrop-like oregano leaves between her fingers and wafted them beneath my nose. "Remember the smell," Nona said.

"Huh?" I blurted, wondering what she meant. It wasn't like I didn't know what these plants were already. I'd helped her put the seedlings in the ground last spring.

She moved to the next row of bushes, like an ambitious bee in search of nectar. "This is rosemary," she informed me, stooping to clip a lush frond stiff with spiky leaves. Again she crushed a couple of leaves between her fingers and made me inhale the scent. "Remember," she said.

Next came the basil plants, light green and dew-kissed glossy, their familiar scent the sweetest of all. We repeated the procedure, me wondering if Nona would ever just get to the point and let me go back to my brooding.

"Very different from the other two, eh?" she pointed out, snipping and tossing a few more bunches of basil into her basket. This time she didn't wait for me to answer. Instead, with me still in reluctant tow, she left the herb plot to gather several ripe tomatoes, a fat-to-near-bursting head of garlic and three purple eggplants.

"We make *Melanzani Parmiggiano* for supper tonight," she announced. "Your favorite."

Back inside the house, Nona tossed me an apron and asked me to rinse off the vegetables. I groaned.

"You got nothing else to do," she said. "You help me make the supper."

When the cleaned herbs and produce sat drying on dish towels, Nona said, "We start with the tomatoes. We peel the skins and put them in a pot to simmer. Look," she said. "They're very different from the eggplants, no?"

No kidding, I thought. *Any dummy can see that.*

She peeled and sliced the eggplant in fat rounds, dipped them first in beaten egg and then in seasoned bread crumbs, then fried them till golden in olive oil flavored with the fresh garlic we'd picked. After laying them flat in a baking dish, she turned her attention back to the simmering tomatoes.

"Now we add the herbs," she said, showing me what to do and how to do it. We stripped the leaves from the stems of each different herb and put them into three separate piles.

"Take a palmful of basil leaves," Nona said, then watched carefully as I obeyed. "Rub them between your hands and toss them in the pot. *Bene.* Don't it make your hands smell good? Now the oregano. Rub those, too. See how tiny the leaves are? *Che bellezza!* Different smell, eh?"

Helplessly, I looked at her and shrugged my shoulders.

"Toss."

I did.

"And now the rosemary," she winked. "Just a little kiss from *Signorina* Rosemary. Smell how strong her breath is?" Nona smiled at my groan. "Good. This dish gonna be perfect. Toss."

I helped her slice the cheeses and then we assembled the casserole in layers of eggplant, cheese and tomato sauce.

And somewhere along the line, much to my amazement, I realized I was enjoying myself.

That evening after the blessing, Nona served the dish we'd made. The casserole's aroma settled around the table like perfume from heaven. My family dug in.

"Well," Nona said, her bright brown eyes snagging mine as I chewed my first hefty mouthful. "What did you learn today, granddaughter?"

"I don't know, Nona. What did I learn?" I teased. Of course I'd learned a lesson today, and she knew me well enough to know I'd gotten her point long before we'd finished preparing supper.

"Okay, smart girl, I tell you. Every person in my garden different," she said.

I giggled. To Nona, plants had personalities, lives uniquely theirs, just like people.

"Nobody the same as nobody else, see? But when you and me put everybody together today, we got something special. Something delicious."

"Yeah, we did," I admitted, a rush of emotion pooling in my eyes.

And that was the shining moment in which I committed myself to taking joy in every one of the unique differences that made me *me.*

"God is very wise," Nona said. "Remember."

Paula L. Silici

My Money Tree

While we try to teach our children all about life, our children teach us what life is all about.

Angela Schwindt

For years I wanted a flower garden. I'd spend hours thinking of different things I could plant that would look nice together.

But then we had Matthew. And Marvin. And the twins, Alisa and Alan. And then Helen. Five children. I was too busy raising them to grow a garden.

Money was tight, as well as time. Often when my children were little, one of them would want something that cost too much, and I'd have to say, "Do you see a money tree outside? Money doesn't grow on trees, you know."

Finally, all five got through high school and college and were off on their own. I started thinking again about having a garden.

I wasn't sure, though. I mean, gardens do cost money, and after all these years I was used to living on a pretty lean, no-frills budget.

Then, one spring morning, on Mother's Day, I was

working in my kitchen. Suddenly, I realized that cars were tooting their horns as they drove by. I looked out the window and there was a new tree, planted right in my yard. I thought it must be a weeping willow, because I saw things blowing around on all its branches. Then I put my glasses on—and I couldn't believe what I saw.

There was a money tree in my yard!

I went outside to look. It was true! There were dollar bills, one hundred of them, taped all over that tree. Think of all the garden flowers I could buy with one hundred dollars! There was also a note attached: "IOU eight hours of digging time. Love, Marvin."

Marvin kept his promise, too. He dug up a nice ten-by-fifteen foot bed for me. And my other children bought me tools, ornaments, a trellis, a sunflower stepping stone and gardening books.

That was three years ago. My garden's now very pretty, just like I wanted. When I go out and weed or tend my flowers, I don't seem to miss my children as much as I once did. It feels like they're right there with me.

I live up in Michigan's Upper Peninsula, where winters are long and cold, and summers are way too short. But every year now, when winter sets in, I look out my window and think of the flowers I'll see next spring in my little garden. I think about what my children did for me, and I get tears in my eyes—every time.

I'm still not sure that money grows on trees. But I know love does!

Ruth Szukalowski

A Son's Harvest

The most important trip you may take in life is meeting people halfway.

Henry Boye

On this scorching, Mississippi-dusty June day in 1989, I had come to my father's home in Meridian to find—I didn't know exactly what. Nervously I walked up the ribbon of concrete toward the little red porch, wondering if this visit was a good idea. But I figured that, after thirty-nine years without any contact, we ought to try to find out whether there was anything between us, anything at all. After all, time was growing short; he was eighty years old, and I was forty-eight.

So, I steeled myself, recalling my childhood years at this house where I had lived before my father and mother divorced, and Mom and I moved to Illinois with her new husband. My stepfather had been as good a father as a son could want. But this man standing on the porch was my birth father. I wanted to know him.

I looked at Ples Mae (he spelled his last name differently from mine), marveling at how thin, how fragile, he had become. His newish overalls floated around him, seemingly holding him up, but his handshake and voice were strong as he motioned for me to join him on the porch while his wife cooked a country feast. There we sat, in two green metal chairs, the kind that spring back and forth. We sprang—and talked about what strangers talk about when they're trying to get to know one another.

"Been a hot one today," I said, wiping my forehead. "Hasn't been much rain."

"Yeah, I been having to water every day," replied my father.

"I've had to water every day, too, up in Washington, D.C.," I said.

Turning to look at me, my father said: "Water? Water what?"

"My garden." We had both stopped springing.

"You mean you're a gardener, too?"

Neither of us had to say it; we both knew it: We were not only kin—we were kindred spirits.

My father and I went to his garden during that first visit. And on each subsequent visit, we took the same walk. During early times, we talked mostly about the joys and heartbreaks of life in the garden, ranging further afield as we got to know each other better, covering everything from politics to relationships to history.

On one of my early visits, I was admiring his amazing crops: all manner of mouth-watering backyard crops, including peas, okra, cayenne peppers, corn, collards, butter beans, even peanuts and watermelons, their vines twirling from used automobile tires.

Seeing my admiration and showing understandable pride, my father stopped his slow stroll through the deep, narrow space, turned to me and asked, "So what are you growing in your garden?"

I began telling him about my rhododendron, Japanese

black pines, azaleas, Japanese maples, bamboo . . . when my father interrupted: "Uh huh, but what do you grow for food?"

"Oh, food. Well, there's rosemary, thyme, sage, cilantro . . ." With a dismissive chuckle, my father just shook his head and walked away, reaching for a hoe to weed around the corn, a *real* crop. I knew what he was thinking: My son's wasting land.

To this day, the memory of that moment brings a chuckle. But, what happened next brought a tear. My father went to his toolshed and came back with a raisin container from the grocery store. Shaking it, he thrust it at me, saying, "Here! Now you can grow some food." The little cardboard box held seeds, of course—pepper, okra, tomato, eggplant, even kernels of corn and some peanuts.

Never mind that any of these crops would overwhelm my postage-stamp-size garden. I brought the container back to the city, and I planted some of the seeds, calling the spot where the pepper and the okra grew the "Ples Mae Patch."

And that tradition continues. Each year, among the rhododendron, the Japanese black pines and all the other ornamentals, there is always a little something to eat. (Tomatoes, if nothing else, because store-bought ones just aren't fit food.) And each year a fundamental truth also grows: No matter how differently we garden, we all share a connection to the earth—and thus, a connection to one another.

That's one of the many reasons nothing keeps me out of my garden. And I'm grateful that nothing—not pride or fear of rejection, not even thirty-nine years of separation—kept me out of my father's garden on that hot June day. The harvest has been priceless.

Lee May

Honest Mike

The only way you can truly control how you're seen is by being honest all the time.

Tom Hanks

Everyone said my tall, thin dad looked like Abraham Lincoln. So when he started growing a beard and began looking for a tall top hat, everyone was sure he would win the prize for the best costume in our town's centennial celebration. But Daddy's resemblance to "Honest Abe" went much further than that.

As a teenager, Daddy had suffered from scarlet fever and rheumatic fever, leaving him with faulty heart valves and frail health. He had to drop out of high school because he couldn't climb the steep steps to his classes.

However, he was able to convince his doctor to let him do "light work," and he got a job as a timekeeper at a local factory.

As Daddy grew older, he found that the minimum wage he earned was not enough to support a family, but his heart condition and lack of education kept him from getting a better job. To stretch his income, he planted and tended a huge vegetable garden. Mom, my sister and I would help plant and harvest. We canned corn on the cob, shelled peas, picked raspberries and rooted in the soft soil for potatoes. Most of what we produced went into the cellar to feed us through the winter, and we sold the rest.

During the year of the centennial celebration, though, we weren't able to harvest our crop. A railroad track ran behind our property. A tanker car carrying a poisonous liquid sprang a leak and sprayed its contents on the vegetation all along that stretch of track. The railroad company issued a warning not to eat any of the produce from our gardens. They sent a notice to homeowners asking them to list the types and quantities of plants they had lost, so they could be reimbursed.

The day after we received our notice, we heard a knock on the door. Several neighbor men appeared, asking to talk to Daddy. They were afraid that the reimbursements would be far less than their actual losses, so they had decided to turn in claims three times bigger than they really were. These neighbors were aware of our financial situation and our dependence upon our garden. They had come to share their decision with Daddy, so he would not be left out.

That night, Mom and Daddy discussed the neighbors' suggestion. But even though Daddy did not know how we would survive without the garden, he was not able to lie to the railroad. On the insurance form, he honestly and accurately reported the plants he had lost. That decision left a huge burden hanging over my parents, yet Daddy had faith that honesty was always the best way.

And it was. I remember the excitement at our house the day the mailman delivered the check from the railroad company. Not only had we been paid for the cost of the seeds and plants we had purchased, but we were also paid for all the food we could possibly have harvested, plus a lot more.

As the town's centennial celebration drew closer, my dad began to look more and more like "Honest Abe." The neighbors who knew how he had refused to lie for his own gain began calling him "Honest Mike." But Daddy didn't live long enough to win that centennial costume prize. His injured heart gave out just a few weeks before the celebration. My sister and I, just eight and nine, cried as we buried Daddy with the candy bar and shaving cream we had planned to give him as birthday gifts.

But we did not bury his beliefs. To this day, whenever I am tempted to change the truth—even just a bit—I remember Daddy's garden and the seeds of honesty he planted there.

Marilyn Diephuis Sweeney

A Couple of Cacti

Adolescence is like cactus.

Anaïs Nin

On a sweltering afternoon, my mother came home from grocery shopping. She stumbled through the door with several paper sacks in one hand and a small, brown paper bag in the other. "Help with these!" she called.

Being a rebellious sixteen-year-old, I slowly sauntered over to her rescue and took the smallest bag from her.

"Be careful with that!" she warned.

"What's in it?" I asked with mild curiosity.

Mother set down the groceries and beamed proudly. "They had a close-out sale on some cacti—poor, pathetic little things. I thought I might try to nurse this one back to health."

I watched as she carefully extracted a sickly fuzzy cactus from the paper bag and set it down gently on the kitchen counter.

I burst out laughing at the fuzzy nub of a plant. "Mom! It looks like Charlie Brown's Christmas tree! I hope you kept your receipt!"

Mother just rolled her eyes at me and carefully set the cactus by the sun window, cooing softly to the ridiculous thing.

By the second week, the fuzzy little cactus had perked up just a little. I didn't pay much attention to it. High school had started, and I was busy with classes and my budding social life. Boys were starting to ask me out on dates, and I was absorbed in a thrilling, but often confusing, new world.

One day, on my way out to school, I found a paper bag sitting on the front steps. My heart sank as I read the brief note. It was a gift from a boy who had a crush on me. I hadn't been very nice to him but didn't know what else to do. I knew I didn't want to go out with him.

I took the bag in the kitchen and, to my surprise, there was another tiny cactus inside. This one was green and straight with lots of prickly spines on it.

"Oh no!" I groaned. "Look, Mom, that guy gave me a cactus! How weird!"

Mother laughed. "Maybe he's trying to tell you something."

"Yeah, something," I mumbled. I knew the two of us weren't meant for each other.

Mother inspected the cactus carefully. "This is perfect. Now the other cactus will have a friend."

"Like, whatever, Mom," I said, mustering up as much sarcasm as I could. I left for school. Mother fussed with the spiny thing and set it next to the other one in the kitchen window.

A couple of months later, I was eating a piece of toast in the kitchen one morning. I glanced at the cacti and noticed that they'd both started bending toward each other like two green bananas. I laughed because they looked sort of . . . happy.

Through the winter, Mother and I watched those two cacti growing closer and closer to each other. They were both bending dramatically and had nearly formed a U shape.

I was a typical teenager, and sometimes our household got pretty turbulent back then. But those two green cacti were always the subject of pleasant conversations between Mother and me. We'd laugh and joke about the imaginary romance they were having.

Mother would be the fuzzy one, and I'd be the spiny one. We'd throw silly one-liners back and forth between the cacti. I'd say things like, "Hey, baby, what's a nice girl like you doing in a pot like that?" Mother would answer, "Hey! Keep your stickers to yourself, young fellow!"

One morning that spring, I went into the kitchen and something truly amazing caught my eye. My spiny cactus had grown a hot pink flower on the top of its head, closing the gap between the two cacti and completing the union between them.

Tears came to my eyes. I realized in that moment that these two cacti had bonded in their own special way. I ran upstairs to get Mother. We both stood there staring at those cacti as big, soggy tears ran down our cheeks.

Later that day, Mother and I went to the garden center. After much discussion, we settled on a beautiful pot, big enough for the two of them.

Without disturbing the cacti's delicate union, we carefully transferred them into their new pot. We were so proud and happy for them. They were in love.

I survived high school and, soon after graduating, moved away to the city and started my own life. Mother kept the two cacti, and I'd always ask how they were doing when I called. "They're still together," she'd tell me.

I felt a sense of security, knowing that our little green couple was happy and healthy.

One day, Mother called to inform me that the fuzzy one had died. "I did everything I could," she told me, "but I just couldn't revive her."

Fighting back tears, I said, "That's okay, Mom. You're the one who saved her ten years ago, remember? Besides, she had a long, happy life . . . and she experienced true love."

The spiny one became ill just months later and passed away. I cried a little when I heard the news. Then I laughed, remembering the happy times Mother and I had enjoyed, watching our spiky sweethearts reach out to each other in our kitchen window. They had helped us keep our hearts connected, too, during my own prickly years.

Kelly E. Reno

Prayer of a Gardening Mother

Those who love the young best stay young longest.

Edgar Z. Friedenberg

Dear God, give me the strength to grow a garden.

Give me the perseverance to find a portion of dirt in my backyard that's free from old popsicle sticks and sand toys, out of range of the swing set, and not used as a tricycle parking lot or a soccer field.

Give me the courage to face the fact that the crate of bulbs that took six weeks to be delivered and three hours of backbreaking labor to plant, can be dug up in five minutes by a two-year-old with a spoon.

Guide me through the backyard over plastic toys, irrigation systems and wire mesh to unravel the dog from the watering hose for the fifteenth time.

Help me accept that everything in my garden is either expensive, high maintenance or unpronounceable, and the only thing that looks the same as it did in the mail-order catalog is the dirt.

Grant me patience when my daughter waters all of the

bulbs with apple juice because "they look thirsty."

Give me the strength to remain silent when my husband puts pans of beer throughout the garden to get rid of the snails.

In your infinite wisdom, show me how to turn off the drip irrigation system that has been on since sometime in mid-March.

Grant me serenity when my son presents me with a bouquet of freshly pulled daffodils crammed into an old plastic sand bucket—and the ability to smile when he tries to put them back.

Comfort me when all of the beer pans in the garden are empty—and the dog is staggering around the backyard trying to do the limbo with the low branches on the apple tree.

And if I ask too much, God, just give me the foresight to know that, no matter what I do, by the end of summer the flowers will be run over by plastic roller skates, the gardening stakes will be used for goal posts, and the fertile soil will, once again, be filled with old popsicle sticks and sand toys—and I wouldn't have it any other way.

Debbie Farmer

Let's Go Thump a Melon

Integrate what you believe in every single area of your life.

Meryl Streep

Daddy was a simple farmer. But he had a magic method of handling life—he'd go "thump a melon."

As kids growing up on our truck patch of Texas Black Diamonds, we all learned how to rap on a melon and listen for the telltale, hollow "thuk-thuk" of ripe perfection. But sometime during my tenth summer I began to sense other, less literal meanings of Daddy's familiar suggestion: "Let's go thump a melon."

That summer I had the worst case of work-fed-upness among us kids. My back ached, and I had spent too many hours weeding those hills of melon with their fruit-bearing runners.

By July my hatred for hoeing had ripened with the melons. Then came one of those smothering days when clouds hung low overhead. The hoe slipped in my sweaty hands, making blisters. I startled at every dry whir of grasshopper wings in my face.

Just as I was ready to burst into tears, Daddy, working nearby, sensed the situation. "Let's go thump a melon and bust it in the shade!" he called, throwing down his hoe with a decided thud.

"But, Frank," Mama protested, "right in the middle of a workday?"

"Best time!" Daddy smiled as he took off his straw hat, mopped his brow and replaced his hat exactly backward on his head. This gesture was Daddy's cue to the family that he was ready for some fun. Not even Mama could resist that plea to lay aside work.

By the time we left the hot, dusty fields with our carefully chosen watermelon cradled in Daddy's arms, we had almost forgotten the sticky afternoon's breathlessness.

Later, lying under the cool shade of an oak, melon melting in my mouth, I remember thinking with surprise, *Daddy knows how important it is to us kids—to everyone!—to lay aside hard work for fun sometimes.*

A couple of weeks later, it came again: Daddy's fun call to thump a melon. We'd been loading the hefty emerald balls onto trucks all day when Daddy suddenly dusted off his hands from the last melon on a load and turned away an empty truck backing into loading position. "That's all for today!" he called, jauntily tilting his straw hat backward. "I'm fixing to hold a melon-thumping contest here," he announced, "and you contestants had best get your entries ready." With that, he turned over a wooden carrying crate and climbed up on his impromptu judge's stand.

Grabbing a broken hoe handle as a microphone, he imitated the lilting voice of a radio announcer. "Ladies and gentlemen! Coming to you from this field of fat, green pigs"—then, at our laughter—"I see some of the contestants here don't believe those are green pigs." He pointed to the melons. "Don't you see those green piglets—their corkscrew tails and heads burrowing under shady leaves?" I looked down and was delighted to see the whole field of melons turn into fat, green pigs.

But melon-thumping wasn't just for fun times. From mid-May until late August, I'd often awaken with Daddy sitting in a rocker near my bed. With the morning chores done, he'd be reading the Bible. When he was sure I was awake, he'd glance over his spectacles at me. "How's about if we go thump a melon and put it in the cistern for noon?" he'd ask.

In my gingham gown I'd traipse out after him into the dewy depths of those green vines. We'd stand together, appreciating the morning hush and the glowing pink horizon. Then we'd thump melons, cool and damp against our faces. We'd pull the perfect one from the vine and lower it into the icy depths of the cistern. At noon we'd hoist up the dripping melon and quench our thirst with its frosty red sweetness.

Melon-thumping was useful in hard times, too. One day in September, when I was fourteen, I came home from the county fair crying. I'd seen Robert Honnycut there, holding hands with my best girlfriend. Robert's wavy, yellow hair sent butterflies flitting through my stomach. Of course, I'd never mentioned that to anyone and never would. However, Daddy studied my reddened eyes and said, "Let's go thump a melon."

"But all the good melons are gone," I protested, trying to take him literally. "And what's left have gone to sugar—you know that."

"Let's go thump one anyway," he said, reaching for his straw hat on a peg and motioning me out the door, away from the prying eyes of my sister.

He'd never say, "Let's have a talk" or "Let's take a walk." But I usually came back from thumping melon feeling better—even if there was no melon worth thumping or no happy ending to the talk.

Some years later, I came home to visit when Daddy was battling emphysema and heart failure. In bed, surrounded by doting relatives, Daddy gazed longingly out the window at the melon patch, overgrown with burrs and thistle. Watching his pinched face, I found it hard to tell which smothered his breath more—his illness or his well-wishers.

I knew that Daddy loved his sisters, but I also knew those well-meaning ladies could "talk him to death," as he sometimes put it. I figured it was my turn to sound out the situation. "Want to go thump a melon?" I asked him.

"In April?" Daddy's sister Bertha exclaimed. But Daddy smiled broadly as I got his old straw hat from its hook and set it jauntily backward on his head. Then I helped his fragile frame out to the porch chair and closed the door securely behind us.

For some moments we sat silently, gazing at the gold and violet ribbons stretched across the late-afternoon sky. Then I told him what I'd observed. "Your sisters are babbling because they don't know what else to do," I said. "They don't want to mention death to you, because they think you might fear it. Do you?" I heard a gentleness in my voice that was surprising, even to me.

Daddy smiled, shaking his head. "Look out yonder," he said, pointing to the multi-hued horizon. Squeezing my hand, he chuckled. "Beyond that is the Creator of it all," he said. "Don't you just know him and me are gonna thump SOME melon!"

Jeanne Hill

$\overline{9}$

POTPOURRI

Kind hearts are the garden,
Kind thoughts are the roots,
Kind words are the blossoms,
Kind deeds are the fruits.

John Ruskin

The Christmas Tree

Man is related to plants as all living things are related.

Josephine Von Miklos

Trees just do not grow up here on the high plateaus of the Rockies—everybody knows that. Trees need good soil and good weather and up here there's no soil and terrible weather. People do not live here. Nothing can live up here and certainly not trees. That's why the tree is a kind of miracle.

The tree is a juniper, and it grows beside U.S. 50 utterly alone, not another tree for miles. Nobody remembers who put the first Christmas ornament on it—some whimsical motorist of years ago. From that day to this, the tree has been redecorated each year. Nobody knows who does it. But each year, by Christmas Day, the tree has become a Christmas tree.

The tree, which has no business growing here at all, has survived against all the odds. The summer droughts somehow haven't killed it, nor the winter storms. When the highway builders came out to widen the road, they

could have taken the tree with one pass of their bull-
dozer. But some impulse led them to start widening the
road just a few feet past the tree. The trucks pass so close
that they rattle the tree's branches. The tree has also survived the trucks.

The tree violates the laws of man and nature. It is too
close to the highway for man, and not far enough away
for nature. The tree pays no attention. It is where it is. It
survives.

People who live in Grand Junction, thirty miles one way,
and in Delta, Colorado, fifteen miles the other way, all
know about and love the tree. They have Christmas trees
of their own, of course, the kind of trees that are brought to
town in trucks and sold in vacant lots and put up in living
rooms. This one tree belongs to nobody and to everybody.

Just looking at it makes you think about how unexpected life on Earth can be. The tree is so lonely and so
brave that it seems to offer courage to those who pass it—
and a message. It is the Christmas message: that there is
life and hope even in a rough world.

Charles Kuralt

Buried Treasure

No act of kindness, no matter how small, is ever wasted.

Aesop

My mother, Eloisa Ferrer y Uria, was born in Trinidad, Cuba, during the Depression. It was a place and time where nothing was wasted. During her childhood, containers of all sorts were hoarded and reused. Broken clothespins and scraps of cloth were made into toys. The silk threads used to tie cement sacks were crocheted into beautiful bedspreads and shawls. And any bare patch of soil could be a garden. In the central courtyard of her family's old Spanish-style home, her father planted mangoes, orchids and chili peppers, filling every nook with beautiful and useful plants.

On Valentine's Day 1947, my mother met Martin Mondrus, a visiting artist from Los Angeles who had seen photographs of picturesque Trinidad and had decided to paint its colonial architecture. They fell in love and were married.

When my mother moved to California with my father,

her thrifty habits persisted. She scrubbed out empty bleach bottles and cut holes in them to make birdhouses and planters. Balls of string became embroidered ornaments. Bits of cloth turned into elegant patchwork quilts and garments.

Outdoors, abalone shells and river rocks were set into homemade stepping stones. The decorative pathways wound through a tangled mass of wild castor beans. There, my mother put to work the gardening lessons she had learned from her father in Cuba. Gradually, she transformed the wilderness, tackling the dense clay soil of Los Angeles with shovels and hoes. The steep hillside that served as our backyard was transformed into a beautifully terraced garden filled with avocado, almond and guava trees, roses, nasturtiums, amaryllis and cymbidium orchids.

For years, as she worked in the garden, my mother would unearth abandoned toys. There were tiny plastic soldiers holding broken weapons, miniature cowboys mounted on horses with smashed legs and glossy, rainbow-hued marbles streaked with hairline cracks.

Most people would have tossed these damaged playthings into the trash; my mother saw them as precious. When my sister and I teased her about saving someone else's trash, she shook her head gently and smiled.

"Just think," she marveled, "this house has a history. Somebody's children grew up here." It was easy for her to imagine adventurous little boys building cardboard forts in their castor bean wilderness.

With the mud lovingly wiped off, the salvaged toys went into a shoe box on a shelf above the washing machine. Year after year, they took up space and gathered dust, but my mother just couldn't get rid of them. She knew that a child had once treasured the shabby soldiers, cowboys and marbles. That made them important enough to save.

One day, long after my sister and I had grown up and left home, a middle-aged stranger knocked on my parents' door. My mother greeted him. He introduced himself with some embarrassment.

"I grew up in this house," he explained apologetically. "I'm in town for my father's funeral, and I've been feeling nostalgic. Would you mind if I looked around outside?"

My mother sighed with sympathy and relief.

"I believe I have something that belongs to you," she said. She went to the back of the house, unearthed the box and handed it to the stranger. Puzzled, he lifted the lid—and then gasped in surprise at the bits and pieces of his boyhood so lovingly preserved. Overwhelmed by the rush of memories, his eyes misted over. He could barely stammer his thanks.

Mother just smiled. She had always known that, sooner or later, her garden's buried treasures would be needed again. Like dormant seeds, the memories held in those tiny fragments of plastic and glass were just waiting for the right time to sprout.

Margarita Engle

The Farmer and the Preacher

A preacher was driving down a country road when he came upon the most magnificent farm he had ever seen in a life spent in rural preaching. The farm stood out like a diamond; it sparkled. While it was by no means a new farm, the house and outbuildings were finely constructed and freshly painted. The garden around the house displayed a collection of beautiful flowers. A fine row of trees lined each side of the white-graveled drive. The fields were beautifully tilled and a fine herd of fat dairy cattle grazed knee-deep in the pasture. All this comprised a beautiful painting of what the ideal farm should look like and the preacher stopped to drink in the sight.

It was then he noticed the farmer on a big, shiny tractor, hard at work. As the farmer approached the spot where the preacher stood beside his car, the preacher hailed him. The farmer stopped his tractor, idled down the engine and shouted a friendly hello.

And the preacher said to him, "My good man, God has certainly blessed you with a magnificent farm."

There was a pause as the farmer took off his billed cap and wiped the perspiration from his face with a bandana. He studied the preacher for a moment and then shifted in his seat to take a look around his pride and joy. Then he turned back to the preacher and said:

"Yes, he has, and we're grateful. But you should have seen this place when he had it all to himself!"

Earl Nightingale
Submitted by Debra Sue Poneman

A Hard Act to Follow

Good gardening is very simple, really.
You just have to learn to think like a plant.

Barbara Damrosch

Mother's Day was fast approaching and, as usual, I was lacking the funds to buy Mom something really special. Knowing how she loved her garden, I decided to go to the local nursery and buy her some flowers.

I was ecstatic to find a yellow rosebush, her favorite, for under $10.

When I presented it to Mom the next day, she loved it! She and Dad planted it right next to the lamppost out in front of the house—a place of honor where everyone passing by could admire it.

After a couple of weeks, the rosebush was growing out nicely—all lush and green. Mom asked Dad if we had any fertilizer. "There's an open bag of 5-10-5 in the garage," he replied. Mom found it and sprinkled a good handful around her rosebush and watered it well.

At first, Mom's rosebush thrived. But after a few weeks of her fertilizer regimen, it started to turn yellow and lose leaves. Eventually, to her dismay, it up and died.

Dad knew how much she loved that rosebush. "I'll find you another one to replace it," he promised. "First, though, I'd better dig up the dead bush and get the spot ready for the replacement." He got his shovel from the garage and started to dig when, all of a sudden, "Clang!" *Hmm, it must've been a rock that killed it,* he thought. He kept digging . . . and digging. He dug around and around the bush to free the rock. But the rock got bigger and bigger until, finally, he had to get a crowbar to help get this huge mass out! He examined it more closely and noticed that the roots were actually going into the rock! "What the heck did she do?" he muttered.

Dad marched into the house and called out, "Ma, what did you sprinkle around the rosebush?"

"The fertilizer you told me to use!" she said innocently.

"Show me," he said.

They walked out to the garage and Mom showed Dad the bag of fertilizer she had been using. Well, I think the whole entire neighborhood heard Dad burst out laughing. Back then, 5-10-5 was a gray granular mix and not multi-colored like it is today. There was also another open bag in the garage—a bag of cement. Because she hadn't read the label, all along Mom had been using the wrong bag. She'd been adding cement to the soil, watering it in—and lovingly cementing her rosebush right to death!

When Dad showed us all that huge mass lying on top of the ground with a dead rosebush cemented in it, even Mom had to laugh.

That plant may be dead and gone today, but in our family, the story of Mom's cemented rosebush is going to live forever.

Susan Gilman King

"Let's plant it right here!"

The Wreath

*Children are God's apostles, day by day sent
forth to preach of love, and hope and peace.*

James Russell Lowell

For their Christmas holiday project, Cassie's Blue Bird troop planned to visit a nursing home.

"Folks in nursing homes are often too old or too sick to be home alone," Mrs. Peters, the group leader, told the little girls. "Maybe they have no relatives; maybe families are far away or unable to help. We're going to cheer them with carols and bring them gifts we've made."

Placing the last flower on her wreath, Cassie wondered about the person whose name she drew—Mabel—somewhere between sixty and eighty. Not yet ten, Cassie had difficulty identifying with "old." Her grandparents played golf, traveled a lot and had plenty of loving relatives.

Outside, a car horn blared. Cassie scooped up her wreath and rushed to join her friends. The Blue Birds, a junior version of Camp Fire Girls, soon arrived at a modest cottage. A matron greeted them enthusiastically.

"The folks are just so looking forward to your visit," she said with a smile.

Stepping onto the cottage's smooth linoleum floor, Cassie sniffed a strong disinfectant odor. Mrs. Peters sounded a pitch on her harmonica and led the troop in "We Wish You a Merry Christmas."

Singing along, Cassie gazed at one wrinkled face after another: some smiling, some sad, some apathetic. One elderly woman turned her face to the wall. As the matron announced the little girls would be circulating among the residents with gifts, a man in a wheelchair spun forward. He wagged his finger fiercely at the visitors.

"What right do you have coming here, reminding us of families we don't have?" he shouted. "Once a year somebody comes here. Take your do-gooding pity and get out!"

Wide-eyed, some of the girls backed away, but Mrs. Peters coaxed them forward again as the matron calmed the grumbling man.

Shaken but determined, Cassie asked a group of card-players, "Please, where can I find Mabel?"

A lady with bright orange hair gestured toward the window.

"Over there," she said cheerfully. "And don't pay these grouches any mind. You kids are okay."

Timidly clutching her wreath, Cassie approached the straight-backed figure surrounded by soft winter light.

"Mabel?"

The gray head with a proud French roll at its crown didn't move. Mabel—if this was Mabel—continued gazing out the window at the darkening California desert. Cassie set her wreath on the worn, polished surface of a table by her side. Taking a deep breath, she stared at it, as if memorizing every leaf.

"I made this wreath for you," she said. "I know it's just

homemade, but there is a story for every twig and flower. I came to tell you about them.

"The base is made from pine branches—some were easy to bend, and some I had to soak in water to shape the frame. It's all natural and gathering the flowers was fun, because I remember where each one grew."

Her courage up now, Cassie talked faster, touching the wreath as she spoke.

"The wild sunflowers are from a vacant lot by my house. Someone is going to build new homes there, so by spring the sunflowers will be all gone. These dried desert flowers—the mustard, sage and lavender—smell so good, and they'll last a long time. Rabbit foot fern is from my patio garden, and so is the baby's breath. I caught the gold and red maple leaves when they blew across our lawn. I found a few little pinecones, too. And in the center is a star white cactus flower. Mom says it's kind of unusual for this time of year."

Slowly, Mabel turned around. Eyes undimmed by age searched Cassie's.

"I sit by this window," she said quietly, "because I miss the outdoors so. Thank you for bringing it inside."

A trembling hand, clustered with brown spots, reached over and grasped Cassie's. "I, too, remember where the flowers grew. Merry Christmas, child."

Sherri Andervich

A Few Strings Attached

Good fences make good neighbors.

Robert Frost

Grandma's pride and joy was three acres of flower gardens surrounding the family farmhouse in eastern Oklahoma.

When a neighbor's rare game hens began escaping from their pens and invading Grandma's carefully tended flower beds, she was frantic. These birds ate seeds and small bedding plants and even damaged shrubs.

Pleas to the marauders' owner brought apologies, but no fence-mending. Now, Grandma was a lady, but if pushed too far, her temper could match her red hair.

One morning after she discovered her seed beds destroyed once more, Grandma sat down and fiercely scribbled something on several pieces of paper. She then threaded yellow corn on pieces of string, and to each string she tied one of her notes.

The next day, several game hens were back in her garden. The birds eagerly gulped down the strings with the corn and went running off with notes dangling from their beaks. And that was the last we saw of invading game hens!

"Grandma," I asked later, "what did you do? Did you write something rude about those birds?"

Her blue eyes twinkling, she answered, "Why, no, honey. I just invited their owner over for a few meals of exotic chicken—roasted, barbecued and fried—and gave the dates!"

Marcia E. Brown

A Gift of Grace

The supreme happiness of life is the conviction that we are loved.

Victor Hugo

As the nurse had instructed, I walked up and down the halls of Mercy Hospital over and over again. I was seventeen—and pregnant. This was the last place I ever imagined myself. I had planned to become an interior designer and move to New York. *Not anymore,* I thought glumly. As I walked past room after room filled with husbands and wives, giggles and encouragement, I was only reminded of how alone I was.

I couldn't help but notice the bright bouquets in so many of the rooms. One woman had at least fifty pink roses on her nightstand. The florist deliveryman seemed to live on this floor of the hospital. Every time he arrived, I said a little prayer, hoping he'd walk into my room in the back corner, but he never did.

I got pregnant the summer before I was to leave for college. My boyfriend, three years my senior, was leaving for medical school at the same time. He left on schedule in the fall, and I never heard from him again. My parents were almost as unsupportive. They begged me to "consider all the options." But even in my pain, I knew that having my baby was the right decision. They were infuriated and gave me money to have the baby in another state, "so you won't be embarrassed."

I moved in with my grandparents. They were well up in age and weren't able to go to the hospital with me. So, on that rainy day when the contractions began, I drove there by myself.

I had never felt so lonely. I wanted desperately to have my hand held by someone who wasn't trying to prick my finger or take my temperature. As I continued to walk, I passed a room so filled with people, it looked like they were having a party, not a baby. I stuck my head in to see what all the commotion was about and heard a pleasant voice come from the bed.

"Hi! It looks like you're getting ready to have one of these!" The new mother was holding a beautiful baby in a white gown and a pink cap.

"Let's hope so," I said, trying to sound cheerful. I was mesmerized by the tiny baby she held with such confidence and pride.

"My name is Laura. Would you like to hold her?"

I was so touched by the woman's kindness, all I could do was nod yes. Getting to her was the hard part. Laura had more balloons and flowers in her room than I had seen all day. She had beautiful orchids and lilies, too. The whole room was so inviting partly because of the flowers' gentle scent.

As I held the precious infant in my arms, she cooed and strained to open her eyes.

"Are you having a boy or a girl?" Laura asked.

"I don't know yet. I'm crossing my fingers I'll find out tonight." I delicately handed her back her gorgeous child, praying mine would be as healthy and alert.

"Well, good luck. You're going to be a great mom."

In my nine months of pregnancy, no one had ever said that. It was the nicest thing I had ever heard.

Hours later, I lay in my own hospital bed, alone, waiting to deliver a child whom I could offer only love. I was beyond scared. As tears fell down my face, I heard a knock at my door. A nurse came in and sat down next to my bed.

"I have a surprise for you, Amanda."

For a passing second, I thought my parents would stroll in, but instead, another nurse walked in with a bouquet of flowers. It was the most beautiful arrangement I had ever seen. It was filled with daisies and lilies and baby's breath and even roses! I was so excited I could hardly keep from jumping out of bed. When I thought it couldn't get any better, another nurse came in, her arms full of more flowers and balloons. Nurse after nurse came in until the room was completely filled with every flower imaginable. I felt like I was in a florist shop!

I was in shock. Who would have gone to so much trouble to send me such thoughtful gifts? I hurriedly looked at the cards and found that they all said the same thing, written in the same handwriting: "You are loved and created with a special purpose. For love."

I had no idea who they were from, but suddenly I *did* feel loved—and ready to bear and love a baby of my own. That night I gave birth to a beautiful baby girl. I named her Grace. A few days later, I walked around the hospital, as proud as only a new mother can be. I stopped by Laura's room to visit and saw that all her flowers were gone.

"What happened to all your flowers?" I asked.

She smiled and said, "You are loved and created with a special purpose. For love."

I fought back the tears, as I realized who had sent my flowers. Only God could have put me in the hospital at the same time as such an angel. Laura told me she had given birth alone years earlier. She said she could sense I was hurting when I passed by her room, so she gave me her flowers to lift my spirits. Little did she know how much her gift had meant: It had given me the strength to deliver my beautiful Grace.

Laura has been my best friend for almost ten years now. To celebrate our friendship, every year on our daughters' birthdays, we send each other flowers. And every year I thank God again, for his grace—and for mine.

Amanda Dodson

One at a Time

If I had two loaves of bread, I would sell one and buy hyacinths, for they would feed my soul.

The Koran

It was a bleak, rainy day, and I had no desire to make the drive from the beach to the cold mountain at Lake Arrowhead where my daughter Carolyn lived.

A week earlier, she had called and insisted that I come see the daffodils some woman had planted at the top of the mountain. So, here I was, reluctantly making the two-hour journey.

By the time I saw how thick the fog was on the winding road toward the summit, it was too far to go back, so I inched my way up the perilous Rim of the World Highway to my daughter's house.

"I am not driving another inch!" I announced. "I'll stay and have lunch, but as soon as the fog lifts, I'm heading back down."

"But I need you to drive me to the garage to pick up my car," Carolyn said. "Can't we at least do that?"

"How far is it?" I asked cautiously.

"About three minutes," she answered. "I'll drive. I'm used to it."

After about ten minutes of driving, I looked at her anxiously. "I thought you said it was three minutes away."

She grinned. "This is a detour."

We were back on the mountain road, in fog like thick veils. *Nothing could be worth this,* I thought. But it was too late to turn back. We turned down a narrow track into a parking lot beside a little stone church. The fog was beginning to lift a little, and gray, watery sunshine was trying to peek through.

Carolyn got out of the car and I reluctantly followed. The path we followed was thick with old pine needles. Dark evergreens towered over us, and the mountain sloped sharply away to the right.

Gradually, the peace and silence of the place began to relax my mind. Just then, we turned a corner, and I gasped in amazement. From the top of the mountain, sloping down for several acres across folds and valleys, between the trees and bushes, following the terrain, were rivers of daffodils in radiant bloom. Every hue of the color yellow—from the palest ivory to the deepest lemon to the most vivid salmon-orange—blazed like a carpet before us.

It looked as though the sun had tipped over and spilled gold in rivulets down the mountainside. At the center of this wild color cascaded a waterfall of purple hyacinth. Throughout the garden were little meditation platforms graced with barrels of coral-colored tulips. And, as if this bonanza of color were not enough, over the heads of the daffodils Western bluebirds darted and frolicked, their magenta breasts and sapphire wings like a flutter of jewels.

A riot of questions filled my mind: Who created such beauty—such a magnificent garden? Why? Why here, in this out-of-the-way place? *How?*

As we approached the mountain home that stood in the center of the property, we saw a sign: *Answers to the Questions I Know You Are Asking.*

The first answer was *One Woman—Two Hands, Two Feet, and Very Little Brain.* The second was *One at a Time.* The third, *Started in 1958.*

As we drove back home, I was silent. I was so moved by what we had seen I could scarcely speak. "She changed the world," I finally said, "one bulb at a time. Just think. She started almost forty years ago. And the world is forever different and better because she did a little bit with consistent effort."

The wonder of it would not let me go. "Imagine—if I had had a vision and had worked at it, just a little bit every day for all those lost years, what might I have accomplished by now?"

Carolyn looked at me sideways, smiling. "Start tomorrow," she said. "Better yet, start today."

Jaroldeen Edwards

More Chicken Soup?

Many of the stories and poems you have read in this book were submitted by readers like you who had read earlier *Chicken Soup for the Soul* books. We are planning to publish five or six *Chicken Soup for the Soul* books every year. We invite you to contribute a story to one of these future volumes.

Stories may be up to 1,200 words and must uplift or inspire. You may submit an original piece, something you have read or your favorite quotation on your refrigerator door.

To obtain a copy of our submission guidelines and a listing of upcoming *Chicken Soup* books, please write, fax or check one of our Web sites.

Please send your submissions to:

Chicken Soup for the (Specify Which Edition) Soul
P.O. Box 30880, Santa Barbara, CA 93130
Fax: 805-563-2945
Web site: *www.chickensoup.com*

You can also visit the *Chicken Soup for the Soul* Web site on America Online at keyword: chickensoup.

Just send a copy of your stories and other pieces to the above address.

We will be sure that both you and the author are credited for your submission.

For information about speaking engagements, other books, audiotapes, workshops and training programs, please contact any of our authors directly.

More Garden Stories?

Would you like to read more stories like the ones in this book that share the humor and heart of gardening? Then subscribe to *GreenPrints*, "The Weeder's Digest," the only magazine that shares the human side of gardening.

Published by Pat Stone, one of the coauthors of this book, *GreenPrints* has been sharing stories of the joy, humor and heart of gardening for over ten years. Pat is offering a special one-year subscription price of $19.97 to readers of *Chicken Soup for the Gardener's Soul.* That's $3.00 off the regular $22.97 price—and along with a full subscription to this unique garden quarterly, it includes a free copy of the sixty-four-page special, "The Weeder's Reader: GreenPrints' Greatest Stories."

Send your name, address and payment to:

GreenPrints—Dept. CSGS
P.O. Box 1355
Fairview, NC 28730

For credit card orders, you can also call 800-569-0602 or visit the magazine's Web site at *www.greenprints.com.*

Helping Gardeners Help Others

"I've never yet met a gardener who wasn't kind enough to share," says the author of our story, "Lean Times." We at *Chicken Soup for the Gardener's Soul* know that's true. We're proud to join the *Chicken Soup for the Soul* tradition in sharing part of the proceeds from this book with the following nonprofit organizations. Please join us.

America the Beautiful Fund

America the Beautiful Fund (ABF) is a nationwide nonprofit organization started in 1965 to save the natural and historic beauty of America and improve the quality of life. Since then, over 65,000 projects involving 10 million volunteers have been developed in all fifty states. These projects are supported through ABF's Rediscover America, American Landscapes, and Operation Green Plant programs.

Operation Green Plant distributes surplus seeds to more than 60,000 community action committees, hunger relief projects, community gardens and environmental projects. It provides food, instills community pride, encourages ecologically sound habits, and revitalizes and beautifies otherwise derelict property.

To apply for a grant of free seeds for a community project, send a self-addressed, stamped envelope to Katie Rehwaldt at America the Beautiful Fund, 1730 K St. NW, Suite 1002, Washington, DC 20006, or download the application at: *www.freeseeds.org*.

The American Community Gardening Association

The American Community Gardening Association (ACGA) was formed in 1978 to help community gardening and greening groups. This educational organization provides information through publications, networking and informal mentors. It encourages the creation of new community gardening programs by connecting interested people and providing good old-fashioned hand-holding. Through its "From the Roots Up" Leadership Training program, it offers workshops and publications to strengthen leadership in local programs.

ACGA's members are individuals and groups who use community greening as a tool for beautification, community development, education, exercise, growing good food and never having to garden alone.

To learn more about ACGA or to receive their booklet, "How to Start a Community Garden," contact them at: 100 N. 20th Street, 5th Floor, Philadelphia, PA 19103-1495; Phone: 215-988-8785, Fax: 215-988-8810; e-mail: *smccabe@pennhort.org.* Web site: *www.communitygarden.org.*

Be The Star You Are!

Every day, we are bombarded by media filled with heart-wrenching tales of violence, abuse and battered lives. Be The Star You Are! believes that information infused with inspiration has the power to change lives.

Be The Star You Are! is a nonprofit positive-message media library committed to providing strong role models for youth and adults. Through its Web site, fundraisers, radio and TV programs, and Reach Out Reading literacy programs, Be The Star You Are! promotes and distributes informative, empowering and positive videos, audio-tapes, books, art and music to groups in need of hope and tools for daily living.

A tax-deductible contribution is an investment that could change the face of tomorrow from one of despair to one of hope. Consider asking your company for matching contributions. Call 877-944-STAR for more information or go to the Web site at *www.bethestaryouare.org* or write to P.O. Box 376, Moraga, CA 94556.

The radio program Be The Star You Are! with host Cynthia Brian airs Sundays 4–5 P.M. PST on Business Radio 1220 AM, streamed live from *www.bethestaryouare.org.*

Home Gardening Project

U.S. Department of Agriculture figures show that mil-lions upon millions of people—our mothers and fathers and children—do not have adequate sustenance. In 1984, The Home Gardening Project began building free raised-bed vegetable gardens at the homes of the aged, the dis-abled, single-parent families and caring institutions. The gardens are easy to manage and highly productive. The director, Dan Barker, has personally built over 1,400 gar-dens, has helped initiate and support garden-building projects in eighteen states and abroad, and is presently working to initiate 200 new projects throughout the country.

That's where the money goes—to build gardens.

Donations can be sent to Home Gardening Project, 8060 Upper Applegate Rd., Jacksonville, OR 97530. On behalf of the recipients, thank you for your compassion.

Who Is Jack Canfield?

Jack Canfield is one of America's leading experts in the development of human potential and personal effectiveness. He is both a dynamic, entertaining speaker and a highly sought-after trainer.

He is the author and narrator of several bestselling audio- and videocassette programs, including *Self-Esteem and Peak Performance, How to Build High Self-Esteem, Self-Esteem in the Classroom* and *Chicken Soup for the Soul—Live.* He is regularly seen on television shows such as *Good Morning America, 20/20* and *NBC Nightly News.* Jack has co-authored numerous books, including the *Chicken Soup for the Soul* series, *Dare to Win* and *The Aladdin Factor* (all with Mark Victor Hansen), *100 Ways to Build Self-Concept in the Classroom* (with Harold C. Wells) and *Heart at Work* (with Jacqueline Miller).

Jack is a regularly featured speaker for professional associations, school districts, government agencies, churches, hospitals, sales organizations and corporations. His clients have included the American Dental Association, the American Management Association, AT&T, Campbell Soup, Clairol, Domino's Pizza, GE, ITT, Hartford Insurance, Johnson & Johnson, the Million Dollar Roundtable, NCR, New England Telephone, Re/Max, Scott Paper, TRW and Virgin Records. Jack is also on the faculty of Income Builders International, a school for entrepreneurs.

Jack conducts an annual eight-day Training of Trainers program in the areas of self-esteem and peak performance. The program attracts educators, counselors, parenting trainers, corporate trainers, professional speakers, ministers and others interested in developing their speaking and seminar-leading skills.

For further information about Jack's books, tapes and training programs, or to schedule him for a presentation, please contact:

The Canfield Training Group
P.O. Box 30880 • Santa Barbara, CA 93130
Phone: 805-563-2935 • Fax: 805-563-2945
To e-mail or visit our Web site: *www.chickensoup.com*

Who Is Mark Victor Hansen?

Mark Victor Hansen is a professional speaker who, in the last twenty years, has made over 4,000 presentations to more than two million people in thirty-two countries. His presentations cover sales excellence and strategies; personal empowerment and development regardless of stages of life; and how to triple your income and double your time off.

Mark has spent a lifetime dedicated to his mission of making a profound and positive difference in people's lives. Throughout his career, he has inspired hundreds of thousands of people to create a more powerful and purposeful future for themselves while stimulating the sale of billions of dollars worth of goods and services.

Mark is a prolific writer and has authored *Future Diary, How to Achieve Total Prosperity* and *The Miracle of Tithing*. He is coauthor of the *Chicken Soup for the Soul* series, *Dare to Win* and *The Aladdin Factor* (all with Jack Canfield), *The Master Motivator* (with Joe Batten) and *Out of the Blue* (with Barbara Nichols).

Mark has also produced a complete library of personal empowerment audio- and videocassette programs that have enabled his listeners to recognize and use their innate abilities in their business and personal lives. His message has made him a popular television and radio personality, with appearances on ABC, NBC, CBS, HBO, PBS and CNN. He has also appeared on the cover of numerous magazines, including *Success, Entrepreneur* and *Changes*.

Mark is a big man with a heart and spirit to match—an inspiration to people of all ages who seek to better themselves.

For further information about Mark write:

MVH & Associates
P. O. Box 7665
Newport Beach, CA 92658
Phone: 714-759-9304 or 800-433-2314
Fax: 714-722-6912
Web site: *www.chickensoup.com*

Who Is Cynthia Brian?

Cynthia Brian has been a garden aficionado since she was a little girl. Born on a farm in the Napa Valley, the eldest of five children, she was a 4-H'er who raised chickens and sheep, drove tractors and picked fruit to finance her college education. Named The Outstanding Teenager of California, she was a teen ambassador to Holland for eighteen months, working as a foreign correspondent.

Cynthia's passion for traveling and people is matched by her enthusiasm for acting and modeling, which she has done professionally for twenty-five years as a SAG/AFTRA performer of films, TV, commercials and print ads. She currently hosts two TV series, *Live Your Dreams* and *The Business of Showbusiness,* and a personal growth radio program. Her book *The Business of Showbusiness* has served as a popular guide for thespians. Through her company, Starstyle Productions, Cynthia offers private success coaching and dynamic presentations. Cynthia and her daughter, Heather Brittany, also cohost TV's and radio's *Animal Cuts.*

Cynthia, a California certified interior designer and professional member of ASID and IDS, is also president of Starstyle Interiors and Designs, an interior and garden design firm. Her designs have been featured in books, magazines, newspapers and television shows.

Cynthia is the author of *A Gardener's Calendar* and the books *Be The Star You Are!, 99 Gifts to Living, Loving, Laughing, and Learning to Make a Difference* (Ten Speed Press) and *Miracle Moments.* Her syndicated column, "Business Bytes," is read in newspapers worldwide.

Cynthia also founded the 501(c)(3) charity Be The Star You Are!, providing positive-message books, audiotapes, videotapes and music to other charities and those in need of tools for daily living *(www.bethestaryouare.org).*

Cynthia gardens on four acres and plays with her animal menagerie including poultry, goats, rabbits, horses, dogs, cats and birds on the mini-farm she shares with her husband and two children in Northern California.

To book Cynthia as an actress, spokesperson or speaker contact:

Starstyle Productions
P.O. Box 422, Moraga, California 94556
Web site: *www.star-style.com*
Phone: 925-377-STAR

Who Is Cindy Buck?

Cindy Buck got her start as a gardener when a friend gave her and her husband, Rob, a whole gardenful of divided perennials as a wedding present. She has been cultivating a green thumb ever since and is proud to have recently graduated to planting from seed. Inspired by the stories she read in compiling this book, Cindy holds regular gardening and storytelling sessions at a local senior care center.

A writer, editor and trainer, Cindy is the author of over forty software manuals and tutorials. She has designed and presented software training programs for numerous companies, including Leaf, Inc., AMC Theaters, Boatman's Bank and the Iowa State Court System. Cindy also writes promotional materials for businesses and freelance articles for magazines and newspapers. Recently she has contributed stories and her editing talents to other *Chicken Soup for the Soul* books.

A professional speaker since 1974, Cindy has spoken extensively about personal growth and self-development. Audiences find her dynamic presentations inspiring and enjoyable. Through Yes to Success Seminars, she has shared tools for self-discovery and greater personal and professional effectiveness. She also teaches stress management programs to the general public.

Cindy is a frequent performer with the Iowa Theatre Company and a volunteer coach for ITC's "In the Schools" program. She also serves as a judge at the regional and state level for the Iowa High School Speech Association. You might hear her voice on the radio as she performs in commercials for the award-winning Hedquist Productions, for which she also reads stories for the *Chicken Soup for the Soul* audiobooks.

Drawing on her personal experiences and the stories of thousands of gardeners, Cindy presents programs on topics such as tending the gardener's soul to cultivate joy and reap success. For more information, you can reach her at:

908 E. Adams St.
Fairfield, IA 52556
Phone: 641-472-7586
E-mail: *cbuck@kdsi.net*

Who Is Marion Owen?

After eight years at sea as a seaman and merchant marine officer, Marion Owen found a home ashore in 1984 in Kodiak, Alaska. Switching her focus to the land, Marion became a master gardener and passionate organic gardener. Now she has thirty raised beds filled with flowers, vegetables and herbs—a teaching garden, where visitors are welcome to explore and learn.

Marion is known as "The Compost Queen." In her columns for newspapers, magazines and Web sites, her articles cover everything from organic gardening techniques, to environmental issues, composting, cooking and healthy living. She also enjoys developing "sneaky nutrition" recipes such as "Out of This World Chocolate Beet Cake," as a way to get nutritious food into family meals. Marion also developed and patented PlanTea, an organic fertilizer in convenient tea bags for the home gardener (*www.plantea.com*). PlanTea is brewed like regular tea to make a liquid concentrate.

Marion's garden is also where she finds beautiful subjects to photograph. For over fifteen years, her award-winning photographs have been featured in *Better Homes and Gardens, Organic Gardening, The Nature Conservancy, Patagonia, Audubon, TIME, Alaska* magazine and *Business Week.* She likes to capture a different view in her photographs: raindrops splashing off flower petals, closeups of snowflakes and salmon swimming underwater.

A gifted teacher, Marion developed a popular series of photography and gardening courses through the University of Alaska. She combines her motivational speaking, gardening and photography skills in slide presentations for master gardener conferences, garden clubs, business seminars and more. She encourages her audiences to discover what they love to do, and then to do it!

Born and raised on Puget Sound in Washington State, Marion and her husband Marty enjoy exploring Kodiak Island on their boat.

Marion loves sea-kayaking, weight lifting, hiking, fishing, reading, scuba diving, cooking and spending time with family and friends.

Marion can be reached at:

P.O. Box 1694 • Kodiak, AK 99615-1694
Phone: 907-486-5079
E-mail: *marion@ptialaska.net*

Who Is Pat Stone?

Pat Stone is a Christian, a husband and a father. He feels blessed to have a wonderful wife (Becky), four terrific children (Nate, Jesse, Sammy and Tucker), and to live as part of a caring community in the mountains of western North Carolina.

Pat has a garden media career that spans two decades and includes everything from "Mother Earth News" to "CBS This Morning." But his pride and joy is being the editor and creator of *GreenPrints*, "The Weeder's Digest," the only magazine that shares the human side of gardening. One day back in 1990, he noticed that there are over 100 how-to garden publications . . . but not one about the joys, humor and heart of gardening.

So, with the help of his family, Pat created it. *GreenPrints* continues today to be an inspirational and heartfelt "Weeder's Digest" of personal garden stories. One reader described it as "a hyacinth for the soul."

Pat is also a professional gardening storyteller, "the Garrison Keillor of Gardening."

For more information about *GreenPrints* magazine or engaging Pat as a speaker, contact him at:

GreenPrints
P.O. Box 1355
Fairview, NC 28730
Phone: 828-628-1902
Web site: *www.greenprints.com*
E-mail: *greenprints@cheta.net*

Who Is Carol Sturgulewski?

Carol Sturgulewski's favorite garden has no boundaries. Growing up in coastal Alaska, she was surrounded by forest. She remembers hunting for wild sourdock with her grandmother, and nibbling cow parsnip stalks and spruce tree tips with neighbor children. As a young woman, she began collecting books on wildflowers and plants, learning how native peoples used nature's harvest for food and medicine. She became an ardent berry-picker. And to her neighbors' dismay, Carol's fondness for native plants prompted her to transplant some of her favorite "weeds" when she recently moved from Kodiak Island to mainland Alaska.

In her professional life, Carol is an award-winning writer on the state and regional level, and former president of The Alaska Press Club. She spent nearly twenty years as a writer and editor for Alaska's three largest newspapers and several smaller papers, specializing in features and education. She also worked as a newspaper magazine writer in Michigan before returning to her Alaskan roots.

When not occupied as a full-time mom, Carol continues to do freelance writing and editing for newspapers and other publications, such as *Alaska* magazine. Carol has also led writing workshops for students from grade school through college, and taught journalism for the University of Alaska. Her familiarity with her native state has helped in her work for regional guidebooks, including *Frommer's* and *Alaska's Best.*

Carol firmly believes that every person can make a difference in the world. A committed volunteer, she has served on boards supporting public broadcasting, literacy, education, and the interests of children, women and senior citizens.

Carol and her husband, Roe, now live in Anchorage, Alaska with their sons, Ben, Ted and Hugh. Their backyard is popular with kids, moose, bears, rabbits, squirrels, wild berries—and a few select "weeds."

You can reach Carol at:

5120 Manytell Ave., Anchorage, AK 99516
Phone: 907-345-2363
E-mail: *carolben@gci.net*

Contributors

Several of the stories in this book were taken from previously published sources, such as books, magazines and newspapers. These sources are acknowledged in the permissions section. However, some of the stories were written by humorists, professional speakers and workshop presenters. If you would like to contact them for information on their books, audiotapes and videotapes, seminars and workshops, you can reach them at the addresses and phone numbers provided below.

The remainder of the stories were submitted by readers of our previous *Chicken Soup for the Soul* books and others who responded to our requests for stories. We have also included information about them.

ahansen is currently serving as CEO of the Mobius Corporation, a group of demented quantum physicist/designers who patent and develop such projects as ambient temperature superconductors, elemental transmutation technologies and exotic materials that exhibit transdimensional capabilities. She also enjoys growing roses—and her beloved lummox of a son.

Dyann Andersen lives in Burnsville, Minnesota and is the proud mother of one married daughter and one granddaughter, both of whom "are just a joy to be around." She loves gardening, is studying both writing and radiologic technology, and lives with her husband, their Schipperke and an alley cat.

Joan Wester Anderson is the author of more than a dozen books about people's experiences with angels, heaven and miraculous events. *Where Angels Walk, True Stories of Heavenly Visitors,* was on the *New York Times* bestseller list for a year. Her most recent book is *Forever Young,* the authorized biography of Hollywood star Loretta Young.

Sherri Andervich enjoys raising native plants, vegetables, herbs and flowers in a rural area abounding in wildlife and wildflowers. She and her husband Jim have five children and two grandchildren, and often volunteer at youth activities, nature reserves and an arts center.

Susan Antler has taken her personal passion for the environment and built an environmental marketing business, Visions of Utopia, to pursue her interests. Among her clients is The Composting Council of Canada, the central resource and network for the composting industry in Canada. To find out more, visit *www.compost.org.*

Dan Barker founded The Home Gardening Project in 1984 to provide self-reliance and joy to the poor and disabled. He is working to help establish similar projects in 200 cities. Dan can be reached at 8060 Upper Applegate Rd., Jacksonville, OR 97530; *hgpf@teleport.com* or *www.teleport.com/~hgpf*.

Claire Beynon was born in South Africa and has lived in New Zealand since 1994. A full-time artist who also writes poetry and short fiction, she is fascinated by the powerful relationship between images and words. Claire is married and has three enthusiastic children.

Marcia E. Brown became a full-time freelance writer when family stories she wrote for her son began to sell. Her work has been published in the *Los Angeles Times, Mother Earth News, Mature Living, Backwoods Home, The Ozarks Mountaineer* and elsewhere. Her e-mail address is *Wordeez@aol.com*.

Joanne Bryan was born in Maryland and moved to Florida at a very young age. At age eighteen, she entered and made a career in the U.S. Air Force. She raised a daughter and now has a wonderful grandson. She is a disabled veteran and spends time volunteering at the local VA hospital greenhouse. Joanne's e-mail is *joannelbryan@hotmail.com*.

Stephanie Welcher Buckley developed a love for gardening through membership in Oklahoma City's Carefree Rose Garden Club. A syndicated newspaper columnist, inspirational writer and speaker, Buckley hosts State of Change, a radio program featuring people who've experienced adversity or prosperity and are changing their community. Reach her at: P.O. Box 1502, Edmond, OK 73034, *stateofchange@netzero.net*.

Bernice Bywater has written poetry since she could hold a pencil. She has also written fiction, nonfiction and advertising copy, which she maintains is a combination of both. She lives near San Francisco, where she writes, paints, designs, gardens and keeps in touch with her four children and nineteen grandchildren.

John M. Capozzi is the author of *A Spirit of Greatness,* in which "Romeo Sets the Stage" appears. Mr. Capozzi also wrote two bestselling business maxim books: *Why Climb the Corporate Ladder When You Can Take the Elevator?* and *If You Want the Rainbow You Gotta Put Up with the Rain!* His latest book, *GET A GRIP!* is a fun collection of golf maxims and cartoons. For more information: *www.jmcpublishingservices.com*. To order books: 800-910-4944 or 212-439-4338.

Gary Carter is a woodworker who lives with his wife on the side of a mountain in Marin County, California. He divides his time between working wood, working words and teaching sailing on San Francisco Bay.

Martine Caselli is an award-winning freelance writer and a frequent contributor to *GreenPrints* magazine. She lives and works in Stony Brook, Long Island, and can be reached at 4 Chalmers Place, Stony Brook, NY 11790.

David M. Cooney is a cartoonist and illustrator. Through the scientific journals featuring his work, his cartoons are seen in over fifty countries. His cartoons run in numerous newspapers under the title "Twisted View." An avid gardener, David lives with his wife Marcia and two children in Mifflinburg, Pennsylvania. His Web site is *www.davidcooney.com*. Reach him at *david@davidcooney.com*.

Reverend Max Coots has lived almost all his life in rural small towns—and loves it. He is retired after thirty-five years as a minister in the college town of Canton, New York, where he devotes himself to gardening, sculpting and the pleasures of small-town life.

Christie Craig is a writer, photographer and teacher with over 400 magazine credits and one published novel to her name. Her work has appeared in such magazines as *Reader's Digest, St. Anthony's Messenger* and *Woman's World*. Known for her inspiration and encouragement, she can be reached via e-mail at *ccraig@comwerx.net*.

Edie Cuttler has been writing since high school, loving the outdoors since childhood and gardening for more than twenty-five years. She is moving from Long Island to the West Coast, where she expects to find more adventures to live, more gardens to sow and more fodder for tales.

Diane C. Daniels is forty-seven years old, a customer service representative for a major health insurance company by day and a writer by night. A passion for writing, especially poetry, has consumed her since childhood. She lives in Sacramento, California, with her son, Charles, and two dogs.

Amanda Dodson is a full-time mother to her beautiful daughter, Grace. A freelance writer, she is working on her first book. Amanda also volunteers twice a week at a local nursing home, where she slows down and enjoys smelling the roses with some of her closest friends.

Jenny Gore Dwyer was born and raised in Ketchikan, Alaska. In 1996, she was diagnosed with cancer of the appendix. Now a four-year cancer survivor, Jenny spends her days enjoying laundry, cooking, PTA and eating cheesecake. She has been married for fourteen years and has two amazing kids. She dedicates this story to Brenna and Sean, and Joey, Cliff and John. Contact Jenny at 6439 N.E. 188th St., Kenmore, WA, 98128 or *jdwyer1987@aol.com*.

Margarita Engle is the author of two novels, *Skywriting* (Bantam) and *Singing to Cuba* (Arte Publico Press). Educated as an agronomist and botanist, she has published numerous articles in landscape and gardening magazines. She lives with her husband, son and daughter in Clovis, California.

Jane Eppinga is presently writing two books, *Arizona Folklore* and *Images of Tucson*. Her first award-winning book was *Henry Ossian Flipper: West Point's First Black Graduate*. Jane also has written for *Good Housekeeping, Chicken Soup for the Cat and Dog Lover's Soul*, and 200 other publications.

Laura Esserman, M.D., is the director of Carol Franc Buck Breast Care Center and associate professor of surgery and radiology at the University of California, San Francisco. She serves on the executive committee of The Center for Integrative Medicine at UCSF and is an affiliate faculty member of the Institute for Health Policy Studies and the Medical Informatics Program. She is also the coleader of the Breast Oncology Program at the USSF Cancer Center.

Debbie Farmer writes an award-winning column, "Family Daze," published weekly in over two dozen newspapers. Her essays have also appeared in 100 parenting magazines around the country. For information on having "Family Daze" appear in your newspaper, e-mail *familydaze@home.com* or visit the Web site: *www.familydaze.com*.

George M. Flynn is a husband, father of three, freelance writer and seventh-grade English teacher. He is also an avid gardener and the author of *Maggie's Heart and Other Stories,* a collection of twenty-four heartwarming gardening stories. The book is available by contacting him at 23 Kemah-Mecca Lake Road, Newton, NJ 07860. E-mail George at *gmcflynn@ptd.net.*

Jean Jeffrey Gietzen is author of *If You're Missing Baby Jesus, Questions and Answers for Catechists* and *A People Set Apart.* She has also written for *A Second Chicken Soup for the Woman's Soul, Reader's Digest, Catholic Digest, Virtue* and more. A wife, mother and grandmother, Jean lives in Tucson, Arizona and Milwaukee, Wisconsin. She leads writing workshops in both states. You may reach her at 520-296-1550 or 414-352-2009.

James P. Glaser lives on Island Lake, south of Northome, Minnesota, with Charmaine. A master gardener, Jim gives talks on what gardening can do for families and communities. He also builds garden accessories, rock gardens and starter gardens for others. Jim can be reached at P.O. Box 102, Northome, MN 56661, 218-897-5329.

Connie Goldman explores challenges, changes and continued growth in the mid-life years and beyond. She offers information, insights and inspiration through her public radio specials, audiocassette tapes, books, articles and speeches. Information is available by writing Connie at Goldman Productions, 926 Second St., Suite 201, Santa Monica, CA 90404; on the Web at *www.congoldman.org* or via e-mail: *congoldman@aol.com*.

Jaynell Grayson is a public relations specialist for IBM Global Services. Food from the 'Hood is a student-owned business located at Crenshaw High School in Los Angeles, California. Company profits provide college scholarships for the student owners, who donate 25 percent of their crop to feed the needy in their community. For more information, contact Aleyne Larner at 323-295-4842. To contact Jaynell, write to: IBM Global Services, Rte. 100, Bldg. 4, Somers, NY 10589; phone: 914-766-4107; fax: 914-766-8494; e-mail: *jngrayso@us.ibm.com*.

Donna Gundle-Krieg is a freelance writer and human resources consultant who lives in Milford, Michigan, with her husband Dennis and two children, Steven and Elizabeth. Between kids' activities and working, Donna tends several gardens and is involved in many community activities. She can be reached at *dgk8859@tir.com.*

Anirban Gupta spent his childhood in Bombay, India, before moving to Calcutta. He edited his school and college magazines, and is currently studying at Calcutta Medical College. Anirban occasionally writes short stories and poems. His recent prize-winning stories include *The Valley Children* and *When Shadows Stand Mesmerized, Searching for Walls.*

Peter Guttmacher's books include *Elvis! Elvis! Elvis! The King and His Movies, Crazy Horse: Sioux Warrior Chief, The Incredible Jeep, Legendary War Films, Legendary Westerns, Legendary Comedies, Legendary Love Stories, Legendary Horror Films,* and *Legendary Sci-Fi Cinema.* His father is his story's real-life protagonist. Peter can be reached at *pguttmacher@earthlink.net.*

Mary Harrison Hart has been happily married to her first love, Tom, for twenty-three years. They have two daughters, ages seventeen and twenty-one. Mary is a self-taught graphic artist, working from home to create logos and T-shirt designs with flair. She also works part-time at Home Depot's garden department. Her passion is to create a backyard sanctuary on a shoestring!

Janice Hasselius is a wife, mother, grandmother, prize-winning watercolorist, published author and a master gardener. She encourages us all to "Keep your hands in the earth, your eyes on heaven and your heart with the Lord."

Maureen Heffernan was raised in Perry, Ohio, graduated from Fordham University and studied horticulture at the University of Alaska-Fairbanks and Ohio State University. She is the director of public programs at Cleveland Botanical Garden and a garden writer. Maureen is also author of the book *Burpee Seed Starter.*

Jeanne Hill is an author, an inspirational speaker and a contributing editor to *Guideposts* magazine. Her award-winning short stories and articles are often chosen for anthologies. She has also authored monthly columns in magazines and published two inspirational books: *Daily Breath* (Word Books) and *Secrets of Prayer-Joy* (Judson Press). Jeanne resides in Scottsdale, Arizona.

Meredith Hodges is a freelance writer who lives with her husband in Fairfield, Iowa. Together they run a cashmere business over the Internet, offering one of the most complete selections of Pashmina products in the world. You may reach Meredith at: *info@ahah-pashmina.com,* or Royal Cashmere, 802 North Tenth St., Fairfield, IA 52556.

Bunny Hoest is one of the most widely read cartoonists today, reaching nearly 200 million diverse readers every week. She has produced *The Lockhorns, Agatha Crumm, What a Guy!* and *Hunny Bunny's Short Tale,* which is distributed internationally by King Features; "Laugh Parade" for *Parade* is seen by more than 80 million people every Sunday. She has twenty-five bestselling anthologies.

Arlene West House, a former New York advertising executive, lives with her husband, two dogs and two cats in Coupeville, Washington. She gave up high heels and power lunches for jeans and Penn Cove mussels served by the sea. She is currently working on her second novel, *Dancing at Nancy White's Party.* Arlene's e-mail address is *rwriter@whidbey.net.*

Georgia A. Hubley chose to leave twenty years in financial management to write full-time. She joined the Pebbles writers group at the renowned Thunderbird Bookshop in Carmel, California, creating the stimulus for many published stories that draw on her childhood memories of rural life. Contact her by e-mail at *GEOHUB@aol.com.*

Molly Bruce Jacobs lives in Maryland with her sons, Garrit and Bradford. She holds a law degree from Columbia University. Her writing has appeared in many publications including *Redbook* and *Sojourner.* A 1996 piece about her sister published in *Baltimore Magazine* won awards for public service and excellence in journalism. Molly is now writing a book about her sister. Contact her at *bjacobs@toad.net.*

Ted Key created the "Hazel" cartoon in 1943. It appeared in the *Saturday Evening Post* until 1969 (King Features 1969–present). The *Hazel* TV series starring Shirley Booth (NBC-TV 1961–65; CBS-TV 1965–66) was based on the same character. Ted, who has twenty-one books to his credit, created "Peabody and Sherman" for "Rocky and Bullwinkle," and Disney has produced three of his movies.

Adam Khan is the author of the book, *Self-Help Stuff That Works,* a collection of articles Adam wrote while a columnist for Rodale Press's newsletter *At Your Best.* He was voted the readers' favorite. Write to him at *adamkhan@aol.com* or P.O. Box 1703, Bellevue, WA 98009.

Emily King gardens and writes from her home in "The Rose City," Portland, Oregon. Her work has appeared in *The Oregonian, The War Cry, Living Solo, Keys for Kids, Warner Press,* and several gift books. She is currently seeking a publisher for her first children's book. Write to her at *daveandemily@juno.com.*

Susan Gilman King was born and raised in Adams, Massachusetts. She lives on a five-acre organic farm in Stephentown, New York, and raises crops, turkeys, beef cows, pigs and chickens. She resides with her soulmate, Bill, her dog, Nathan, and cat, Thomas. Contact her at 303 Madden Rd., Stephentown, NY 12168, 518-733-6723.

James A. Kisner, author of *Sweet Dreams and Tender Tears,* writes poetic stories based on true-life events. His poetry reflects his life, and the lives of those who read his Internet pages and submit their stories to him. For information on his Web pages and books, e-mail him at *POPPYK1@aol.com.*

Carin Klabbers-Ouwens lives at the Koninginneweg 75, 2982 AH in Ridderkerk, the Netherlands. She is an amateur story writer, and has published some of her fanfiction. She writes for fanzines and combines her household duties with volunteer work. Philip, her husband, works in chemistry and molecular biology.

Tom R. Kovach was born and raised in north-central Minnesota. He studied journalism at the University of Nevada-Reno and at Bemidji State University in Minnesota. He traveled with the U.S. Army in Vietnam, Korea and Germany. A freelance writer, Tom writes for magazines including *Field and Stream, Backwoods Home,* and many others.

Charles Kuralt's job for twenty-eight years was to drive the back roads of America in a CBS camper. More than 600 episodes of *On the Road with Charles Kuralt* were filed from every state in America. Audiences will long remember the rich, slow, mahogany tones of his voice on *Sunday Morning with Charles Kuralt.* He leaves us seven bestselling books, so many stories and so many memories.

Jean Little was born in 1931 in a little gray shingled bungalow across the road from her grandfather's farm. She began writing poetry when she was about nine years old. Many of her poems are about her wonderful childhood experiences in the country and the simple things in life. Jean lives in Leslie, Michigan.

Jeff Lowenfels ran away from New York to practice law in Alaska. His column has appeared in the *Anchorage Daily News* for over twenty-five years—the longest-running gardening column in America. He also does horticultural TV and radio, and is a past president of the Garden Writers Association of America.

David Clinton Matz (also known as Cliff, Malls and White Zombie) makes his publishing debut here. A freelance student of the audio and visual arts, David is an entertainer and counselor on the streets, where he sometimes resides. He is currently working on several spiritual essays. Contact him at 830 Boyd St., Lancaster, OH 43130, 740-653-5571.

Lee May, gardening columnist for *The Atlanta Journal-Constitution* and for *Southern Accents* magazine, is author of *Gardening Life,* a collection of essays, and a memoir, *In My Father's Garden,* from which "A Son's Harvest" was adapted. He cultivates life in Atlanta and in the rocky hills of north Georgia.

John McPherson is a syndicated cartoonist and creator of "Close to Home," a single-panel cartoon that appears in 650 newspapers worldwide, including the *Washington Post,* the *Los Angeles Times* and the *Tokyo Times.* He may be contacted by e-mail: *closetohome@compuserve.com*; Web site: *www.closetohome.com.*

Doris Meyer works in the Los Angeles jails as a correctional education school administrator. She has a national reputation for creating programs for incarcerated men and women, specializing in parent education, child visitation and domestic violence. An avid weekend gardener, she and her husband Paul are parents to Greg, Paula and Matthew.

ViAnn Meyer lives in beautiful Spokane, Washington, with her extended family, as well as a motley collection of cats and Ziggy the pup. The menagerie enjoys working, playing and living in a magical place dubbed the Meyer Cat Garden, which is always open for tours. ViAnn is a secretary at the local Air Force base and devotes her free time to her garden club.

James A. Michener, one of the world's best-loved writers, was known for his trademark epics exploring major themes and cultures, beginning with *Tales of the South Pacific*, which won the Pulitzer Prize in 1947. He devoted much of his life to public service and in 1977 was awarded the Medal of Freedom.

Jonita Mullins, a freelance writer and editor, discovered gardening after purchasing an older home in the historic district of Muskogee, one of the oldest towns in Oklahoma. She serves on the board of directors of the Founders' Place Historic District and the Three Rivers Museum of Muskogee, and is active in her church, First Assembly of God of Haskell.

Hillary Nelson is an award-winning columnist for *The Concord Monitor.* She writes and farms in Canterbury, New Hampshire, where she lives with her husband and two children.

Earl Nightingale was at one time the most listened-to man in the history of the broadcast industry. His audio program, "Lead the Field," was the first spoken recording to earn a gold record, and remains a bestseller to this day. For more information on "Lead the Field," as well as the largest collection of personal development resources in the world, visit *www.nightingale.com* or call 800-525-9000 for a complimentary catalog from Nightingale-Conant Publishing.

Jay O'Callahan is a writer and a performance artist of international renown. He has performed his dramatic works at Lincoln Center, The Abbey Theatre in Dublin, The Fine Arts Complex in London, and throughout the United States. For more information on his work and audio recordings, call 800-626-5356.

Linda O'Connell, a St. Louis resident, has been a preschool teacher/director for twenty-four years. She also teaches a variety of adult education classes in the St. Louis public schools' Community Education Centers. She and her husband, Bill, enjoy travel, camping and spending time with their children and grandchildren.

Mark Parisi's "off the mark" cartoon appears in over 100 newspapers worldwide. His offbeat panel can also be found in magazines, Web sites, newsletters, books and on greeting cards and T-shirts. Mark has published two compilation books and is chairman of the NE Chapter of the National Cartoonists' Society. View his comics at *www.offthemark.com.*

Lee Paton is the director of clinical services at Resources Connectors, Ltd., a health-care management and consulting firm in Portland, Oregon. She is a frequent lecturer in the United States and in Asia on topics related to pain, suffering, death and dying, and palliative care.

Mike Peters, political cartoonist for the *Dayton (OH) Daily News,* is recognized as one of the most prominent cartoon artists in the U.S. His work appears in newspapers worldwide, national publications, galleries and on television. In 1981 he was awarded the Pulitzer Prize for editorial cartooning. He also taped a fourteen-part PBS series, "The World of Cartooning with Mike Peters." In 1984, syndication began for Peters' comic strip "Mother Goose & Grimm."

Beth Pollack is a senior in high school and already very ambitious. She dreams of becoming a professional writer and, in December 1999, her first published article appeared in *Newsweek* magazine. Pollack has also completed her first novel, which fits into the genres of suspense, drama and historical fiction. She is currently seeking a publisher for this work.

Ursel Rabeneck and her husband, André, have made the beautiful Laurentians in Quebec their home for the past thirty years. They have four married children and continue to enjoy tennis, skiing, reading and gardening.

Carol McAdoo Rehme grew children instead of a garden. Now she is busy sowing other seeds. A professional storyteller and speaker, she specializes in original pioneer vignettes. Her freelance writing appears in books and magazines such as *Heart-Stirring Stories of Love, Whispers from Heaven,* and *Shining Star.* You can contact her at: *crehme@verinet.com.*

Kelly E. Reno is a professional writer who has authored thirteen books, both fiction and non-fiction. She writes freelance articles for several magazines and newspapers. She lives in Los Angeles with her husband, Fred, and son, Nicholas.

Lucy B. Richardson's love of flower gardening blossomed when she moved next door to a delightful elderly lady, a member of the Garden Club of Frankfort, Kentucky's largest and oldest garden club. She joined the club and became president, as well as holding other offices in the Kentucky Garden Club organization, and serving as a nationally accredited flower show judge.

Lon J. Rombough is a horticulturist, consultant and writer working with unusual fruits, especially grapes. His book on growing grapes will be published in early 2001 by Chelsea Green Press. For information and a list of more than 130 grape cuttings, go to *www.hevanet.com/lonrom* or write to P.O. Box 365, Aurora, OR 97002.

Dan Rosandich is a full-time illustrator and cartoonist, who will draw artwork for any project. Call him at: 906-482-6234. To see color samples of his work, go to *www.dirill.com* and click on his name.

Erica Sanders lives in the country with her husband, three boys, various animals and a garden overflowing its bounds. She is currently in school studying to become a counselor.

April Pulley Sayre is the author of thirty-seven books for young readers, including the picture books *If You Should Hear a Honey Guide, Home at Last: A Song of Migration,* and *Turtle, Turtle, Watch Out!* She and her husband love to garden and watch birds. They coauthored *Hummingbirds: The Sun Catchers* and travel to speak about hummingbirds and gardening with native plants. You can contact Sayre through her Web site: *www.aprilsayre.com.*

Charles Schulz, the late cartoonist of the comic strip "PEANUTS," made an inexorable contribution to our cultural landscape for fifty years, enthralling the world with his magical microcosmic world of a group of wise-beyond-their-years children and their beloved dog, Snoopy.

Kathy Shaskan ditched a successful career as a marketing executive to pursue her interest in humorous writing and illustration. This fact alone prompts people to burst out laughing. Her weekly cartoon, "Blossom Fuller," can be viewed online at *www.blossomfuller.com.*

Bernie Siegel, M.D., originated Exceptional Cancer Patients, a therapy that facilitates personal empowerment, lifestyle changes and healing. He has written *How to Live Between Office Visits, Prescriptions for Living* and other books. For information about his books, tapes and schedule, contact ECaP at *www.ecap-online.org* or 814-337-8192.

Paula L. Silici is an award-winning author who resides in Parker, Colorado. She is a regular columnist for the National Writers Association's quarterly publication, *Authorship,* and is currently working on her fourth historical novel. Her poetry, nonfiction and short stories have appeared in regional and national magazines. She can be reached at *silici@attglobal.net.*

Sheila Stroup writes a Metro page column for the *New Orleans Times-Picayune* and likes to tell stories that are full of hope. She believes each of us has the responsibility of making the world a more beautiful place and that a garden is one lovely way to do it.

Maggie Stuckey is the author of eight gardening books, including *Gardening from the Ground Up, The Complete Herb Book* and *The Complete Spice Book.* Her newest book, coming in spring 2001, is a complete guide to growing good things to eat (vegetables, herbs, fruits and edible flowers) in a container garden.

Bertha M. Sutliff lives in the mountain regions of northern Arkansas. She has been writing professionally for four years. Her accomplishments include various short stories, novellas and articles for online magazines. She is currently working on an anthology of World War I and II veterans' stories and a historical novel.

Marilyn Diephuis Sweeney currently juggles five careers: teaching college composition, fitness and piano, directing a children's choir, and managing marketing for an electronics firm she and her husband, Don, own. She has published articles in professional journals and newspapers and given presentations at writing conferences. She and Don live in Glenview, Illinois, where, carrying on her father's tradition, they enjoy gardening.

Ruth Szukalowski, fifty-five years old, is a housewife and mother and has been married for thirty-five years. She has five children and three grand-children. Ruth makes wildlife quilts and quillows (quilt-in-a-pillow). She enjoys gardening, fishing, archery, reading and birding. She can be reached at R.R. 3 Box 191, Cornell, MI 49818-9409.

Ann Pehl Thomson is an avid gardener and has taught horticulture to students of all ages. After four decades in the sunny Southwest, a recent move to the Northwest is challenging her to learn successful gardening under gray, soggy skies. Currently, Ann lives with her husband and two sons near Seattle, Washington.

Skye Trimble is a freelance writer working in the documentary film industry in the Washington, D.C. area. She originally wrote "A Million Trees" for the book, *Stone Soup for the World* by Marianne Larned, which features inspirational stories about humanitarianism. Contact her at: 2546A South Walter Reed Dr., Arlington, VA 22206 or by e-mail at: *Mskyet@aol.com.*

Stuart C. Vincent is a 1923-born Santa Rosa, California, native and lifelong resident. He agrees with Luther Burbank that it's "the city designed for living." He and his wife, Geets, teach elders autobiographical writing through the local junior college. They're freelancers and members of the Bay Area Travel Writers and Sonoma County Press Club. Contact them at *geets@sonic.net* or via fax at 707-528-0749.

Pamela Waterman taught high school English for seventeen years. After leaving teaching she took up garden writing and photography. She writes a column for the *Pasadena Star News* and gives slide lectures on gardening topics. She is currently working on a book about Pasadena gardens. She can be reached at 585 Laguna Road, Pasadena, CA 91105, or by fax: 626-799-4336.

Nita Waxelman, retired freelance advertising copywriter and newspaper columnist, is currently working on her memoirs, *Pocketful of Sunbeams,* which includes the story "Iva Mae's Birthday." Now living in the Missouri Ozarks, she enjoys gardening, trout-fishing, one grumpy cat and a husband who looks like a skinny Santa Claus.

Ken Weber has been a newspaper writer, editor and columnist for more than thirty-five years. Currently he is a nature/wildlife columnist for the Providence (R.I.) *Journal* and editor of a newsletter for the Audubon Society of Rhode Island. The author of several books on hiking, canoeing and nature subjects, he lives in Greenville, Rhode Island.

Marion Bond West is an inspirational author and speaker. She has written for *Guideposts* for twenty-eight years and is a contributing editor. She's also authored six books and written for about fifteen other magazines. She may be contacted by calling 706-353-6523 or writing 1330 DaAndra Dr., Watkinsville, GA 30677.

Valerie Wilcox is a native Minnesotan who has left the long, bitter cold winters for the more tropical Zone 5 (upstate New York). However, she misses Minnesota very much. When she isn't trying to plant things she has no business putting in the ground, like stuff from Zone 6, she raises organically-grown cut flowers for local markets in Stone Ridge, New York.

Tom Wilson launched his cartoon, "Ziggy," America's loveable hapless hero, in 1971 in fifteen newspapers. Ziggy now appears in 600 newspapers, countless books and calendars, and in more than 50 million greeting cards purchased each year. The televised animation special, "Ziggy's Gift," won an Emmy for Outstanding Animated Special.

Rayne Wolfe keeps busy penning a syndicated career advice column "What Works," scribbling short stories to read on NPR, teaching writing and working on a book about living with a cop. Rayne's stories have been published nationwide. She recently left executive recruiting to become a cub reporter (at age 44!) for *The Press Democrat* in Santa Rosa, California. You can reach her at *RayneWrites@aol.com*.

Nicolle Woodward is a resident of beautiful Bennington, Vermont, and just beginning her writing career. She has always been an avid reader, but started to write poetry and short stories seriously just a few years ago. Her theory? Enjoy each day and thank God for his blessings.

Bob Zahn has had thousands of his cartoons in all the leading publications including *Woman's World, Better Homes & Gardens, Reader's Digest, First,* and many others. Hundreds of his greeting cards have been published by major greeting card companies. Six of his humor books have been published. Bob's e-mail address is *zahntoons@aol.com*.

Linda Jin Zou is currently working on her first fiction under the working title of *Her Choices,* portraying a Chinese woman as she confronts changes and moral dilemmas brought about by the new economic and political landscape in China. She can be reached at 3712 Benthaven, Fort Collins, CO 80526, or at *imark@webaccess.net*.

Permissions *(continued from page vi)*

Street Smarts. Reprinted by permission of Lucy B. Richardson. ©2000 Lucy B. Richardson.

A Veteran's Garden. Reprinted by permission of James P. Glaser. ©2000 James P. Glaser.

Gardening in Our Blood. Reprinted by permission of Jean Little. ©1967 Jean Little.

Butter Beans and Bulldogs. Reprinted by permission of Marion Bond West. Originally appeared as *Jerry's Garden* in *Clarity*, a *Guideposts* publication, issue February/March 2000.

Ladies of the Garden Club. Reprinted by permission of Stephanie Welcher Buckley. ©2000 Stephanie Welcher Buckley.

I'll Plant Anything. Reprinted by permission of Valerie Wilcox. ©2000 Valerie Wilcox.

The Rose Babies. Reprinted by permission of Georgia A. Hubley. ©2000 Georgia A. Hubley.

Of Moose and Men. Reprinted by permission of Peter Guttmacher. ©2000 Peter Guttmacher.

A Garden Is to Grow and *Angel of Mercy.* Reprinted by permission of Erica Sanders. ©1990 and 1991 Erica Sanders.

The $100,000 Stray Cat. Reprinted by permission of ViAnn Meyer. ©2000 ViAnn Meyer.

As Thyself. From *Rediscovering American Values* by Dick DeVos. ©1997 by Compassionate Capitalism, Inc. Used by permission of Dutton, a division of Penguin Putnam Inc.

Ruby's Roses. Reprinted by permission of Donna Gundle-Krieg. ©2000 Donna Gundle-Krieg.

Garden Meditations. Reprinted by permission of Reverend Max Coots. ©1980 Reverend Max Coots.

An American Beauty. Reprinted by permission of Arlene West House. ©1999 Arlene West House.

The Man Who Lived in a Box and *A Few Strings Attached.* Reprinted by permission of Marcia E. Brown. ©1995 Marcia E. Brown.

The Tulip Tradition. Reprinted by permission of Doris Meyer. ©1999 Doris Meyer.

The Golden Girls. Reprinted by permission of Linda O'Connell. ©2000 Linda O'Connell.

A Healing Place. Reprinted by permission of Laura Esserman, M.D. ©2000 Laura Esserman, M.D.

A Row for the Hungry. Reprinted by permission of Jeff Lowenfels. ©1999 Jeff Lowenfels.

The Timely Letter. Reprinted by permission of Lon J. Rombough. ©2000 Lon J. Rombough.

A Million Trees. Reprinted by permission of Skye Trimble. ©1998 Skye Trimble.

Iva Mae's Birthday. Reprinted by permission of Nita Waxelman. ©2000 Nita Waxelman.

Luther Burbank and the Disappearing Raspberries. Reprinted by permission of Stuart C. Vincent. ©1999 Stuart C. Vincent.

Brian. Reprinted by permission of Jay O'Callahan. ©1990 Jay O'Callahan.

Gone Fishin'. Reprinted by permission of David Clinton Matz. ©1999 David Clinton Matz.

A Garden So Rich. Reprinted by permission of Christie Craig. ©1997 Christie Craig.

The Sock Garden. By April Pulley Sayre, reprinted from the August 1999 issue of *Ranger Rick* magazine, with the permission of the publisher, the National Wildlife Federation. ©1999 by the National Wildlife Federation.

My Mother's Cure. Reprinted by permission of Jean Jeffrey Gietzen. ©1985 Jean Jeffrey Gietzen.

Mike and the Grass. Excerpted from the book, *Forever, Erma* ©1996 by the Estate of Erma Bombeck. Reprinted with permission of Andrews McMeel Publishing. All rights reserved.

God's Mountain Garden. Reprinted by permission of Bertha M. Sutliff. ©1999 Bertha M. Sutliff.

Rusty Nails. Excerpted from the book, *The World Is My Home* by James A. Michener. ©1992 by James A. Michener. Reprinted by permission of Random House, Inc.

Flowers for a Newborn Child. Reprinted by permission of Claire Beynon. ©2000 Claire Beynon.

The Day the Lilies Bloomed. Reprinted by permission of Jane Eppinga. ©1999 Jane Eppinga.

The Bubbup Bush and *Nona's Garden.* Reprinted by permission of Paula L. Silici. ©1999 Paula L. Silici.

A Hug from Heaven. Excerpted from *Where Wonders Prevail* by Joan Wester

Anderson. ©1996 by Joan Wester Anderson. Reprinted by permission of Ballantine Books, a Division of Random House, Inc.

A Garden for Four. Reprinted by permission of Rayne Wolfe. ©1999 Rayne Wolfe.

Roses for Rose. Reprinted by permission of James A. Kisner. ©1998 James A. Kisner.

Buddies. Reprinted by permission of Maggie Stuckey. ©2000 Maggie Stuckey.

A Lesson in Love. Reprinted by permission of ahansen. ©1997 ahansen.

Garden Crime. Reprinted by permission of Ursel Rabeneck. ©2000 Ursel Rabeneck.

Black Tulips. Reprinted by permission of Carin Klabbers-Ouwens. ©1999 Carin Klabbers-Ouwens.

Downwind from Flowers. Reprinted by permission of Lee Paton. ©2000 Lee Paton.

The Next Best Thing. Reprinted by permission of Ann Pehl Thomson. ©1999 Ann Pehl Thomson.

Tough Love. Reprinted by permission of Mary Harrison Hart. ©2000 Mary Harrison Hart.

A Tree House for Everyone. Reprinted by permission of Maureen Heffernan. ©2000 Maureen Heffernan.

Mandela's Garden. Excerpted from the book, *Long Walk to Freedom* by Nelson Mandela. ©1994 by Nelson Rolihlahla Mandela. By permission of Little, Brown and Company (Inc.).

You Forgot Something. Reprinted by permission of Bernie Siegel, M.D. ©2000 Bernie Siegel, M.D.

Lean Times. Reprinted by permission of Dyann Andersen. ©2000 Dyann Andersen.

Hummingbirds in Hell's Kitchen. Reprinted by permission of Hillary Nelson. Excerpted from *Tending the Earth, Mending the Spirit* by Connie Goldman. ©1996 Hillary Nelson.

Sunflowers in Beijing. Reprinted by permission of Linda Jin Zou. ©2000 Linda Jin Zou.

The Burning of the Leaves. Reprinted by permission of Edie Cuttler. ©1996 Edie Cuttler.

The Perfect Garden. Reprinted by permission of Molly Bruce Jacobs. Originally published as *A Letter to Annie,* in *Baltimore* magazine ©1996.

Celebrate Your Family Tree

Chicken Soup for the Mother's Soul II

Code #8903 • Quality Paperback • $12.95

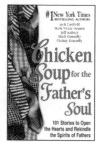

Chicken Soup for the Father's Soul

Code #8946 • Quality Paperback • $12.95

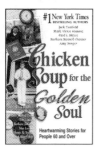

Chicken Soup for the Golden Soul

Code #7257 • Quality Paperback • $12.95

Chicken Soup for the Teenage Soul Letters

Code #8040 • Quality Paperback • $12.95

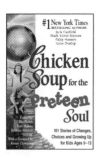

Chicken Soup for the Preteen Soul

Code #8008 • Quality Paperback • $12.95

Chicken Soup for the Little Souls

Code #8121 • Quality Paperback • $12.95